Published in conjunction with
The Institute For Psychohistory

# CHILDHOOD AND HISTORY IN AMERICA

## Glenn Davis

*The Psychohistory Press*

Division of Atcom, Inc., Atcom Building
2315 Broadway, New York, N.Y. 10024

D
16
D32

4/63 12.95

90417

Library of Congress Catalog Card Number: 76-27774

International Standard Book Number: 0-914434-04-7

To Lloyd de Mause and the
Institute for Psychohistory

# CONTENTS

FOREWORD

During the summer of 1973, browsing through several journals in a bookstore, I noticed an early issue of *History of Childhood Quarterly: The Journal of Psychohistory*. As I had recently completed the manuscript of a psychohistorical article on Theodore Roosevelt, the temptation to send Journal editor Lloyd deMause a copy was irresistible. Expecting the usual months of delay any academic accepts as part of the editorial process, I was surprised to receive an invitation to lunch in a matter of days.

During that lunch, deMause explained to me his work on the history of childhood, which was still in press, and the outlines of his psychogenic theory of history. Its simplicity was as disconcerting as the breadth of its scope. Since individuals are formed in their early years, he said, and individuals, not "broad forces," form history, all history is first determined in the infancy and childhood of individuals. Moreover, the evolution of history is caused by the lawful evolution of childhood itself. All progress has its origins in advances in parenting. What I anticipated would be a modest effort to neatly add yet one more interdisciplinary field to the study of history turned out to be a one-man movement seeking to create a totally new theory of historical motivation, one which held traditional history to be pure narration and sociological theory to be pure tautology.

The man had none of the symptoms of madness. His manner, though enthusiastic, was not obtrusive. Patiently listening to my questions, he handled them with a disturbing facility. Moreover, his facial expression lacked the qualities one associates with grandiosity. I guessed that he simply felt he had made a discovery.

After lunch, deMause continued to break the rules of academic formality. I was offered unlimited access to his files, the fruit of years of research in primary sources in the history of childhood. There was no inquisition as to my personal qualifications or intentions, but just the tacit acceptance of our shared interest in Theodore Roosevelt's psychology and psychohistory. DeMause listened to my rapid-fire criticisms of his work, often surprising me with this simple rejoinder: "I hadn't thought of that."

As I rode back to Connecticut, I thought about the encounter. He did ask me questions I was not prepared to answer—always a challenge. He was curious as to who took care of the infant Teedie, showing an intense interest in his first few months of existence. He wondered why I barely mentioned the boy's mother, asked for an in-depth characterization of the child before adolescence, and inquired as to what I knew of the broader American childhood experience of the 1850s and 1860s. I knew the answer to none of these questions. Who wrote of infancy? Historians almost never bothered and, besides, a strain of psychoanalytic thought culminating in Erik Erikson sought to broaden the time period for personality formation and de-emphasize early childhood. I found few sources concerning Roosevelt's mother, and few biographies, even psychobiographies, contained much hard information in this area. Why bother with a prepuberty characterization when a characterization of the young man was much more accessible? The thought of also handling the childhood of his contemporaries in an article-length study jarred my sense of focus and order.

Yet I knew of no better way to satisfy my curiosity concerning deMause's theory than to continue my Roosevelt research along childhood lines. What began as just one additional trip to the manuscripts at Harvard University ended with an additional year of full-time research and writing. The experience proved that I'd missed the essential Roosevelt in my earlier article—that the core of the individual had been formed by the time the boy wore britches. Detailed reconstruction—made possible through a wealth of preserved diaries, letters, and other primary materials—allowed a presentation of the sequential stages of development. Moreover, a study of the childhoods of others during the 1850s and 1860s showed that the Roosevelt household captured all the essentials of other modal families of the time. When I viewed the adult history of this generation in early twentieth-century America, I had to admit it was possible that its major themes had their origin in these early years.

The bloated 750-page manuscript I produced from the research manifested my own remaining discomfort with the material. The X of childhood did not directly cause the Y of society, as I asserted, but was simply a precursor. I buried the parallels between Roosevelt's experience and that of others in his generation in a section entitled "A Psychobiography in Miniature" and devoted pages to more acceptable notions of national character. I expanded sections on Roosevelt's adolescence and made few overt references to his childhood in later chapters. One conclusion was unavoidable: As I discussed childhood material, I began to think about my own, to reactivate long-forgotten memories, not all of them positive—and I did not enjoy the process. When childhood in the writing moved to the background, so did my own, and it felt better to watch it retreat.

I saw little of deMause during that winter and spring but instead explored personal questions. I examined my own childhood and, upon dealing with personal themes, became better equipped professionally to deal with my research. The more I opened myself to my own early experience and simply saw what had always been there, the more I could see the realities of childhood which were contained in my notes.

By the spring of 1975, I was ready to put the psychogenic theory to a more thorough test. I decided to put one time period under the empirical microscope and determine if, indeed, a detailed study of the evolution of childhood would turn out to explain the evolution of American culture in the twentieth century. I asked deMause if he would coauthor the study. Declining, he instead offered to be of assistance, which came in frequent meetings concerned with both theory and sources and especially in providing the material which forms the bulk of the first chapter.

As I continue to explore childhood in greater depth, the stronger does the psychogenic theory appear. It also proves to be excitingly dynamic, allowing for continual expansion without contradicting initial statements. More importantly, for every question it answers, it asks a new one—questions which previously would not even have been conceptualized. This seems enough to ask of our new science of psychohistory.

Glenn Davis

New York
1976

# ACKNOWLEDGEMENTS

I would like especially to thank the staffs of the New York Historical Society, the New York Public Research Library, and Sterling Library at Yale for their fine assistance during the research stages of this book. Appreciation goes to Martin Quitt, Richard Lyman, Barbara Finkelstein, Patrick Dunn, William Gillmore, Paul Elovitz, Jim Anderson, Henry Martin, and members of the Institute for Psychohistory for their helpful comments on various portions of the manuscript. My mother, Estelle Davis, offered many hours of research assistance, and my wife, Judy Lyon Davis, never failed to offer encouragement. My editors, Bruce Morrison and Henry Ebel, were invaluable in their aid concerning content and expression. And finally, of course, this book could never have been conceptualized if it were not for Lloyd deMause.

# PART I:  INTRODUCTION

# CHAPTER ONE

# THE PSYCHOGENIC THEORY OF HISTORY

During the past five years, an interdisciplinary group of some thirty scholars has met in New York united by two basic concerns: (1) an interest in the application of psychoanalysis to historical change, and (2) the possibility that human beings, both alone and in social groups, are not separate from the natural world and are therefore subject to scientific laws of behavior. This group of scholars, all Research Associates of the Institute for Psychohistory, has devoted a large portion of its time to the discussion of "the psychogenic theory of history." Formulated by the Institute's director, Lloyd deMause, this theory attempts to present an evolutionary, psychoanalytic theory of human history. This opening chapter will summarize deMause's psychogenic theory as he has presented it in recent Institute papers and workshops.[1]

The most important assertion of the theory is that, just as the formation of personality takes place in the individual's early years, so must the evolution of history be traced back to the mass evolution of childhood. Now, statements about childhood in the past have had a variety of meanings. Some historians have viewed the childhood years as a noncausal microcosm of later adult society. Others have attributed to "childhood," in some vague sense, elements of the foundation of adult culture. The psychogenic theory of history upon which this book is based involves the more radical premise that the evolution of childhood within the family is the root *cause* of the evolution of society.

Empirical testing of this radical causal notion is complex and multifaceted, involving (1) an analysis of the stages and processes of the evolutionary history of childhood, (2) a description of the resulting personality types, (3) a conception of broad historical movements as a function of the personalities produced in childhood, and (4) the realization that the embryo of social change is encased within intergenerational dynamics, and that these in turn are the psychic "genes" of historical evolution.

The notion of history and culture as caused by changes in childhood is radical because it departs from two traditions which have so far dominated psychoanalytic and sociological thought. The first is defined by orthodox psychoanalytic views originating with Freud, which see culture as the product of successive severe repressions of instincts, when the needs of the individual come into conflict with and give way to the requirements of civilization. As Freud stated, "the doctrine of repression is the foundation upon which the whole structure of psychoanalysis rests,"[2] and all applied psychoanalysis until now has been dominated by the concept of history as progressively greater repression and personal renunciation. The second tradition, the sociological heritage of Tonnies, Simmel, Weber and Parsons, assumes that social forces and institutions "cause" individuals rather than the converse. Thus, the individual does not create history but is a product of it. Individual emotional life is eventually arrived at, but rather as a precipitation of the study of society—or as one sociological historian phrases it, "that pivotal jump from aggregate data to the personal impact of social change."[3]

Both traditions impose severe limits on the understanding of historical change. Freud's vision of conflict as socially required repression, growing throughout history, is more fully articulated in *Civilization and Its Discontents*:

> The development of civilization appears to us as a particular process which mankind undergoes, and in which several things strike us as familiar. We may characterize this process with reference to the changes which it brings about in the familiar instinctual dispositions of human beings. . . . In most cases the process coincides with that of the *sublimation* (of instinctual aims) with which we are familiar, but in some it can be differentiated from it. Sublimation of the instinct is an especially conspicuous feature of cultural development; it

is what makes it possible for high psychical activities, scientific, artistic or ideological, to play such an important part in civilized life. . . . finally, and this seems the most important of all, it is impossible to overlook the extent to which civilization is built up upon a renunciation of instinct, how much it presupposes precisely the nonsatisfaction . . . of powerful instincts.[4]

Freud had already elaborated this view in 1909 when he wrote that "progress can be described as a repression that progresses over the centuries."[5] Geza Roheim subsequently noted that "I regard the evolution of mankind as proceeding from bad to worse . . . the factor which since the dawn of humanity has been at work at developing civilization at the expense of happiness is the death impulse or destructive impulse as active through the superego."[6] Thus we pay a heavy price for our civilization and its progress: a neurosis largely instigated through suppression of the sexual instincts, "dangerous innate forces which operate without regard to social necessities and moral values."[7] In the words of Freud, "Our civilization is, generally speaking, founded on the suppression of instincts. Each individual has contributed some renunciation of this sense of dominating power, and the aggressive and vindictive tendency of his personality."[8]

So thoroughly rooted in tradition is Freud's view of civilization that the conception of the id-ego-superego is already visible in Plato's tripartite division of the psyche and of society. Thus the well-ordered state, like the well-ordered soul, becomes an often precarious balance between mutually hostile agencies.

Even the ego psychologists, such as Anna Freud, Hartman, Kris, Loewenstein and Erikson, ground their theories on the presence of drive conflict and the universality of instinct, repression, and sublimation. Anna Freud writes:

A man's id remains the same at all times. It is true that instinctual impulses are capable of transformation when they push toward the ego and have to meet the demands of the outside world. But within the id itself little or no change takes place, apart from the advances made from the pregenital to the genital instinctual aims.[9]

The best description of this dependence on the early Freudian "plumbing" model by contemporary ego psychoanalysts is Bernard Apfelbaum's "On Ego Psychology: A Critique of the Structural Approach to Psycho-Analytic Theory." Rather than

abandon the notion of repression as the basis of civilization, the
ego psychologists, Apfelbaum shows, merely extend the drive
psychology of early psychoanalysis by imposing ego structures
*upon* these drives. Rapaport is quoted by way of illustration: "In
contrast to the id, which refers to *peremptory* aspects of behavior,
the ego refers to aspects of behavior, which are *delayable, bring
about delay*, or are themselves *products of delay.*" Apfelbaum
adds, "The structural approach in this setting no longer refers
primarily to psycho-analytic explanations based on id, ego, and
superego relations. It had mainly come to refer to an emphasis on
what Rapaport calls the 'control of structure over drive.' " As
Rapaport himself states, "It is partly by the hierarchic repetition
of this process of defense-structure formation that drives are
'tamed' into adult motives; and it is mostly the failure at one point
or another of this taming process that gives rise to neurotic,
psychotic, or character disturbances." Apfelbaum concludes,
"Thus maturity rests on the capacity of structural formations to
delay 'the congeries of immediately discharge-directed drives
which is conceptualized as the id.' The assumption here is that
drives do not develop, only structures do."[10]

All these models of the forces of civilization correspond to the
contemporary concept of "socialization," which is the paradigm
for recent child-rearing. The parent's position is *counter* to that of
the child, who possesses impulses in need of molding and
direction. This process assumes the necessity of not only putting
something *into* the child, but placing a lid upon it. Both aspects of
the process are necessarily seen to operate through the imposition
of parental authority.

The second traditional model for historical change, common to
both sociology and anthropology, involves an organic, holistic
concept of "culture" or "society" which involves forces beyond
the individual. First "social" change occurs, in accordance with
economic or other laws, then personality (and family life) changes
to adapt to the "social" changes. The emotions of individuals are
not central to notions of historical causality because they are seen
only as manifestations and symptoms of broad "movements" of
society. Thus John M. Whiting presents us with the following
diagram,[11] a universe in which the environment teaches the child
(a container of raw energy) to mediate basic drives:

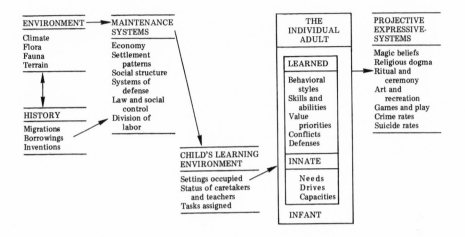

Fig. 1. Whiting's Model for Psycho-Cultural Research

Thus economic and environmental "structures" determine how children will be reared; the quality and goals of the socializing process selectively emphasize or de-emphasize such psychological variables as docility, aggressiveness, destructiveness, competitiveness, etc., and these variables are then projected in the form of a distinctive set of religious, mythical, or ethical beliefs. Joel Aronoff is one of the few sociologists who affords some independent causative function to "psychological variables," but even he weights his model to sociocultural and environmental determinants.[12] The starting point is always the macro, abandoning the personal and the emotional as men and women are denied their roles as the feeling architects of their own fates.

Some recent thinkers have begun to question the primacy of the cultural and institutional merely mediated through individual psychology. The impetus for this challenge has come from several directions, including (1) an increased understanding of the impact of individual emotional development on social change, (2) a realization of the centrality of psychological dynamics other than repression, and (3) the emergence of the "development distortion" model of neurosis as opposed to that of "unsuccessful repression."

Increased understanding of the role of emotions in social change may be illustrated in the area of technological advance. Based on

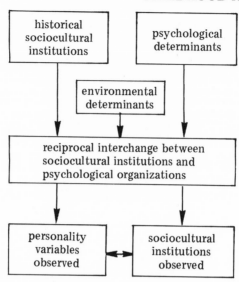

Fig. 2. Joel Aronoff's Revision of Whiting's Model

the purely cognitive abilities of man, the history of technology makes no sense at all. Examples are numerous: it took four millennia, from 3000 B.C. to 1000 A.D., for men to realize that the horse collar choked the horse, and that a collar fitting its shoulder would enable it to pull heavy loads. The ancient Greeks, who probably invented the water mill before the third century B.C., used it for only the most limited purposes. The Pre-Columbian Indians used the wheel for a toy but not for carrying goods or people. The only explanations for historical omissions like these lie in the area of psychology. Thus, Calvin Hall proposes the recognition that inventions are rooted in personal fantasy, not social need:

> Why do such things as faucets exist which can be used to symbolize the penis? No, we are not prankish. ... The motive power for behavior is a wish, not a purpose. The faucet was invented for the same reason that the young man dreamed his penis was a faucet. The inventor of the faucet was acting out *his* fantasy of a penis which could be turned on and off at will. ... Genes do not mutate in order to annihilate or to evolve a species. Nor was the faucet invented in order to supply man with a convenient and controllable source of water, although once in existence it proved to have such a use.[13]

Whether Hall is on the mark in this particular case is not as important as his quantum leap from impersonal to personal and affective sources—the sense that it is the feeling individual and not the inanimate institution or inorganic custom which is the source of change. As deMause has written, a truly psychogenic theory "reverses the relationship between physical and psychological reality, so that instead of material progress setting the pace of history and somehow dragging behind the psyches of its actors, human psychology is made primary—setting Marx on his head and Hegel back on his feet—and material reality is viewed as primarily the outcome of man's decisions, past or present, conscious or unconscious."[14] Writers such as Everett Hagen (*On the Theory of Social Change*) began showing that before the industrial revolution could take place, a new kind of personality, and a new kind of family to produce it, was necessary.[15] Such an inclination to completely reverse one's perspective is the initial radical leap necessary to the formulations of this book, for its empirical evidence is based on information and defined problems which previously would have been ignored.

Secondly, it is only recently that the value of regression has been recognized both in therapy and social process. Growing up for every child is not simply successful repression and channeling of instincts—it involves periodic regression to integrate earlier experiences into an ongoing unity. Unresolved issues and dynamics may achieve more satisfactory resolution through their reexperience. Kenneth Keniston recognizes the recuperative or regenerative nature of regression when he writes of "regression in the service of the ego—that is, the ability of the ego to, as it were, 'shut itself off' and truly remain open to the childish, the sexual, the creative, and the dream-like. The highest creativity, be it biological procreativity or artistic innovation, presupposes an ego that can abandon control of instinct and temporarily renounce a cognitive orientation so as to permit fantasy, orgasm, childbirth, even sleep." He adds, "The term 'regression in the service of the ego' is used to characterize creativity in all its forms, dreaming, openness to the childish and the archetypical, spontaneity of response."[16]

The concept of delegation, as formulated by family therapist Helm Stierlin, isolates the means by which tasks or missions may be transmitted by the older generation to the younger. This kind of task-creation has the child experience or "act out" what parents may envision and yearn for but cannot themselves obtain. As intimate aspects of socialization, the concept of delegation also encourages us to move beyond earlier and simpler concepts of repression.[17]

Finally, further developments in psychoanalytic theory, related to the first two points above, have replaced the "unsuccessful repression" model of neurosis by a new paradigm, a "developmental distortion" view of individual pathology. Based on Freud's later discovery that the ego itself is a source of repression and distortions in development, the model has been expanded through the works of Klein, Winnicott, Balint, Fairbairn, Guntrip, Meltzer, Rheingold, Apfelbaum, and Janov. The developmental distortion model sees the child as not naturally antisocial, but rather as undergoing developmental distortion and pathology only as a result of the continuous inability of the parent to meet its needs. Thus, neurosis or psychosis is always something done *to* the child. This is a more dynamic view of psychology by far, with greater potential for psychohistory, making repression and frustration not inevitable conditions of civilization but symptoms of a particular stage of evolution.

Drawing upon these broad movements, deMause conceptualized and articulated the following paradigm:[18]

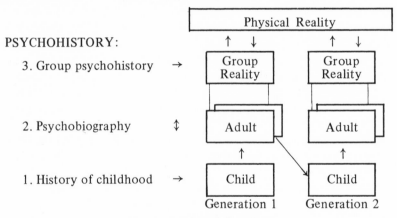

Fig. 3. DeMause's Paradigm

According to this revolutionary view, the evolution of childhood is the ultimate source for all new historical personalities, and the genes of historical change lie wholly in adult-child interactions.[19] The skeletal structure of the theory tracing such dynamics was posited by deMause in his 1974 introduction to *The History of Childhood*,[20] the only history of childhood in the West written expressly for psychohistorical purposes. DeMause there argues:

1. That the evolution of parent-child relations constitutes an independent source of historical change. The origin of this

evolution lies in the ability of successive generations of parents to regress to the psychic age of their children and work through the anxieties of that age in a better manner the second time they encounter them than they did during their own childhood. The process is similar to that of psychoanalysis, which also involves regression and a second chance to face childhood anxieties.

2. That this "generational pressure" for psychic change is not only spontaneous, originating in the adult's need to regress and in the child's striving for relationship, but also occurs independent of social and tehnological change. It therefore can be found even in periods of social and technological stagnation.

3. That the history of childhood is a series of closer approaches between adult and child, with each closing of psychic distance producing fresh anxiety. The reduction of this adult anxiety is the main source of the child-rearing practices of each age.

4. That the obverse of the hypothesis that history involves a general improvement in child care is that the further back one goes in history, the less effective parents are in meeting the developing needs of the child. This would indicate, for instance, that if today in America there are less than a million abused children, there would be a point back in history where most children were what we would now consider abused.

5. That because psychic structure must always be passed from generation to generation through the narrow funnel of childhood, a society's child-rearing practices are not just one item in a list of cultural traits. They are the very condition for the transmission and development of all other cultural elements, and place definite limits on what can be achieved in all other spheres of history. Specific childhood experiences must occur to sustain specific cultural traits, and once these experiences no longer occur the trait disappears.

As deMause has stated elsewhere, whereas repression freezes the historical personality, regression allows the parent and child to invent history anew in each generation. Scholars are prone to lament that man has a longer infancy than other animals; yet this long infancy (and lack of fixed instincts) gives man a history. It is therefore perfectly appropriate, he contends, that "the end result of five billion years of evolution is to produce a helpless baby, completely dependent, whose central instinct is to form an intensely personal relationship."[2][1]

Given this area of supreme importance—childhood—it was then possible to undertake a maiden voyage into the past in order to examine (1) the historical realities of the evolution of childhood, (2) the evolution of culture, and (3) the correlation between the two. DeMause's survey of the history of childhood in the West did indeed illustrate a progressive, clearly identifiable evolution of parent-child relations, a reality which could be documented and charted. The results were expressed in the following graph:[2][1]

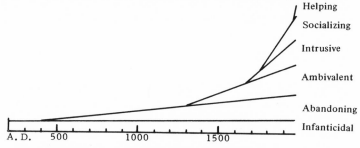

Fig. 4. DeMause's Psychogenic Modes of Childhood in the West

A brief description of the six stages, and the approximate dates when an advanced group of parents first reached each new level of parent-child evolution, is contained in the following summary, taken from deMause's article "The Evolution of Childhood":[2][2]

1. *Infanticidal Mode (Antiquity to Fourth Century A.D.)*: The image of Medea hovers over children in antiquity, for myth here only reflects reality. Some facts are more important than others, and when parents routinely resolved their anxieties about taking care of children by killing them, it affected the surviving children profoundly. For those who were allowed to grow up, the projective reaction was paramount, and the concreteness of reversal was evident in the widespread sodomizing of the child.

2. *Abandonment Mode (Fourth to Thirteenth Century A.D.)*: Once parents began to accept the child as having a soul, the only way they could escape the dangers of their own projections was by abandonment, whether to the wet nurse, to the monastery or nunnery, to foster families, to the homes of other nobles as servants or hostages, or by severe emotional abandonment at home. The symbol of this mode might be Griselda, who so willingly abandoned her children to prove her love for her husband. Or perhaps

it would be any of those pictures so popular up to the thirteenth century of a rigid Mary stiffly holding the infant Jesus. Projection continued to be massive, since the child was still full of evil and needed always to be beaten, but as the reduction in child sodomizing shows, reversal diminished considerably.

3. *Ambivalent Mode (Fourteenth to Seventeenth Centuries)*: Because the child, when it was allowed to enter into the parents' emotional life, was still a container for dangerous projections, it was their task to mold it into shape. From Dominici to Locke there was no image more popular than that of the physical molding of children, who were seen as soft wax, plaster, or clay to be beaten into shape. Enormous ambivalance marks this mode. The beginning of the period is approximately the fourteenth century, which shows an increase in the number of child instruction manuals, the expansion of the cults of Mary and the infant Jesus, and the proliferation in art of the "close-mother image."

4. *Intrusive Mode (Eighteenth Century)*: A tremendous reduction in projection and the virtual disappearance of reversal was the accomplishment of the great transition for parent-child relations which appeared in the eighteenth century. The child was no longer so full of dangerous projections, and rather than just examine its insides with an enema, the parents approached even closer and attempted to conquer its mind, in order to control its insides, its anger, its needs, its masturbation, its very will. The child raised by intrusive parents was nursed by the mother, not swaddled, not given regular enemas, toilet trained early, prayed with but not played with, hit but not regularly whipped, punished for masturbation, and made to obey promptly with threats and guilt as often as with other methods of punishment. The child was so much less threatening that true empathy was possible, and pediatrics was born, which along with the general improvement in level of care by parents reduced infant mortality and provided the basis for the demographic transition of the eighteenth century.

5. *Socialization Mode (Nineteenth to Mid-twentieth Centuries)*: As projections continued to diminish, the raising of a child became less a process of conquering its will than of training it, guiding it into proper paths, teaching it to conform, socializing it. The socializing mode

is still thought of by most people as the only model
within which discussion of child care can proceed, and it
has been the source of all twentieth-century psychological
models, from Freud's "channeling of impulses" to
Skinner's behaviorism. It is most particularly the model of
sociological functionalism. Also, in the nineteenth
century, the father for the first time begins to take more
than an occasional interest in the child, training it, and
sometimes even relieving the mother of child-care chores.

6. *Helping Mode (Begins Mid-twentieth Century)*: The
helping mode involves the proposition that the child
knows better than the parent what it needs at each stage
of its life, and fully involves both parents in the child's life
as they work to empathize with and fulfill its expanding
and particular needs. There is no attempt at all to
discipline or form "habits." Children are neither struck
nor scolded, and are apologized to if yelled at under
stress. The helping mode involves an enormous amount of
time, energy, and discussion on the part of both parents,
especially in the first six years, for helping a young child
reach its daily goals means continually responding to it,
playing with it, tolerating its regressions, being its servant
rather than the other way around, interpreting its
emotional conflicts, and providing the objects specific to
its evolving interests.

DeMause's synthesis of the Darwinian and Freudian models
provides us with a new paradigm for the understanding of
historical change. It also enables us to conceptualize idealized
personality typologies associated with the successive child-rearing
modes. Thus, an overview of the evolution of personality is
presented with the understanding that leaps and lags, permutations
and combinations, are always possible. Another crucial point is
that what in one period is considered normative is seen in another
time as psychotic or neurotic.

In his article "The Formation of the American Personality
Through Psychospeciation," deMause presents the following chart
summarizing psychogenic modes with their main historical
manifestations:[2][3]

| Mode | Parental Wish | Historical Manifestations |
|------|---------------|---------------------------|
| Infanticidal | Mother: "I wish you were dead, to relieve my fear of being killed by my mother." | Child-sacrifice and infanticide, child as breast-penis, intolerance of child's anger, hardening, ghosts and magic, child sale, child sodomy |
| Abandoning | Mother: "I must leave you, to escape the needs I project into you." | Longer swaddling, fosterage, outside wetnursing, monastery, nunnery and apprenticeship |
| Ambivalent | Mother: "You are bad from the erotic and aggressive projections I put in you." | Enemas, early beating, shorter swaddling, mourning possible, child as erotic object precursor to empathy |
| Intrusive | Mother: "You can have love when I have full control over you." | Early toilet training, repression of child's sexuality, end of swaddling and wetnursing, empathy now possible, rise of pediatrics |
| Socializing | Mother and Father: "We will love you when you are reaching our goals." | Use of guilt, "mental discipline", humiliation, rise of compulsory schooling, delegation of parental unconscious wishes |
| Helping | Mother and Father: "We love you and will help you reach your goals." | Children's rights, de-schooling and free schooling, child therapy, birth without violence |

Figure 5.  Psychogenic Modes and Their Main Historical Manifestations

Each psychogenic mode, each of the six main family types, corresponds, according to deMause, to a personality type that determines the values and emotional structure for the corresponding historical group:[2 4]

| Infanticidal Mode | Schizoid Personality | Primary-process thinking, symbiotic omnipotence, gender/zonal confusion, splitting and projective identification, sado-masochistic disorders |
|-------------------|----------------------|--------------------------------------------------------------------------------------------------------------------------------------|
| Abandoning Mode | Autistic Personality | Unrelated, narcissistic, exploitive, parasitic, distrustful, oral rage, self weak or grandiose, psychopathic, unable to tolerate delay, lacking in remorse, idealized mother, timeless |
| Ambivalent Mode | Depressive Personality | Guilty and depressed, insatiable in needs for love, status, sex, enormous superego demands, reality of time |
| Intrusive Mode | Compulsive Personality | Pseudorational, cold, detached, self-critical inwardly, phobic, obsessive-compulsive and conversion symptoms |
| Socializing Mode | Anxiety Personality | Less rigid character armor, free-floating anxiety and dissatisfaction with life due to delegate-living, loss of individuality in group, incomplete feelings |
| Helping Mode | | None yet adult |

Fig. 6.  Personality Types by Psychogenic Modes

DeMause's taxonomy of personality types is partially supported by two recent psychoanalytic writers, each of whom confirms a portion of his schema while explaining similar dynamics. Benjamin Wolman describes three main types of families: (1) Narcissistic-Hyperinstrumental (deMause's Abandoning) which produces psychopathic narcissism, (2) Depressive-Dysmutual (deMause's Ambivalent) which produces depressive personality problems, and (3) Schizo-Hypervectorial (deMause's Intrusive) which produces obsessional problems.[25] Similarly, family therapist Helm Stierlin's Expelling, Binding, and Delegating family types correspond to deMause's middle three main psychogenic modes.[26]

Some additional remarks on this skeletal presentation of the psychogenic theory of history are in order. First, the analogy of psychic to physical evolution is obviously not mechanical. The analogy is useful only to the extent that both obey lawful principles and proceed in dynamic, identifiable stages. In both cases, mechanisms may be isolated which help to account for the creation of new forms—whether through through parent-child interactions or the mutation of DNA. In both cases, older fossilized forms continue to coexist with advanced organisms. Some psychospecies, like some biological species, may prove more adaptive and therefore more likely to predominate.

The limitations of the analogy are many. For instance, students in the physical sciences, upon viewing biological evolutionary data, are struck by the "messiness" of the resulting curve, the fluctuations from established pattern that defy clean and facile generalizations, as well as the difficulties in repeating experimental conditions. Such difficulties are also apparent in the area of psychic evolution. This is so for many reasons:

(1) As deMause has pointed out, parenting types readily merge and are "recombined" in marriage.[27] While the genes merge in the gamete, one female and one male set, the genetic materials remain stable and may be traced; yet any type of parent may marry another. Compounding the problem, parents may change, and nonparents may take care of the child.

(2) Whereas in early forms of biological evolutionary development only an inkling of future form is visible, as in the embryonic lung in certain fishes or the beginning of arms in certain amphibious creatures, much more advanced behavior may be seen at times in earlier psychogenic forms. An infanticidal parent, in ancient Greece or in contemporary America, may have moments of empathy toward his or her child, especially when the child is not demanding something; still, the *predominating* effect is

established by the parents' infanticidal "battering."

(3) Another dimension of complexity lies in the very nature of human interaction. Against the gross classifiable "facts" of biological evolution we must set the human psychological spectrum that runs from homicidal and physical acts to symbolism, verbalization, and even unexpressed wishes. Such variety is always difficult to classify.

(4) Psychic evolution is more rapid than physical evolution and continually accelerates its pace. Whereas physical evolution proceeds in the measure of geological time and can therefore be dated according to geological formations, psychic evolution occurs in increasingly narrow bands of time, each mode taking less "space," more advanced forms requiring less growth time before moving to the next stage.

(5) Substantiation of the existence of psychospecies is more difficult than in the case of physical species. Emotions are not recorded in fossil bones, particularly before the invention and perfection of writing, when the record of psychospeciation was nearly obliterated with the deaths of people.


This book seeks to directly apply the psychogenic theory and, in so doing, to illustrate that its power lies in the fact that it is not an invention but a discovery. Part II seeks to understand the evolution of American childhood from 1840 to 1965, thus placing deMause's socializing mode under a microscope. The socializing mode will be found to have evolved in four discrete stages, here defined as submodes. Each submode is approximately a generation (thirty years) in length. The outer ranges serve as guides, not precise borders. The chart below illustrates my submodal conclusions, and their definitions follow.

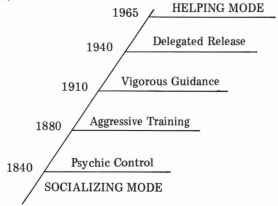

Fig. 7. Socializing Submodes of Childhood in America

(1) *Psychic Control* (c. 1840-1880): Each submode of socialization may be said to have two sides: the hard, socializing, adult-oriented side and the soft, child-oriented side. The soft side of psychic control is the "psychic" aspect, wherein physical, more blatant means of control are replaced by psychological means. The hard or "control" side lies in the intensity of psychological socialization—the child is seen as a dangerous, potentially explosive creature. Intensive psychological authority bonds of parent over child are created, producing guilt as a normative dynamic and a high degree of parental projection into the child. The child thus created is a moralistic-didactic being, compelled to reach out and control its environment, concerned with its own energy and with directing it into the social sphere in order to control and organize society, to regiment it and bring it into a coherent and more viable intimacy. This urge for unity takes on fantasized, unrealistic proportions. The primary missions delegated by the adult generation are directed toward the child's superego.

(2) *Aggressive Training* (c. 1880-1910): The soft side of the second submode lies in the reduction in the intensity of authority bonds and parental projections, in which intergenerational relations rely less on the imposition of open guilt patterns and on stringent emotional and instinctual controls. Distancing measures are reduced somewhat and previously internalized tensions are focused outward and manifested in a new concern with the child's place in society. In the process of child rearing, "the child within the parent" becomes less threatening, requiring less drastic defense structures. The resulting aggressive child has more flexibility and autonomy than his controlled predecessor, is less didactic, wishes to promote societal organization in a more pragmatic manner, has less (though still considerable) compulsion to take personal control and to affirm personal strength through powers of mind or body. Thus the child's social attempts are characteristically more successful, less resembling personal virility-puberty rites. The hard side lies in the fact that though the child is not psychically *controlled*, it is aggressively *trained*. Articulated parental standards of achievement reach new levels of refinement and the aggressive and competitive pursuit of goals is stressed. The discipline earlier associated with control of instinct is now directed to the facility and potency of social interaction. The child must still fight his way to adulthood. The primary delegated missions are those of the ego.

(3) *Vigorous Guidance* (c. 1910-1940): The soft side of rigorous guidance involves a further reduction of authority bonds, a reduction of parental projections, more empathy, and the

emergence of the modern child. It is in this period that a more sophisticated science of child behavior begins to describe the stage of evolution in which the parent can begin to accept behaviors stemming from the internal desires of the child. In sum, psychoanalysis and the new psychology can be seen in reference to the history of childhood as a manifestation of the ability of some to draw closer to their own childhood and to look deeply at "the child within," moving beyond multilayered defense structures and confronting a primal pool of pain, allowing for the reduction of parental projections upon the child and increased empathy. This empathetic ability, at first somewhat conceptual and intellectual, later evolves into a more complete, visceral response. It is during this period that the progressive school flourishes, child labor laws are passed in quantity, and minimal levels of infant treatment are spelled out. But on the hard side, the child, though not aggressive, is a vigorous being of competition and desire to show metal, whether mental or physical. Though less ruled by rigid precepts of conscience than the control child, and less socially competitive than the aggressive child, determination marks the desire to achieve more fluid and complex social interactions. The child's life missions are still primarily derived from the parental ego.

(4) *Delegated Release* (1940-1965): The soft side of this final stage of socialization under consideration involves a further decrease in authority bonding, greater empathy, a further decrease in parental projections, the beginnings of the developmental distortion view of personality formation, and greater childhood freedoms. This submode, the submode of the Spock mothers, is widely considered the liberal method of child care. The hard side involves the delegation of id missions, still placing delegated release within the socializing mode. Distorted parental id expressions and the conscious recognition of parental frustration, especially the limitations imposed upon the mother in contemporary culture and her isolation in the process of child rearing, motivate imposition of id or sensual missions upon the young. It is hoped that the child will experience the expansive, holistic freedoms which the parents were denied.[28]

The hard and soft sides of the four submodes may thus be divided terminologically as follows:

|    | HARD       | SOFT     |
|----|------------|----------|
| 1. | control    | psychic  |
| 2. | aggressive | training |
| 3. | vigorous   | guidance |
| 4. | delegated  | release  |

The evolution of American childhood that I have outlined will be documented by isolating various cultural parameters—the child and religion, fiction, education, infant training practices, maternity-paternity, child sexuality, and, most importantly, the concrete area of actual parental behaviors and perceptions. This is consonant with the psychogenic perspective that "culture" is the manifestation of a level of psychic growth, and that every aspect of it may be traced to its psychic precursor in infancy and childhood. My documentation therefore draws on a variety of source materials: works on the care of infants and children, medical texts, popular medical literature, children's literature and criticism, primary source materials such as diaries, letters, and journals, official government proceedings and reports, psychology texts, secondary sources concerned with parenthood and the family, and recent studies of the historiography of childhood.

The distinction between a submodal evolution of childhood and a narrative history of childhood cannot be overstated. The process of tracing the evolution of submodes involves the identification of innovation—the appearance of forms which did not previously exist. If a submode is to be of evolutionary importance, it begins a trend, draws a growing segment of the population along with it, and eventually forms the basis from which a new submode grows. Yet *submodal analysis does not necessarily say anything about the precise numerical frequency of forms within a culture.*

Rather than a narrative of the history of childhood, or a statistical statement, the four submodes of socialization are the building blocks or elements of the childhood population at any one time. As each new submode grows in numerical frequency, it begins to dominate the literature of child rearing, although the actual number of children being brought up in this new submode remains statistically small. The new child-rearing literature somehow succeeds in reaching the "soft" or "child-oriented' side within each adult even though they still bring up their own children according to older submodes. The reality of childhood culture, then, is an internal architecture of submodal elements undergoing various processes such as evolution, numerical growth, recombination, and decay.

The dating of the evolution of childhood portrayed in these pages centers around identifiable periods of the inception and growth of new child-rearing patterns. The psychic control submode of 1840 to 1880, for example, is not a picture of the childhood experience of the total population, but rather of the introduction of the submode by a radical group of parents—in its infancy around 1840, and setting a pattern of growth by the late

1870s. My selection of materials presented here from the over two thousand primary sources which I examined convinces me that toward the end of each submode the new themes have come to predominate in the literature and to make some inroads in becoming the main trend of childhood culture. Only parents brought up in the predominant submode, in turn, are able to bring up their own children in yet newer submodes.

The knowledge of the submodal elements of society allows for an entirely new perspective on American history, a view of its internal architecture. Part III, "Themes of Twentieth-Century America," seeks to show how the evolution of childhood is the cause of the evolution of American society. Progressivism, the New Deal, and the dynamics of the post-World War II period and the 1960s are shown to be respective evolutionary expressions of the four submodes. Because the term submode describes a childhood experience, and not individuals, the term psychoclass is used in deMause's sense of a group of adults united by the same childhood submode. History can therefore be described as the expression and interaction of psychoclasses.

## REFERENCES

1. The major statements of the psychogenic theory of history can be found in Lloyd deMause, "The Evolution of Childhood," in *The History of Childhood*, ed. deMause (New York: Psychohistory Press, 1974); deMause, "The Independence of Psychohistory," in *The New Psychohistory*, ed. deMause (New York: Psychohistory Press, 1975); deMause, "Minutes of the First Summer Workshop," *Bulletin of the Institute for Psychohistory* I (1975); deMause, "The Formation of the American Personality Through Psychospeciation," *The Journal of Psychohistory* 4 (1976): 1-20.

2. Harry Guntrip, *Personality Structure and Human Interaction* (London: Hogarth Press, 1961), p. 67.

3. Charles Rosenberg, ed., *The Family in History* (Philadelphia: University of Pennsylvania Press, 1975).

4. Sigmund Freud, *Civilization and Its Discontents*, trans. James Strachey (New York: W. W. Norton, 1962).

5. deMause, "Minutes of the First Summer Workshop."

6. *Ibid.*

7. *Ibid.*

8. *Ibid.*

9. *Ibid.*

10. Bernard Apfelbaum, "On Ego Psychology: A Critique of the Structural Approach to Psycho-Analytic Theory,"

*International Journal of Psycho-Analysis* 47 (19660: 451-52.

11. John Whiting, "A Model for Psycho-Cultural Research." Distinguished Lecture at the 72nd annual meeting of the American Anthropological Association, printed in their program.

12. Joel Aronoff, "The Cane-Cutters of St. Kitts," *Psychology Today*, January 1971.

13. deMause, "Minutes of the First Summer Workshop."

14. deMause, "The Independence of Psychohistory."

15. Everett Hagen, *On the Theory of Social Change* (Homewood: Dorsey Press, 1962).

16. Kenneth Keniston, *The Uncommitted: Alienated Youth in American Society* (New York: Harcourt, Brace and World, 1960.

17. Helm Stierlin, *Separating Parents and Adolescents* (New York: Quadrangle, 1972).

18. For more on the differences between the models of "unsuccessful repression" and "developmental distortion," see Apfelbaum, "On Ego Psychology."

19. deMause, "The Independence of Psychohistory," p. 12.

20. deMause, "The Evolution of Childhood," p. 3.

21. deMause, "Minutes of the First Summer Workshop."

22. deMause, "The Evolution of Childhood," pp. 51-52.

23. deMause, "The Formation of the American Personality Through Psychospeciation," p. 4.

24. *Ibid.*

25. Benjamin B. Wolman, *Call No Man Normal* (New York: International Universities Press, 1973).

26. Stierlin, *Separating Parents and Adolescents.*

27. deMause, "Psychospeciation," p. 23.

28. For a discussion of the Helping Mode, see *The History of Childhood*, pp. 52-54. Secondary literature on the history of childhood in America is not extensive. For an idea of the extant materials, see Faye Sinofsky et al., "A Bibliography of Psychohistory," *History of Childhood Quarterly* (Spring, 1975). For unpublished materials not likely to appear in published bibliographies, see: Helen H. Davis, "Conceptions of Child Nature and Training from 1825-1880 (unpublished Master's thesis, University of Cincinnati, 1936); E. A. Wilson, "Hygienic Care and Management of the Child in the American Family Prior to 1860" (unpublished Master's thesis, Duke University, 19400; Iris Culver Meadow, "Concepts of Child Nature in American Life and Education, 1800-1900 (dissertation, University of Missouri, 1951); Elaine Damis,

"The History of Child Rearing Advice in America, 1800-1940" (Honor's thesis, Radcliffe College, 1960); Geoffrey Steere, "Changing Values in Child Socialization" (dissertation, University of Pennsylvania, 1964); Ernest Belden, "A History of the Child Study Movement, 1870-1920" (dissertation, University of California, 1965); Anne Trensky, "The Cult of the Child in Minor American Fiction" (dissertation, City University of New York, 1969); see also, Anne S. Macleod, "For the Good of the Country" (paper read at the Children's Literature Association, Storrs, Connecticut, March, 1974) and "Children's Fiction and American Culture, 1820-1860" (dissertation, University of Maryland, 1973); Peter Slater, "Views of Children and of Child Rearing During the Early National Period" (dissertation, University of California, 1970); Michael Sulman, "The Freudianization of the American Child" (dissertation, University of Pittsburgh, 1972); Jimmy Chapman, "Changes in the Concepts of Childhood Education" (dissertation, University of Texas, 1972); Ray Hiner, "Images of Youth on the Eve of the Great Awakening" (paper read at the American Educational Association, Chicago, 1974); Lynn Bloom, "It's All For Your Own Good" (paper read at Popular Culture Association, Milwaukee, May, 1974).

PART II: THE EVOLUTION OF AMERICAN CHILDHOOD

1840-1965

CHAPTER TWO

PSYCHIC CONTROL, 1840-1880

The meaning of "psychic control"—a state characterized by intensive guilt, repressive of personal feelings, a strong authority bond between parent and child, and low parental empathy—is most clearly revealed in the detailed child-rearing records kept by two pioneering parents during the 1830s: the ministers Bronson Alcott and Francis Wayland.

Bronson Alcott kept detailed records of his three daughters from their births: Anna in 1831, Louisa in 1832, Elizabeth in 1835. By 1836 he had twenty-five hundred pages of manuscript, the first such record by a parent in history, and a telling testimony to the new interest being taken in the child. In a sweeping experiment, a leap into the realm of psychic control, Alcott resolved to abandon the use of the rod. This was a novel approach to the rearing of children, which had traditionally involved "breaking the will" through force or neglect. Moving much closer to the child than was the common practice, Alcott insisted on close, intimate contact during the first years of life. Even servants were not permitted to handle Anna.

These novel resolves were no indication of leniency or of a willingness to forego stringent parental control. Rather, they symbolized the institution of a more intensive and thoroughgoing *moral* control in which the child's drives would be severely held in check. Though Alcott takes the liberal position that the child is not born damned, and that to a certain degree the child's animal nature must be tolerated, his language must be read cautiously. For example, he wrote in seemingly advanced language that "The *child* must be *treated* as a *free, self-guiding, self-controlling* being. He must be allowed to feel that he is under his own guidance; and that all external guidance is an injustice which is done to his nature unless his own will is intelligently submissive to it."[1] Yet, Alcott's meaning becomes clear only in the context of his other notes, which indicate that a radical conscience must be bred into the child and be so rigidly developed that little outside guidance would be necessary after a certain point of maturation. In the words of one childhood historian, "Alcott expected nothing less than moral perfection from his daughters, and to that end . . . child-rearing must go forward under perfect parental control."[2] Alcott devised rigid schedules for his daughters, who were expected to rise at six in the morning, wash and dress, and breakfast at seven. There followed study, play, more schooling, and bedtime at 7:30 in the evening. The sisters were kept apart from each other much of the day to ensure their serious development. The price of any move toward independence was the severe withdrawal of approval and love, a classic technique of psychic control. The family had become what historian Stephen Kern would later refer to as a hotbed of intimacy, a unit insulated from the rest of the world and one in which close-knit, intimate relationships are bound by the dynamics of guilt and insecurity. The result is the substitution of moral for physical coercion, a subtler though still total domination of the child's inner life through conditional love and the institutionalization of a uniquely effective inner policeman.

Another early mother writes in her diary about the process of training her young daughter in the ethic of stoicism, and is obviously pleased at the child's ability to control her impulses:

> Our little daughter . . . was born January 5th, 1832. . . . Before she was quite a year old, we began to correct her for crying. This has been a severe but wholesome discipline. It has taught her a command over her feelings, which we trust may be of great service in her subsequent life. Now, when she is grieved or displeased, unless she is in a bad humor from Godly suffering, she will suppress the disposition to cry, often with a very perceptible struggle and effort. But, even when she is unwell, and blurts into a loud cry, we generally correct her, until she suppresses it. . . . In this discipline, we

sometimes used the rod; but more frequently shut her in a room alone, until she became quiet.[3]

Here we see another instance of the transition to psychic control: the hesitation concerning the use of corporal punishment, the threat and enactment of separation from the intimacy of the family, both bent on the goal of repression of the emotions.

The experience of Francis Wayland during the same decade was very similar, as shown in an anonymous letter to a periodical in 1831, later discovered to be written by Wayland.[4] (Wayland's major literary work was *The Elements of Moral Science*, 1835.) Wayland's mode of child rearing, actually more severe than Alcott, illustrates the border line between physical and psychic control—the minister resorting to both methods on occasion as his mood took him. His writings contain older, overt dictates of authority: "The *right* of the parent is to *command*; the *duty* of the child is to *obey*. Authority belongs to the one, submission to the other."[5] "In infancy the control of the parent over the child is absolute; that is, it is exercised without any due respect to the wishes of the child." Wayland elaborates:

In as much as the present state of man is morally imperfect, and every individual (young and old) is a sharer in that imperfection, it is the duty of the parent to eradicate so far as in [his] power the wrong propensities of his children. He should watch them with ceaseless vigilance for the first appearance of pride, obstinacy, malice, envy, vanity, cruelty, revenge, anger, lying.[6]

Wayland, who was president of Brown University from 1827, had his first child in 1826. He lost another child in the first year of his presidency, and his wife died in 1834. He filled his writings with the preachings of both physical control and the progressive measures of an emerging psychic control. In the letter with which we are here concerned, he describes his use of the older physical mode, as opposed to the newer psychic control, when his child Herman refused to eat. He proceeded to make the fifteen-month-old child fast, a condition which lasted for thirty-six hours, until the child's will was broken and he finally submitted to taking food from his father. Along with such physical brutality came the Alcott kind of moral control—concern with discipline, training, and schedule. The same boy who had been starved by Wayland later illustrated a massive degree of reaction formation and repression in his letters to a brother in 1852, when his father was fifty-six: "Do you ever, Frank, look forward to that time when we must part with Father? I can hardly bear to do so and yet I sometimes for a moment have done so. It is sad to think of standing by his bedside or having him stand by ours and bidding him goodbye for the last time . . . unless you are concerted, that gulf is between you and Father forever." After his father's death, Herman wrote: "Did you ever remark the resemblance between his character and that of Jesus of Nazareth. I speak with reverence. His unselfishness, his care for others, his courage, for righteousness and justice, his sympathy for the suffering, his pity for the fallen, his prayerfulness."[7]

Such is the level of repression at the dawn of psychic control, in which feelings of aggression toward the parent are buried deeply in the unconscious and are expressed, if at all, only in displaced forms or on the symbolic level. Idealization of the parents and a massive lack of self-worth demanding continual effort are the common result. It is this massive superego which is the staple product of psychic control, its omnipresence diffusing itself throughout mid- to late-nineteenth-century American life.


## RELIGION AS CONTROL

The inbreeding of conscience and moral fervor through psychic means is extremely evident in the cultural parameter of religion. Religion affords a unique glimpse into the issues of authority and submission, and it will be argued that all religion in the mind of the child is a reflection of intergenerational dynamics. Religious developments in this period illustrate that the parent has moved from the role of policeman of an essentially evil being, to that of a creator of societal progress who imposes the most total, subtle, and effective controls. Whereas in the eighteenth century's intrusive mode the child is *relegated*, he is now *delegated*, bound to specific goals and aspiration—often latent and unconscious—entirely defined by the parental world. The following stanza may be considered the paradigm of the religious parameter of psychic control:

Remember, children of the earth,
Each house is in its way
Bearing its own report to heaven,
Of all you do and say.[8]

Religion served to bind the child to his own developing superego, transposed upon him by a vigilant adult generation.

The diary of twelve-year-old E. M. Olcott illustrates this aspect. The youth begins, "God has spared my life to another year, but I fear I am not thankful enough to Him for it. But I trust He will make me more so." For young Olcott, God is a consciously personified entity, described as an authoritarian adult, an adult whose good feelings are forthcoming in strict relation to proper behavior: "Oh, how much I enjoy being in Sabbath School. . . . I think God has helped me more tonight. For I feel conscious of being more kind to the children and I know my lessons. But I must not be proud and give God my thanks."[9] There is a painful awareness of conditional affection, of a love which may be turned abruptly off; yet, even beyond this is a more fearful realization that God (the idealized parent) may continue to love *in spite of* the child's transgressions, leaving the crime (as fully defined by society) unpunished and the guilt intensified. *Days at Muirhead*, a typical didactic novel, describes a naughty school boy, concerning whom the author writes: "God had forgiven him, it was true; but do you think *he* ever forgot that he had made his father and mother ashamed and sorrowful, and given such pain to the kind hearts that were so bound to his? We can't sin alone—others will suffer, must suffer, through our sins."[10]

Young Olcott writes, "It seems strange to me. It seems impossible that I *do not* love Christ who has done so much for me; yet I am sure I do not." In relaying a sermon, Olcott has understood that transgression can never be unintentional but that one must take full responsibility: "The apostle Paul does not tell us when we sin against God that we are careless or negligent—but he says that we *trample on the son of God*. Everyone was moved to tears."[11]

In order to reinforce a system in which the child must take full responsibility for transgressions, fearful consequences are necessary. These horrid punishments must be as inscrutable as the authority which invokes them, and they must be so powerful that mere nuance from the parent conjures their spectre. The slightest adult projection upon the child may precipitate an atmosphere of fear. Nothing is more suited to this purpose than the most inscrutable aspect of existence: death. Thoughts of deaths and their function in reinforcing authority bonds are a daily fact of life, experienced most intensely on Sunday; the spectre of death surrounds the child. One youth asks, "Oh, where will I be this time next year? Perhaps I will be living but oh! Perhaps I shall be in eternity." Another records, "I can count in our family during the past two years, seven deaths. Oh what a warning it should be to me! Last night after having been to the funeral it seemed as if I heard a *voice* whispering warnings into my ear and telling me to prepare to die." Olcott's journal includes a description of a life imprisoned within morose emotions, relating information about a friend Katie who expects to die soon, "May God promise her life." The journal dutifully records cases of children who have died, interspersed with resolutions to conquer the temptation to sin.[12] The Reverend James Janeway earlier reminded children that a fate of premature death could mean the ultimate disaster: damnation. "Every mother's child of you are by nature children of wrath," and, "Oh! Hell is a terrible place; that is worse a thousand times than whipping." The reverend's popular writings are obsessed with the child's relation to death, so that thirteen chapters of a book are each devoted to a child who died. One child was good, feared wicked company, and read the Scriptures regularly; yet he "grew weaker and weaker . . . and at last did cheerfully submit his spirit unto the Lord. . . ." Janeway asked his youthful readers, "How do you know that you may be the next child that may die?"[13]

We see the same obsession in the diary of Louis P. Gratalap, age twelve, of Staten Island: "Death had not touched us. O! How kind, how merciful, has God been." He adds that his mother kept working through hard times, continuing to keep off disaster.[14] James Black composed a book (c. 1861) in the typical didactic-anecdotal style of writing popular during the period, including a vignette in which a mother states, "True enough! yes Richard, the great God has made such a close connection between sin and suffering, that if you break any of his laws . . . you will be sure to suffer . . . for sin has a strange faculty of punishing itself."[15]

The use of death and religion is crucial as a means of control, as a vehicle for expressing a level of psychological maturation requiring an intensive authority bond over the child in order to retain stability. Several documents are illustrative here. The Massachusetts Sabbath Society's contribution, a short piece for girls entitled *Broken Idols* and evidently composed by a pastor, chronicles a nightmarish course of events. A young girl commits the "crime" of continuing to read rather than watch after a young sister—who subsequently crawls about, catches a draft, and almost dies from a severe relapse of fever. Fear of a terrifying inscrutable God who can only be interpreted by parents, who in comparison to God seem gentle, prompts a full and intensive confession to the mother: "Well, Mama, can't I love him [God], too? I want to love him, so I won't be afraid of the dark. He won't let anything hurt me." The mother retorts, "Feeling cross isn't wrong, my dear, if you don't give way to it, for you can not always help the feeling. The sin is in giving way to the wrong feeling, and acting as it prompts you." Thus comes repression, and punishment is integrated into the plot. The girl eventually goes blind, yet never loses faith in a just and merciful deity.[16]

The Congregationalists offered *Above and Below; or, Why the Baby Died*, in which the possible dangers of unbridled aggression and uncontrolled emotion are illustrated. An angry boy pushes his young sister, who hits her head and almost dies. His mother chides him, repressing her grief and quietly reminding the boy that angry children do not go to heaven. To make the moral stew more potent, the child has a younger brother already in heaven and is reminded by his mother that his sibling could be looking down upon him. The boy is dismissed, his mother quietly stating, "I think you had better go to your own chamber, and think about your sin . . . and ask your heavenly Father to forgive you."[17]

The concept of death as a fearful retribution, rendering the child completely impotent, was simply a part of daily life. A child is quoted in a contemporary magazine: "Mother, why don't you get somebody to *kill* little Isaac." The article continues to describe the creation of a powerful childhood superego: "In his solitude, the child had contemplated his misdemeanor as a sin against goodness, until self-loathing came over him, and he imagined the heaviest doom did not transcend his doubts."[18] Another source quotes a girl as follows: "A little girl was discovered lying on the bed in her own room passionately weeping . . . 'Oh dear! I am so afraid I shall live till everybody is dead that I love, and not a creature will be left to cry at my funeral.' "[19] Another child writes, in a morbid diary typical of many of the period, of her gratefulness for life, recounting how a girl in Sabbath class was struck by melancholia, crying aloud suddenly. God is such an immediate experience that the girl attributes her slightly elevated spirits to God's intervention, for "God has helped me more tonight," but the thought of the future, the dawn of 1854, is seen as a possible termination: "Perhaps I shall be in eternity." A few years later, still alive, the child thanks God for her outlasting a bout of measles, noting that a friend died of fever and adding of an ailing companion, "May God preserve her life!"[20] Another remembers that "whenever there is a funeral in a church, we children like to go to it," and relates the sad story of a friend who was cross to her sister and promptly witnessed the sister's death (implying guilt through association). The girl vividly portrays how she would cry upon hearing her friends repeat the story.[21]

The most explosive issue concerning the child and religion was the question of infant damnation. Under the dominion of earlier modes, there was never any question: physical control always implied the belief that the child must be restrained to prevent his evil nature from wreaking havoc. Now a new dynamic put in its appearance: the ability to move beyond original sin, but only at the price of considerable anxiety. If a child's fate is not to be considered as predetermined, it is the parents' awesome responsibility to determine it.

The older view of the child did not suddenly disappear under the onslaught of the newer views. One does not have to comb many sermons for evidence of a surviving Calvinism. Thus Rev. S. M. Kuhns states in the *Lutheran Quarterly* that the doctrine of infant damnation still holds and that children must manifest some sign of conversion before they can be considered for Church membership. Jacob Burns writes: "Never forget that they possess a depraved nature, prone to all evil. . . . a child left to his own way will bring ruin on himself, and sorrow and disgrace his parents. . . . You cannot begin too early. Long before your child can speak, he is susceptible of moral training." B. F. Barrett illustrates the tensions between old and new in concluding by way of compromise that the child has evil "tendencies." Another writer states that children born of evil parents may be saved in heaven.[22]

It is not surprising that Horace Bushnell's *Christian Nurture*, a statement of the soft side of psychic control, created a storm of controversy. It was shocking to many to have a clergyman commit to writing the notion that infant damnation was an erroneous doctrine, that the child may simply have bad tendencies or, more radically, be a blank slate. It follows logically that parenting (called Christian nurture) rises in importance; it is never too early to begin since the early years are "most pliant to good." Education may triumph over evil, even over that which points toward natural depravity. Bushnell writes: "But virtue is more a state of being than an act or series of acts: and if we look at the causes which induce or prepare such a state, the will of the person himself may have a part among those causes more or less important, and it works no absurdity to suppose that one may be even prepared to such a state, by causes prior to his own will." Bushnell adds that the parents' influence is most profound.[23]

THE LITERATURE OF PSYCHIC MANIPULATION

The assertion that there must be a unified underlying force behind the changes in nineteenth-century childhood requires evidence of its complete permeation into every parameter of culture. Psychic control is as pervasive a theme in the secular literature of the period as in religious texts. Literature for children took on new import, a writer for *The Southern Literary Messenger* noting that "no trait in the literary development of the age is more striking than the importance which seems suddenly to have attached to what we call juvenile books for children. ... At no former period has there been any involvement of similar description so observable as the present one."[24] The number of periodicals increased geometrically, from 700 in 1865 to 1,200 in 1870 to 3,300 in 1885.[25] This expanding output emphasized the creation of severe superego controls, reinforcement of guilt, binding of the child to the parent, and more subtle yet personalized means of distancing and control. Concern with a new discipline so that the child may become an adequate parental delegate and the acting out of the projective fantasies upon the child are as clear in literary sources as in religious ones.

As the birch rod was replaced by the carefully modulated tongue, numerous more subtle interactions between infant and mother became normative for a progressive segment of the population. Written materials reflect both the potentials and difficulties of the newer strategies. *The Son Unguided, His Mother's Shame* (1848) is emblematic of the new importance of the child: "Its character is as yet of wax."[26] A popular novelist of the era puts the same thought in a vivid nutshell: "the impress of the older and wiser mind should be placed upon the child from the earliest dawn of its intelligence, so that the little one's character shall be determined, instead of being left to chance."[27]

The word "impress" becomes significant and is consonant with such other key usages as "mold," "form," and "shape"– all used in reference to character formation by means of psychological impressment. The intensely formed superego is expressed in pure form through the first-person narrative of one Guy Dennis:

Now and then, I hear a sermon that makes me feel bad; sometimes, when I wake in the dead of the night, I have awfully solemn thoughts about death, and what will come after it; but I try to get to sleep; and the next day I am hard at work, and forget everything disagreeable. I don't like to think: it makes me uncomfortable.[28]

The theme of the child as the parents' superego delegate is made even more manifest in fiction than in the area of religion. One novel traces the experiences of Adeline, "disliked from being disobedient, idle and passionate"—three sins implying rebellion against authority.[29] *The Bobbins Boy: How Nat Got His Learning*, another piece of instructive fiction designed for both youthful and parental eyes, puts into the school teacher's mouth long speeches concerning the proper virtues of perseverance and hard work: "The motto of every youth should be 'upward and onward.' " The youth must "resist temptation." Work may lead one, regardless of natural ability, to untold heights, for "the dullest scholar in the room may distinguish himself by application . . . while the brightest may fail of success by wasting his time."[30]

Rebellion against delegated paths of behavior can only lead to ruin. A novel entitled *The Mischief Maker: Ralph Rattler* is a story of the chronic bad boy—not the Huck Finn of Twain's consciousness, but a youth with an ardent temper who causes his parents pain. The boy is filled with warnings to the recreant child, for "one sickly sheep infects the flock and poisons all the rest." The author resorts to diatribe: "A fierce lion in the place would be better than such a boy; for at worst, a lion can only kill the body. But a bad boy can make the heart unhappy, and lead the souls of his schoolmates to death . . . a wicked boy becomes a living scourge, a tempter of others; and therefore every child, who would escape an evil snare, *must avoid an artful, mischief-making boy.*"[31]

Glance Gaylord's *The Boys at Dr. Murray's* portrays a confrontation between the indomitable Dr. Murray and an incurable young thief. When stern measures are not sufficient to curb the boy's passion, he is struck with a serious illness and his suffering prompts reform.[32] Unwillingness to obey is almost the definition of wickedness. In *The Brother and Sister*, Martha blames herself when her stepsister almost drowns while in her care. Damning herself further, she succeeds in alienating her father and is cut off from the family and sent away. It is outside the nurture of the home that the girl becomes sick (sickness is almost always depicted as the result of alienation from the adult world, or rebellion, or moral transgression); and it is only after her stepmother's death, an event which exacerbates her self-loathing to a point of total submission, that the girl can be united with her father. The author adds this coda: "There is no peace, no rest, no real happiness . . . until we have come to Jesus."[33] Similar is the overt statement of control in John Habberston's *Budge and Loddie*: "The impress of the older and wiser mind should be placed upon the child from the earliest dawn of its intelligence, so that the little one's character shall be determined, instead of left to chance."[3 4]

In *The Poor Woodcutter and Other Stories*, T. S. Arthur traces the exploits of a young boy who leaves home along with his dog. Yet the dog's homing instinct is evidently stronger than the youth's, and it returns home in time to save the boy's sister from drowning. The action is wrong because it is "disobedience," and the mother's reconciliation involves an analysis of her child's dreams. There are two types of dreams, she explains: the "fantastic" type, which are of absolutely no import, and the "correspondential" type, which function as modes of instruction, often messages from God to be meditated upon. In other words, even the child's own fantasies must be seen as messages from an authority.[3 5]

Catherine Sedgwick's best-seller, *Home*, likewise explicitly illustrates the dynamics of psychic control. Here a boy, Wallace, throws a cat in boiling water for having torn his kite to bits, which is of course a horrifying manifestation of aggression to his onlooking family. But even such extreme behavior is not disciplined by physical means. There is no show of anger, but rather a confinement of the boy's activities to his room, so that he may think about "how much worse than consumption is a moral disease." He is ostracized in a quiet and effective way. Finally, the son repents to his father, promising that he now has his passionate temper under control and proving it when taunted at school by avoiding fights. His father preaches to him: "We must remember, my son, that virtue and vice produced by circumstances is not to be counted to the individual. It is the noble struggle and resistance against them that makes virtue."[3 6]

Between 1865 and 1881, a minimum of 250 children's books was published each year, an upsurge which hastened the development of children's book reviewing into a craft—which often became a forum for the reviewer's own beliefs about children. Samuel Osgood's *Books for Our Children* (1865) is both a telling criticism and a tangible journalistic evidence of the new pressure of socialization—the demand that the child rise in the world by controlling and disciplining his instincts and energy:

> He grows up in the midst of excitement, with an average amount of privilege and prosperity unknown heretofore to the mass of children in any community. . . . Adults often push infancy prematurely into childhood, childhood into youth, and youth into maturity. . . . school is the forerunner

of rivalry of business, society and politics. Our heads are apt
to be much older than our shoulders. . . . He is a precocious
little creature, with rare susceptibilities and powers, whose
very . . . high aptitudes, and whose great exposures should
move us to temper not a little our pity for his failings with
admiration for his excellence.[3 7]

Dr. Josiah Gilbert Holland, who instituted the magazine *St.
Nicolas* (one of the most popular children's periodicals) listed the
*raison d'etre* for his work, stressing the hope that the publication
would "cultivate the imagination in profitable directions,"
"prepare boys and girls for life as it is," and, of most interest,
"stimulate their ambitions."[3 8] The *McGuffey* reader, a periodical
which reached over one hundred million children between 1850
and 1900, encapsulated the tenacity aspect of psychic control in
the following:

> Once or twice though you should fail
> Try, Try, Again;
> If you would at least prevail,
> Try, Try, Again.[3 9]

And Horatio Alger, Jr. urged children to *Strive and Succeed*
(1872).[4 0]

We are a far cry from Sidney Lanier, Howard Pyle, Bret Harte,
William Dean Howells, Samuel Clemens, Thomas Aldrich, and
Frances H. Burnett, writers who would later bring in what some
term the "golden age of children's literature" in the latter part of
the century. The emphasis here is on didacticism, an impetus for
control which itself was uncontrollable. Lydia Sigourney's *Sayings
of the Little Ones, and Poems for Their Mothers* summarizes
concisely the dynamics evident in both religious and fictional
works:

> A boy who paid close attention to the Scriptures . . . had a
> great admiration of physical strength and vigor, and a
> corresponding desire to obtain them. He was observed very
> frequently to wash his hands. On almost every occasion,
> when he could obtain water and when there seemed no
> necessity on the score of neatness, he would be zealously
> practicing this ablution. To an inquiry into the cause of this
> almost constant hydropathic exercise, his reply was:
> I wish to go strong. . . . Does it not say that "he who hath
> clean hands shall wax stronger and stronger?"[4 1]

Here one can see all the elements: strength and vigor (not innate, but as an object of achievement), self discipline as a means of obtaining strength, a belief in the absolute truth of ideals handed down to the child—all superimposed on a substratum of intensive guilt.


## PARENTS AS THE INSTRUMENTS OF CONTROL

Religion and fiction are important aspects of culture; yet no parameter goes so close to the heart of the psychic reality from which all aspects of culture originate as the mother-child relation. This is difficult terrain. More crucial than maternal behaviors, even more crucial than maternal intentions (conscious or unconscious), are the perceptions of the infant. The ideal—both for psycho-historical and clinical purposes—would be a transmitting device, relaying the reality of the child's emotions but translated from the child's preverbal modes of thinking and feeling. However, existing evidence, with all its imperfections, does show the dynamics of psychic control evident in religion and fiction.

One surveys thirty years of *The Mother's Magazine and Family Circle* in conjunction with other popular magazines (e.g., *The Child at Home, The Mother's Journal and Family Visitant, The Mother's Assistant*) and finds a fairly homogeneous ideological definition of the maternal role. It evolves only slightly as the thirty-year period progresses. As early as 1833, the charter of the association that was to begin publishing *The Mother's Magazine* declared that one reason for its formation was "to show the best method of regulating the temper and disposition of children" and communicate to mothers "the full importance and responsibility of their tasks." The first volume warns against physical control: "too often an effort is made to greet it, by throttling, and tossing and turning it from side to side, or throwing it rudely from lap to lap."[42] As the stage of childhood was elevated in correspondence with the emergence of intensive socialization through psychic control, so the position of the mother was defined as chief molder of the child. Though the father remained absolute sovereign in the household, the final and often the only vote concerning the management of worldly affairs, yet it was the mother who was now entrusted with the monumental task of intimate socialization. Of course, this movement in the direction of intimacy carried an implicit danger: the mother risked a reactivation of the painful pool of her own early traumas. Such dangerous feelings were staved off through the distancing measure of control and through the fantasy of maternal omnipotence. In a process repeatedly encountered in the history of childhood, each move towards the child is also a move toward the parent's own childhood and arouses precisely the anxieties that earlier modes of child rearing—including the infanticidal and the abandoning modes—were defenses against. Psychogenic progress occurs to the extent that the parent is able to cope with these anxieties without recapitulating onto the child the traumas of his or her own early years. Hence is is only superficially paradoxical that the extreme control fantasies we have been tracing, with their morbid and apparently sadistic overtones, should in fact have been progressive by comparison with the practices of an earlier generation.

The literature written for and about the mother, often biased toward the dominant middle-class culture, is filled with a concern for tying the child to the mother as tautly as possible. We can get some inkling of the bond in the following passage: "A sigh, a single sentence, a message received, a book loaned or given, and even a look, has, in thousands of instances, changed the entire character of a life, and placed a man where he never would have been, but. for that single circumstance."[43] Another mother's magazine communicates precisely the same emotion: "The destiny of a nation is shaped by its character; and that character, the aggregate character of all its individual citizens, will ever be found to be molded chiefly by maternal hands."[44] There is incessant reminder of the importance of the mother's every move: "As the first impressions on the mind of a child are the most permanent, so are they also exceedingly important. The mind of a child may be likened to a piece of . . . paper, the surface of which, being free from every stain, as far as actual transgressions is concerned, may be made to receive whatever impressions we see fit to stamp on it."[45] Another source makes precisely the same point: "Perhaps there is no proposition that is so hackneyed and at the same time so little understood, as that women are the prime cause of all the good and evil in human actions. . . . Yes, mothers, in a certain sense, the destiny of a redeemed world is put into your hands."[46] Others found the influence of mothers no less than "incredible," setting their claims with the excitement of a newly found discovery. The offensive is directed primarily at mothers, but an occasional use of the term "parent" may be considered as a tacit inclusion of the father in certain areas:

No, parent! You may trace on the sandy beach impressions distinct and multiform, but the next rolling wave will wash them out. The spots and stains of a storm that strips nature of its beauty and glory may be repaired ... but, oh remember, and it may be written with a diamond impression on your soul, that the impressions of childhood ... remain forever.... It's utterly impossible to prevent your children from being molded in exact conformity to the bias and impressions you have given them.[47]

After a warning that more than half the diseases from which children suffer are caused "by the injudicious treatment they receive at the hands of those who have no excuse for their ignorance," *The Mother's Journal* includes a poem likening the child to a developing plant: the mother is a "nurturing tree" and it is possible to tell from the "young plant" if its future is healthy and secure.[48] Another poem includes the idea that a pebble in a streamlet may change the course of a river and that a dewdrop on a baby plant may warp an oak forever.[49] A journalist notes that "a word spoken inadvisably, may sink deep within the mind of the child, and when years have passed away, spring up and bear evil fruit."[50] The following passage shows in vivid terms the effect of psychic control:

> Just what it was in the woman's face that filled me with such terror, I have never been able to explain. ... the subtle, more terrifying thing was a certain fixed *stillness* in the face. The steady quiet gaze with its haunting smile always hit me in the same way and followed me to every corner of the room.... There was never any suggestion of her *doing* anything to frighten ... and it was this very quiet, so unchanging and unreal, that added an uncanny haunting element to the fear.[51]

The feelings induced in a mature man by the face of a woman vividly convey the sense of controlling power and maternal omnipresence so characteristic of the nineteenth century.

A section from the 1857 diary of the mother of an important child psychologist—G. Stanley Hall—reflects this widespread perception of the maternal role in all its lofty standards:

> With what prayerful carefulness should I order my speech, my every tone of voice, all the particulars of manner which go to make up the general deportment. I have regarded this matter far too little. I am a mother, and what is my influence on my children whose young hearts are made ineffaceable impressions which have a bearing on their character through

time, and also their future destiny? It is a serious inquiry and
awakens sad reflections.[52]

A popular literary device of the period was to liken a blemish
on the female character—especially the mother—to a spot on the
sun, astronomic in scale, creating intensive repurcussions. "There
is a special need that *maternal influence*—about, if not absolutely,
the mightiest influence God has given to human beings—should be
sanctified, and all on the side of God. That influence lives while
others die."[53]

Such were the ideas that gave rise to a new environmental view
of personality formation. Since the mother surrounded the child,
she *was* the environment. Individual differences within the same
family—even in relation to physical health and mental
abilities—were mainly attributed to impulses of the mother. The
responsibilities of motherhood had now increased geometrically,
for mothers were now the cause of moral, physical, and emotional
development.

The nub of psychic control was its intensive subtlety, avoiding
the Scylla of temper and the Charybdis of apathy. The mother is
to speak gently, to rule by love rather than fear: "A word—a
look—has crushed to earth many a blooming flower."[54] Because
the child is so susceptible to influences, every move must be
prudently monitored. A subtle, more ultimately successful, mode
of control than grosser earlier forms (in terms of creating a
parental superego delegate), this control draws upon novel tools:
"It is unusual to attempt the management of children either by
corporal punishment, or by rewards addressed to the senses, or by
words alone. There is no other means of government, the power
and importance of which are seldom regarded—I refer to the
human voice." The same journal reports that few cases of corporal
punishment succeed, that the mother must create an "affability
mixed with firmness."[55] Mrs. L. C. Tuthill tells the mother that
"system is everything," from the early rising which will promote a
long life to the submission of the child to parental will—"all the
moral obligation of which he is capable."[56]

In producing a child—an object "on loan, to be rendered back
with interest," an immortal soul—the mother must be in total
control. Temptations of bodily pleasures and sloth must be
resisted so that habits of order and industry may be fixed.
*Harper's* ran a story concerning a woman who transgressed the
bounds of family life, became a *belle dame*, foregoing the duties of
motherhood for the pleasures of society, and came to resent her
husband's interest in her child. Subsequently, the child died of

fever, producing a guilt the woman transcended only by again becoming pregnant.[5][7] Indeed, control commonly began with pregnancy, necessitating the avoidance of anger, jealousy, terror, and grief, for the woman's state during pregnancy could actually abort the child. Reading between the lines, the stereotyped pastoral ideal of the American wife and mother is a myth created by a culture afraid of its underlying intensive emotions, a lid placed upon a seething foundation. "A fitful temper," says one writer, "will lessen the quantity of milk, make it thin. . . . Fits of anger produce a very irritating milk, followed by gripping in the infant, with green stools."[5][8]

Two means of keeping the mother's more intensive emotions subliminal and of reinforcing her ability to control the child were the ethic of feminine delicacy and the directing of the finite quantity of female energy into her most useful function, the raising of children. Woman was considered highly vulnerable, in need of the protection of the household and the quiet and peace of domesticity.

*The Physical Decline of American Women* (1860) traced the fragilization of the American woman, to the point where she had become a "doll," and chastised her for directing her energies away from motherhood, as well as condemning the use of contraception and the resort to abortion. Personal "abuse" (masturbation) is condemned mainly on the grounds of loss of energy, a directing of energy away from the vital procreative sphere. A pregnant woman is a delicate being, has a very tenuous existence, her power for good or evil balancing on a precipice. The mother's powers are so great that she contains a "soul substance" which may be altered by feelings, thoughts, and behavior. If a woman is impregnated by a male under the influence of strong drink, infant physical deformity may result. Paradoxically, the delicate woman's powers approach omnipotence, and her every action is as subject to scrutiny as an omen from the gods. Sex is to be avoided during gestation, and—an interpretation indicative of competition between father and offspring, with the latter now winning precedence—sexual activity is seen to hinder lactation. An earlier work shows a respected physician taking with some seriousness the tale of a black child born to white parents because the mother dwelled too incessantly upon the *thought* of an Ethiopian.[5][9]

Entire medical textbooks were devoted to the subject of feminine sexual disease. The author of one of these characteristically stresses that as the reproductive function lies at the center of existence, the energies involved in the process must not be wasted. Another work states that "the organs of reproduction are the center round which the whole ... of the female revolves and as such regulate the life and machinery of her being." There is a curious stress upon the sexual organs, in paradoxical concurrence with the desexualization of the "good" woman (wife and mother). It is now established as fact that clitoridectomies were performed in the late nineteenth century for such mild symptoms as chronic itching of the vulva. Since many saw the function of sex as purely reproductive (maximizing the direction of energy toward child-molding) the clitoris was an expendable organ, disturbing the valence of the maternal bond. That which stimulated the clitoris in effect deprived the infant, for a swollen, impassioned clitoris involved misdirection of a pregnant woman's vital forces.

In sum, the ideal mother was obsessed with her maternal functions and homemaking, was self-controlled and deliberate, above worldly affairs, morally pure, optimistic, gentle but controlling. Psychic control now had its mediator.

The subject of the realities of paternity during this period is a more difficult one, since far less was written about the paternal role. The material which does exist—sporadic articles in women's magazines, an occasional reference in an article or book otherwise directed at women, journal records and autobiographical accounts—indicates that the father was a sovereign who especially kept his distance during the crucial early stages of personality formation, and only afterward moved a step closer to the child. Yet, during the first years, the father was not to be completely discounted. *The Young Husband's Book* (1843) states: "The same law which imposes upon the husband the duty of supporting his wife, gives him a general and paramount claim to her obedience." But the new husband-father is advised: "Let him resolve, from the very first, *never to spend an hour from home*, unless business, or at least, some necessary and rational purpose demand it"—another instance of the binding, consolidated institution of the family.[60]

An English text popular in America answers a young woman's inquiry: "Dear Mrs. Randolph, you could only do the first thing which God requires—submit yourself to your husband." One minister declares, "Wives, submit yourselves to your husbands as unto the Lord," and continues, "For the husband is the head of the wife, even as Christ is the head of the Church."[61] Murray Nicholas' *The Happy Home* uses political terms in describing the home, the necessity of "submission" to parental authority, the view that every parent is "constituted a family governor" of the "family commonwealth."[62] Following a description of the ultimate evil of refusal of submission to parental authority, of the necessity of training diligence and industry in the child, as well as temperance and control of passionate emotions, he states: "The father is a sovereign, but not the despot; he is not merely a counselor; he is a legislator; his will is law, not advice. He is the king of the family commonwealth and would make all feel that obedience is at once their duty and his due."[63] All profit by the relationship, a series of interrelations determined in form and content by almighty powers. Distanced from the intimate care of the child, delegated the most absolutist of familial powers, the literary ideal of the father is one of a benevolent dictator.

One source has it that "A father speaks by command; he is the ultimate authority." *The Child at Home*, the publication of the American Tract Society, quotes a child reporting to his mother: "I thought if I climbed the tree I should be certainly killed, but when I thought again *if I was killed in obeying father, it would not be bad for me.*"—an attitude considered by the publication as a mark of true courage.[64] There was an overt relationship between paternity and religious matters. As noted earlier, one minister speaks of the holy sanction of the father as head of the wife, as Christ is the head of the Church. *The Mother's Journal* emphasizes that in the death of a child, the father cannot realize the depths of the mother's grief, which are a result of her more intimate contact. The distance and worldliness of the father is even lamented by one journalist: "It is one of the special faults of our time, and particularly of our country, that the paternal influence is too little felt in the family." *The Mother's Magazine* saw complementary functions between the father and the mother, the mother demonstrating all-powerful influence in the early years of grace, gentleness, and love, while the father stresses power, might, and fear; yet both are benevolent, creating "therefore a mingled confidence of awe, affection, submission and respect."[65]

Personal remembrances in the form of memoirs and diaries add to the dimension of childhood perceptions of the father, indicating the tendency to idealize the father and to strictly repress the impact of his authoritarianism. In addition, the incidence of a close yet distant father allows for adulation and longing. Even though the autobiographies of individuals such as Theodore Roosevelt, Clarence Darrow, Richard Ely, Frederick Howe, William Allen White, Samuel Gompers, and Terence Powderly are not monolithic in their respect for their parents, still the paradigm is Ely's remark: "I always thought my father was a superior man," accompanied by feelings of self-deprecation.[66] Most common is the sense of distance from the father, an emotional vacuum more extensive than in later periods; one must search in these writings for subtle clues of ambivalence, and of the child's rage experienced on the unconscious level. Even a writer with the perceptive gifts of G. Stanley Hall fails in the attempt to reach his own true feelings toward his father. He writes that he felt kindly toward the man and harbored no lasting antagonisms, and he even says that "I was never able to cherish the least resentment, and do not think I ever had a lasting antagonism, save one or two, toward anyone in my life." Yet later, within the same text, Hall speaks fleetingly of negative feelings and resents that "we children were incessantly exhorted to make good, to succeed as they had fallen by the way."[6][7] Charles Francis Adams comes closest in breaking through the screen of repression when he writes that he did not like his own father—though he cannot explain exactly why.[6][8]

Analysis of the paternal role broadens our understanding of psychic control. The child can now be seen as a tabula rasa with untold potentialities and almost limitless educability, intimately bound and molded by a devoted mother, with a benevolent yet stern paternal figure moving closer to the child as he matures—all within the framework of a relatively progressive move away from blatant control and toward emotional bonding, reinforced by patterns of guilt and latent incestuous ties.

## THE REPRESSION OF CHILD SEXUALITY

The views expressed in this period toward child sexuality can help test the thesis of psychic control and illustrate in greater depth the manner in which the child was manipulated and controlled. Cautions against masturbation were directed more and more to the child and infant as well as the adolescent, and the concern with control was in complete consonance with other parameters of culture. In addition, the fear that the body had a fixed quantum of energy which could be squandered by "pollution" permeates the literature.

The desire to prevent masturbation knew few bounds. Between 1856 and 1932 the Government Patent Office awarded thirty-three patents to inventors of sexual restraints. The first patented masturbation lock, dated June 1870, bears the preamble:

My invention is a device for so covering up the sexual organs of a person addicted to the vice of masturbation, from his own touch and control that he or she must refrain from the commission of the vicious and self-degrading act. . . . It is

. . . well known to physicians, and to some heads of families, that multitudes of children of both sexes injure their moral and physical natures for life by the practice of this vice.[6][9]

So great was the fear of masturbation that by the 1860s the hypothesis was presented that the "vice" may actually cause insanity; and a list of symptoms, easily recognized and directly stemming from the practice, was proposed. Popular writers of the period like O. S. Fowler catalogue such symptoms as ruined memory, epilepsy, hysteria, gastric difficulty, and back pains; and Fowler cites as signs of the masturbator a certain expression in the eyes, an evasive glance, poor posture, timidity, and lack of memory.[70] R. L. Trall's *Sexual Diseases* (1858) has as its main theme the problem of "pollution" and the dissolution of energy. He writes in the tone of a preacher: "None but the experienced medical man can trace the deplorable consequences to feeble, malformed, puny, and imperfectly organized offspring; and no one but the profound physiologist can clearly see all the external works, exhausted vitality and . . . decay, stamped indelibly on thousands of our young men and maidens, otherwise in the bloom of youth, health and beauty." Trall elaborates his inventory of consequences and symptoms: consequences include irregular sleep, headache, nervousness, and swelling; treatment may involve "mental management exercise," good diet (mainly vegetarian), exercise, early to bed and early to rise, and mechanical devices to prevent erection. Symptoms of masturbation include weakness in the joints, paralysis of the lower extremities, insanity, early aging, spitting of blood, impaired vision, pimples on the face, nymphomania, shrinking of the genitals, eruptions on the genitals, and cancer of the uterus. It is clear by the conclusion of the work that almost any sexual disease can be caused by masturbation. Trall also stresses the concept of the period that there is a fixed quantum of energy in the body which must be guided into proper areas: "If the constantly accumulating energy of the nervous and muscular systems is not expended in regular and appropriate exercise or labor, it will seek an outlet in some less rational way," and frequently in "fitfull and violent" eruptions of the sexual organs.[71]

In direct connection with the necessity of establishing control over the child, one writer indicates that masturbation is a symptom of the child's unwillingness to work at appointed tasks:

A doctor discusses the necessity of *control* of impulses: But though the intellectual powers are imperfectly developed, the

feelings and the impulses are stronger, or at least, less under
control, than they become with advancing years; and one
great object of education is to bring them into proper
subordination. Mental disorders, then, show themselves in the
exaggeration of those impulses; in the inability or the
indisposition to listen to that advice or to be swayed by those
. . . which govern other children.[72]

Masturbatory taboos produced such shyness that, as one physician
indicates, it was common for patients to travel hundreds of miles
in order to be certain that they were medically examined only by
a complete stranger.[73]

Other authorities, such as Rosch, Napheys, Wright, and Dixon,
present a fairly unified view that child sexuality is a hotbed of
dangers. Edward Dixon's *Woman and Her Diseases from Cradle to
the Grave* (1847) declares that sex is exclusively for the purpose of
procreation, urging early education of the young girl as to the
proper uses of the uterine system and the dangers of subverting it
in early life. Dixon adds an ominous note: "It would be improper
to enter into further detail on this subject, in a volume like this;
but when it has been said by others as well as ourselves, that this
vice is of such frequency as to constitute one of the greatest
drawbacks to the preservation of youthful life, we feel that a less
decisive mention of it, on our part, would have been
inexcusable."[74] Heywood Smith (1878) reminds the girl that "the
organs of reproduction are the center around which the whole
cosmogony of the female revolves and as such regulate the life and
machinery of her being." Masturbation, he adds, may cause
inflammation of the ovaries or enlargement of the clitoris;
clitoridectomy is recommended in extreme cases, and pregnancy is
cited as a cure for hysteria.[75]

Writers outside of the purely medical realm did not always
speak of child sexuality in such frank terms. In the pages of *The
Mother's Magazine* one finds euphemisms such as: "A habit which
is considerably present in almost every family, of allowing children
to sleep with older persons, has created nervous problems." And,
in even more opaque terms: "Children compared with adults, are
electrically in positive condition. The rapid changes which are
going on in their bodies, abundantly generate and as extensively
work up its vital . . . fluids. But when, by contact for long nights,
with elder and negative persons, the vitalizing electricity of their
tender organization is absolved, they soon grow pale, languid and
dull, while their bed companions feel a corresponding
invigoration."[76] Another writer speaks of the "restless wild" who
need to be "calmed and consolidated into manly force by brave

exercise."[77] At times, descriptions of childhood diseases resemble comments concerning child sexuality. Diseases must be broken up by keeping the patient still.[78]

Some balance is clearly necessary in reading these accounts. Thus, William Lyon Phelps noted of his school life in New Hampshire—a school which harbored every social class—that he was surrounded by language which would have made a "sailor blush."[79] Even in the nineteenth century, control could sometimes be avoided or circumvented. Yet it is difficult to overstate the unanimity with which the ideal was preached and reinforced. James P. Walker's sermon of 1863 may be taken as a summation of the themes we have traced:

> Character and God are alike in several particulars. . . . By self-denial the pennies increased till they changed into silver, and . . . they were changed into the gold pieces. . . . This is labor. Thus you must curb your passions, not indulge your temper, avoid falsehoods as you avoid poison, think twice before you speak, and three times before you act, do the difficult thing, which is right, rather than the pleasant thing, which is wrong. This is self-denial. . . . good, kind, thoughtful habits will change into the silver of good principles, and finally into the pure gold of honest, intelligent, upright, enduring Christian character.[80]

## EDUCATION BY MANIPULATION

The earlier grosser forms of control were, of course, by no means abandoned during these years—nor have they been abandoned by lower-mode parents today. They are especially apparent in the realm of education. A professor remembers growing up in the 1860s and 1870s under the aegis of a particularly sadistic schoolmaster who would hold a peg between his students' upper and lower teeth or compel them to hold a five- to ten-pound log at arm's length for fifteen minutes.[81] Characteristically, however, educators were also drawn into the ideology of control. Thus, Henry Kiddle urged the teacher to "discipline the intellect" and wrote of the "habits" and "noble impulses" needed to build character. Again, the all-seeing eye, the watch against evil, is apparent: "No part of the teacher's duty is more important than a consistent vigilance so as to arrest the formation of deleterious habits." Kiddle wrote of a unique plasticity of mind during childhood and of the necessity of seeing that it is molded in the proper directions. The goals toward which one strives in the school are order and subordination, prompt obedience to authority and submission to rule, the basic preconditions of moral training.[82]

As part of the shift from physical to psychological controls for children, New Jersey became, in 1879, the first state to abolish corporal punishment in the schools. Although the law was leniently enforced (an estimate has it that 9,408 beatings were administered in Newark schools in 1876), the move to legislate is eloquent proof that blatant physical control was no longer a socially acceptable means of coercing children, although physical punishment continued at levels short of severe beatings and whippings. Somewhat earlier, Lyman Cobb wrote: "A boy who *must be beaten,*' at home or at school, on the same principle, *'must be beaten*' when a man, for, if he is not *reasoned* with, and *in kindness* shown the wrong he has done, but is *beaten*, he will not submit to anything but BEATING, when grown to manhood. Can there be a man found, who would commence *beating* another for any supposed injury, unless his feelings had first become HARDENED and callous by witnessing the sufferings or pain of children, who were whipped at home or school."[83]

It is also during this period that the kindergarten came into being, a novel institutionalization of the ethic of early training and socialization. Writers spoke of this new early education in terms of its potential for development. "The kindergarten education," said a contributor to *The Mother's Magazine*, "develops the child physically and mentally," while checking unfavorable tendencies.[84] Punishment is often ostracism from the group, as in the case of the boy who must sit on the girl's side, or the student who is told to wear a dunce cap.[85]

The child's very educability, plus the use of schooling as a control device, made the rise of compulsory schooling inevitable. Many spoke of the fact that before the child may be useful to society in a tangible sense, he must begin training his every movement and breath; every aspect of his or her life, even play, should have some purposeful objective in child development. Education was to serve the purpose of moral socialization. One analysis of the 245 texts used in Connecticut schools in 1846 revealed an obsession with moral concerns, painting a universe which is guided on moral principles.[86]

A variety of sources show education at that time to be concerned with the issues of authority, control, and morality. One journalist remarks that revenge is the very "spirit of the devil" and pounds the words "patience, patience, patience," into his prose.[87] One boy's diary of the 1860s speaks of an incident in which he was put in a wood box for an entire morning with the cover down.

The boy has a hard time of it, not having the courage to confess his shame to his grandmother; he later expresses his admiration for his brother whose qualities far surpass his own.[88] Oliver Wendell Holmes, a schoolboy in the 1860s, remembers his schoolmaster quoting the following poem:

> These children that seem of one note in your eyes,
> So little in size, so little in size,
> What may they not be? And what may they not do?
> The first in the nation was once such as you.[89]

Ralph Rattler is the fictional outcast, the rebel who manifests the sin of temper and is ostracized by his friends and schoolmates. His punishment is the denial of love while the reader is reminded that "one sickly sheep infects the flock." The school rebel is not only pitied but feared:

> A fierce lion in the place would be better than such a boy; for, at the worst, a lion can only kill the body. But a bad boy can make the heart unhappy, and lead the souls of his schoolmates to death. . . . a wicked boy becomes a living scourge, a tempter of others; and therefore every child, who would escape an evil snare, must avoid an *artful, mischief making boy.*[90]

Ellen Glasgow shows vividly the power of the shaming process in the nineteenth-century schoolroom when she recalls her shame upon being put at the foot of her arithmetic class:

> I remember vividly this and I have not forgotten that while I sat there I felt a chill crawling up my spine like a beetle. Sickness, black and chilly attacked the pit of my stomach and all the stamping feet and treble voices coming closer . . . stabbing down into my ears and into my throbbing head. It was the beginning of one of my nervous headaches, and a cold sweat broke out while I struggled not to disgrace myself. . . . If the children had been cannibals, and I a missionary prepared for the feast, my doom would not have seemed more dreadful to me, or more inevitable. . . . I should be in eternal disgrace.[91]

Stories of school life abound with the potentialities inherent in every young individual: if only the child will apply himself and adhere to the dictates of the established institution, then there is no ceiling on his possible achievement. A teacher states that "the dullest scholar in this room may distinguish himself by application and . . . perseverance." There are moral tales of sin and reform, and perfectability is presented as an ideology of existence.[9 2]

## CHILD-REARING PRACTICES

The area of actual child-rearing practices—the nuts and bolts of personality formation—is of central importance, and yet this is one of the most difficult of areas with which to deal. The first problem is to determine, as precisely as possible, how a progressive segment of the population treated its children on a day-to-day basis. The general scarcity of statistical information for the mid-nineteenth century is even greater for areas as personal as toilet training, feeding, weaning, punishment, and control within the home; before the rise of the psychological professions little such information was recorded. A second problem concerns the difficulties of distinguishing between externally reported behavior and the *significance* of that behavior: the crux of the matter is the psychological effect, the emotional reality for the child. A bottle may replace the breast; the same bottle may be administered in a variety of ways and with a myriad of motivations and feelings, all with profound personality implications; a mere catalogue of such overt practices can be seriously misleading. A third problem is implicit in the very concept of evolutionary history. Biological evolutionary theory has familiarized us with the astounding complexity that results from the coexistence of advanced and earlier life forms; a similar coexistence of advanced and "fossilized" child-rearing norms is the rule rather than the exception in psychogenic evolution. A specific set of parents may seem relatively advanced; yet earlier forms of treatment seep into the nursery at every turn, transmitted by friends, relatives, the surrounding society—the carriers are everywhere.

With these reservations in mind, we may cautiously proceed into the area of practices, beginning with modes of feeding—the first and most profound formative influence on the infant. One writer has observed that as Victorian morality arose, nursing came to be seen by many as a sign of indelicacy. An 1836 source indicates: "The mother's milk, a suitable quantity, an under suitable regulations, is so obviously the appropriate food of an infant during the first months of its existence, that it seems almost unnecessary to repeat the fact. And yet, the violations of this rule are enormous and constant, as to require a few passing remarks."[9 3] A popular writer is ambivalent about the process, indicating that although nursing is best for the child, and that mothers should ideally nurse their own children, it could drain the mother's vital energies. Nursing sessions should therefore be regularized; and, until teething, the sole food of the infant should be the mother's milk, the exception being when it is not plentiful enough and wet nurses are available.

The employment of wet nurses declined steadily during the nineteenth century. This was in many ways fortunate for the child, both for emotional reasons and in view of the fact that the wet nurse would sometimes give up to thirty feedings daily to different infants, her nipples often cracking as a result. One writer has dated the advent of rubber nipples to 1861, although the nursing bottle itself has existed since antiquity. Robert Sunley indicates that the wet nurse and the bottle were alternatives mainly for the middle and upper classes, and that impoverished wet nurses were often obtained through newspaper ads. A French writer, popular in American and published by a Boston company, favored the mother doing the nursing herself, as well as schedulized feeding during the first six months on an all-milk diet. Premature weaning may fatigue the child, he points out, and all the issues as to who shall nurse and care for the child should be decided before birth.[94] Schedulized feeding, as reported by doctors, rose from 20 percent in 1800 to nearly 100 percent in 1875. Caleb Ticknor's book, *A Guide for Mothers and Nurses in the Management of Young Children*, is similar to others in calling for a strict milk diet for the first ten to twelve months; he adds that one-third of the infant's time should be devoted to nourishment, the rest to sleep. LeFavre goes so far as to state that the infant should be put to the breast eight or nine hours after birth.

The first solid food for infants consisted of bread soaked in a mixture of sugar and cow's milk, given according to fixed schedules. The wet nurse is usually seen as a viable option, as long as she is in good health, with good, uncracked nipples, and it is an extra plus if she has recently given birth. Weaning is recommended after from six months to one year, depending on the infant; Ticknor warns that the mother is to be firm in her resolve and resist the many machinations the child will perform in order to gain her sympathy.[95]

Information on toilet training is scarce, but the pervasiveness of the control theme in this period leads one to suspect that the omission may indicate, in this case, its importance rather than its insignificance. Where the subject does appear, it is clear that a premium was placed on retentiveness or orderly and schedulized elimination. Ticknor recommends toilet training as early as possible; elsewhere there seems to be a conspiracy of silence, an indication that excrement is even less acceptable as a subject for discussion than sex.[96]

Infant mortality is also a difficult subject for a period before advanced statistical methods. Oscar Dudley's *Saving the Children* does not give precise statistics concerning infant mortality, but it does turn up such items of interest as the fact that Chicago and the state of Illinois, prior to 1877, had no organized protection for dependent children and provided no legal checks on child abuse that stopped short of wanton brutality. It is of note that the Society for the Prevention of Cruelty to Animals was instituted one year before the Society for the Prevention of Cruelty to Children. One doctor recorded that one child out of five died within a year of birth, and one in three before the completion of the fifth year. The federal census of 1850 indicates that child mortality rates were lower then than in the past and higher than in future decades: 9.29 percent of males and 7.94 percent of females are listed as having died under one year of age, 2.5 percent males and 2.28 percent females from one to five, .70 percent males and .63 percent females from five to ten.[97]

Those engaged in the sociological analysis of family structure—though worlds away from the psychogenic perspective—have presented several observations useful in studying the ideology of psychic control. For example, the evidence indicates that families tended to grow increasingly smaller as the nineteenth century progressed. At the same time, between 1850 and 1880, one in three children would have an additional adult besides the parents living in the household (chiefly grandparents, boarders, or servants), which in most cases added another significant relationship. Evidence from the Detroit area indicates that from 1850 to 1880 there was a smaller age difference among children in the same family.[98] Edward Shorter argues that in Europe the effective increase in the number of children conceived before marriage up to 1850 began to decline from that time until 1950, furthering the development of a close-knit nuclear family.[99] Of course, the decline of fertility itself furthered the move toward the tighter nuclear family. Another factor was the dissolution of the extended family clan due to greater mobility, familial fragmentation and intergenerational splitting.

Other significant areas of child rearing include artifacts as rudimentary and potentially revealing of attitude as the cradle and other indications of mobility—for mobility implies freedom. Tuthill (1855) feels that cradles perform a positive function but cautions that anything as extreme as tossing would serve to overexcite the infantile nervous system. One doctor believes that the cradle should be built in the shape of the womb. On another subject, one author proposes one year as the ideal time for the child to walk; another warns against allowing the child to walk about before two years of age.[100] In 1840 the first baby carriage was manufactured in America, providing a means of greater mobility for the child and an opportunity for more visual stimulation.

Some basic conclusions may likewise be ventured concerning toys. After 1860, moving-vehicle toys became more popular at the same time that board games, with their elements of competition and gambling, came into being. Toys became more complex, offering challenge and instruction to the user of clockworks and miniature locomotives—and, in 1859, a new means of expressing aggression: the cap pistol. At the same time that the child was being controlled, parents were providing it with a greater opportunity to control the play world and to strive toward mastery of the environment.[101]

Evidence indicates that in the realm of discipline, psychological means of control replaced physical ones in a manner consistent with our discussion. One writer states that "few cases occur in which corporal punishment need be resorted to." Lydia Child tells parents that anger is an untenable emotion which can only serve to drive the child farther from God ("Speak gently—it is better by far to rule by love than fear"), and Wishy considers the phrase "spare the rod and save the child" an accurate view of progressive views of discipline.[102] Books like Lyman Cobb's *The Evil Tendencies of Corporal Punishment* (1847) appeared telling mothers it is better to rule by love than by fear.[103] David Macrae, a Scotsman who visited America during the 1870s, was amazed at the restraint of American parents; H. H. notes in *Bits of Talk About Home Matters* that it is unfortunate that "breaking the will" is a phrase going out of usage; and Augusta Larned in *Talks with Girls* (1877) notes that whipping has, for some, gone out of fashion. Priorities of means of effecting authority are listed by Larned as follows: (1) love, (2) reason, (3) authority, (4) reproof and appeal to the conscience, (5) threat, and (6) execution of threat. It is of interest that this sequence recapitulates in reverse the general evolution of child-rearing techniques in human development, and that Larned was able to grade such distinctions consciously, recognizing the progressive crudity of forms down the evolutionary ladder.

The control ideal involves means of coercion inculcated in such a thoroughgoing manner that the act of submission itself is seen as "delightful.":

The question as to who is to rule the family, is one which, of necessity, must be early determined. In rare cases, it may be settled without an appeal to any other force than that of authority, but settled it must be. . . . Almost every child makes an experiment of its strength, entering upon a vigorous warfare against parental authority. If the contest ends in a "yielding" to the superior will, it is not often that it has to be renewed. After this conquest, parental vigilance should be on the alert to see that all commands are followed with prompt and unhesitating obedience, until even to the most stubborn will the duty becomes easy if not delightful.[104]

What we are confronted with is a Spartan, authoritarian ethic which tries not to succumb to physicality. It is a mindset fueled by a dynamic set of contradictions, illustrated by the following: "The sooner the children are made to submit to the will of the parent, the better," and "Obedience is its own reward." Another writer concludes that "no eye can be too vigilant, no guardianship too strict." The Spartan side is most observable: "We do not desire to make our boys rigid, unflinching Spartans, yet they should have exposure to discipline" and acquire the hardness without which they will suffer. "Children must be made to obey"; "the child should be trained to live in a world of trial, of crosses and disappointment." Failures—any diversions from the directed course—are seen as the result of improper *training* in childhood. The same writer continues: "Submission to authority is the duty of all, and is promoting the good of all. . . . The refusal of submission to parental authority by children always leads to multiplied evils. . . . As far as the right training of children is concerned, it is impossible to say too much on submission to parental authority." Children must be trained to habits of "diligence and industry" if they are to excel at anything. Idleness is a sin and temperance one of the supreme virtues, especially in regard to the "passions, affections, and appetites." At the same time that parents are put into the role of trainers, they are told never to act as anything but gentlemen and gentlewomen. Insubordination, breaking of the authority bond, is a danger that threatens to increase geometrically unless checked:

Let children grow up with their wills unsubdued, with the authority of their parents continually questioned and resisted and a want of respect for superiors, and reverence for sacred things and sacred names, and sacred places, will almost inevitably ensue. And to what do these lead but to insubordination . . . to gross irreligion and eternal death . . . A cheerful, and uniform and prompt regard to parental authority, wherever the parent may be, is necessary to constitute an obedient child.[105]

The paradox of a simultaneously stern and gentle parent is resolved by the following: the child's conscience is to be so thoroughly inculcated that he may be his own policeman. A writer in *The Unitarian Review* observes that there is an early period in the baby's life when it must be ruled purely by benevolent authority, without reason, but that gradually self-control replaces the need for authority. Each stage is crucial and "we cannot make up fully at any later stage for what was neglected or ill done.[106]

## THE CHILDREN

A final section concerning this period of psychic control illustrates its most important implications of all: the effects on the minds of children. One of the unique and extreme responses to conditions like those I have described has recently been termed by deMause the "reversal reaction," in which the child feels compelled to play the role of the parent and to nurture one or both of his parents. The following mid-century poem illustrates the phenomenon, a product of early socialization.

I must not tease my mother;
And when she likes to read
Or has a headache, I will stop.
Quite silently indeed.
I will not choose a noisy play.
Nor trifling troubles tell
But sit down gently by her side
And try to make her well.[107]

Direct evidence of the reversal reaction is clear in the memoir of one Libbie C., who died in 1857 at the age of twelve. One night, Libbie was heard to groan, but when asked what was the matter she replied, "My tooth aches; but don't tell mother, for she will get up and get cold, and be sick again." Libbie thanks her mother for discipline, when it comes, and describes the care she has provided her in periods of illness.[108]

Another characteristic of mid- to late-nineteenth-century childhood is the frequency with which repressive control finds its only outlet in psychosomatic disorders. The current state of knowledge makes it impossible to state with assurance that the frequency of psychosomatic disorders has increased since that time, but a good deal of evidence points in that direction. The asthma of Theodore Roosevelt, the mysterious headaches of his brother Elliott which brought on fainting spells for no apparent cause (he was sent to the best physicians) but which quickly disappeared when he was sent to a dude ranch in Texas—these are reflective of general family experience in this period, a pattern marked by repressed rage and bodily sickness followed by (if the family possessed the means) a journey outside the confines of the home and, often rapid improvement. Of course, given the habituation to psychic control, an ill-timed separation could be traumatic, as one recollection of the 1850s indicates: "Mother wanted to go East but she did not wish to take me. . . . I was a very healthy child, and the doctor said it would not do me any harm for Mother to leave me. . . . I had been very ill during their absence."[109] One ten-year-old records in a diary of 1849: "I forget to say I have a little neice, nearly as old as I am, and she lives in the country. Her mother is my sister, and her father is a clergyman, and I go there in the summer, and when she comes here in the winter, and we have things together, like whooping cough and scarlatina." She goes on to describe how her parents often take trips without her.[110]

Evidence of the strength of the mother-child bond, along with intensive anxieties over maternal loss and deprivation, is present in the following dream recounted by Lydia Sigourney. A boy, knowing his mother was not well, woke up suddenly one morning after dreaming of his mother and said in a rapturous voice as a smile illuminated his features: "Her hand! It is *her hand*! May I take hold of it? *May I take hold of it?*"[111] The fantasy of reunification with the mother is an intense one; its full implications will be discussed at a later point.

Biographical and autobiographical accounts reflect the ideology of psychic control. Oliver Wendell Holmes' biographer describes his mother's consuming interest in her family. Stanley Hall's *Confessions* illustrates the idealization of mothers, Hall calling his mother "a saintly woman" "whom I knew under the greatest stress never to show a single symptom of anger or even impatience with three children." He lauds her completely modulated and controlled speech, reflecting her complete awareness of each word and action. She could not endure antagonism "and seems to have had nothing less than a passion for getting and keeping in amiable relations with every acquaintance." At the same time Hall refrains from commenting on her passivity, her migraines, and fits of nausea so severe that the family sometimes had to tiptoe.[112] Frederick Howe remembers: "Watchful eyes observed us in all we did. There was a sense of being clamped down, stiff in a mold made for us."[113]

Henry Adams remembers the quiet, nonphysical, yet extremely effective discipline of his aging grandfather, ex-President John Quincy Adams. One day, in about 1845, Henry rebelled against going to school. The President, then close to eighty, without speaking a word, walked him the entire mile to school. Adams remarked, "With a certain maturity of mind, the child must have recognized that the President, though a tool of tyranny, had done his disreputable work with a certain intelligence. He had shown no temper . . . no personal feeling, and had made no display of force. Above all, he held his tongue."[114]

Biographers of Thomas Edison note that, although he was severely treated as a child, he never showed overt hostility towards his father. William Dean Howells writes only laudatory things about his father, how he possessed a "gentle intelligence" and "an instinct for beauty and truth," as well as tolerance and a sense of poetry. Jane Addams remembers the classic family structure of the father who made the major decisions and set policy, while the mother was bound to the intimate care of her children during infancy.[115]

Ray Stannard Baker remembers a firm, vigilant father: "My father had a great affection, based upon a true understanding, for his sons. . . . His discipline was absolute and sometimes harsh. .,.,. He had a piercing eye and when he looked at a boy that boy knew that nothing he had done or thought could be covered up. I say that we respected him: it was more than that: we adored him. He was not only a man of unusual physical strength, but he was strikingly handsome." Remarking upon his delicate and gentle mother, he adds: "My father and God, not altogether indistinguishable from each other, filled by far the largest place in my boyhood."[116]

Ellen Glasgow remembers a handsome father, "entirely unselfish," with a "vital sense of responsibility." At the same time, as is evident in many of the diaries and views of childhood in this period, she believes that she has inherited most of her traits from her mother. When Ellen was ten, physicians attempted to help her mother who was suffering from a "nervous illness" for which they could find no organic cause. Glasgow is mystified as to "why my

mother, who had never known a selfish thought in her life, whose
nature was composed of pure goodness," was victimized by illness.
The mother, who married at twenty-one and bore ten children,
remained close to each one, ultimately venting her anxieties
against herself in the form of mental collapse, at which time Ellen
felt desolately abandoned.[117] This is one of the classic patterns of
maternal psychic control: closeness followed by abandonment
followed by feelings of desolation. The childhood of Emily
Dickinson illustrates similar dynamics. She recalls a mother subject
to bouts of depression and suffering from hypochondria. Emily, it
is argued by one writer, suffered a severe depression as a result of
having to deny the rage she felt toward a mother who withdrew
after initial contact.[118]

Diaries are filled with descriptions of psychophysical states
related to emotional smothering or abandonment, as in William
Lyon Phelps's entry of 1880 in which he describes "melancholia
which lasted some weeks. I felt dreadfully, awful bad. Somehow I
was glad when Lizzie came."[119] Hutchkins Hapgood, born in
Chicago in 1869, remarks after killing a bird: "I could not, while
the thought of the dead wren was upon me, bear to be alone.
Painful consciousness was then too intense." Likewise he connects
the discovery of sexuality with feelings of intense guilt and
misery.[120] Henry James had a dream as a child while his family
was visiting France (similar to a dream of Theodore Roosevelt,
while his family was in Europe, in which the devil carried him
away) in which he found himself frantically defending himself
against someone attempting to break into his room. He pressed
against the door while someone was pressing down against the
lock; he was lucky and the intruder left.[121]

Recurrent themes in the diaries of young children may now be
seen in a more significant motivational context. Lucy Larcom
vividly portrays feelings of fragmentation: "Inwardly, I objected
to the idea of being an infant; it seemed to me like nothing in
particular—neither a child nor a little girl, neither a baby nor a
woman. Having discovered that I was capable of being wicked, I
thought it would be better to grow up at once, and assume my
own responsibilities. It quite demoralized me when people talked
in my presence about 'innocent little children.' "[122] Ten-year-old
Catherine Havens of New York writes of her fascination with
funerals, stating that she is intensely drawn to them. She records
the story of a friend who recently passed away.[123]
Twelve-year-old Louis Gratalap of Staten Island writes that "the
hand of Death had not touched us," and another child tells of her
friend Tissie who was struck with convulsions while her parents
were away from home.[124]

The following may be interpreted as an instance of repression of a sensual experience, avoiding, even within the confines of a personal diary, the simple admittance of reality. An adolescent girl writes: "Ally is a *nice child.* We have slept together every night but one for a week. O Horrible. What a pen! And what ink! I cannot read this writing myself. Naughty girl that I am I have not written my dear brother for more than a month." Next she resorts to symbolic expression by copying out several stanzas from a poem concerning a couple who put their candles out and get into bed until they spy six figures in "uncouth garb" just outside the door:

There was one *stately form* who their leader did seem,
Enveloped in a bright scarlet gown,
She moved her long arm to and fro in the air
And flourished her hips up and down.

At this point, the figures take mysterious compounds from the floor and imbibe them until they can be heard no more. The stanzas continue with a terrible scream and then even more terrible laughter:
Oh! Who are those creatures who wander by night?
Are they beings of good or of ill?
Oh! Tell us in pity—we die of a fright—
And we know you can say—if you will.


In this process of externalization, we see that the stigma of sensuality is placed upon others, but fear is only shown in terms of a wish for detachment and control. The girl's next diary entry tells of her loneliness at boarding school and her disappointment that her mother experienced headaches upon visiting the school, headaches which would recur upon the girl's return home.[125]

Most children's diaries are dreary, obsessed with personal failings, guilt, the spectre of death and retribution, an ominous fear that one has sinned without knowing how. There is a general sense that if one submits enough, salvation may be obtained: "Can't I love Him, too . . . I want to love him, so I won't let anything hurt me."[126] Helen Lansing Grinnell kept a diary addressed as a letter to her son Frank from 1859 to 1867 (the years he was five to fourteen years old), and she begins affectionately: "You are the very personification of mischief . . . I hope . . . you will grow up to be a good man, a comfort to your parents, and a blessing to society." Although she writes of whipping Frank, she says that she is ready to cry at having to do it in order to make the boy sober;

but whipping is soon abandoned in favor of words. She reasons with the boy after a beating, "appealing to your affectionate heart, and your . . . ambition, and love of being excited."[127]

## THE CHILDHOODS OF THEODORE ROOSEVELT
## AND WOODROW WILSON

Because of the remarkable paradigmatic significance of Roosevelt's and Wilson's childhoods, they are here presented in some detail. This will also lay a foundation for chapter six, which will deal with the emotional history of the progressive years.

Historians are generally aware that something in Roosevelt's personality was characteristic of America in the late nineteenth century. In Sidney Hook's words, he was "an expressive symbol and instrument of social and historical forces." Erik Erikson conceives of historical actuality, in which an individual's development coincides with the development of the community, so that his personal conflict resolutions are either an idealized or actual microcosm of a workable resolution for society. Roosevelt's contemporaries were already aware that he had his representative quality: "He embraces more sides of American character than any other statesman who has arisen since Abraham Lincoln." A merchant friend said that "Roosevelt can best be understood by saying that he was a symbol of America. He had all the qualities developed to almost ideal form. Another commented, "He was America."[128]

Roosevelt's childhood, in all its detail, was typical of psychic control. His mother, Mittie, was a delicate southern belle, an ornament who was pampered and of whom few demands were made. Having fallen in love with Theodore Roosevelt, a wealthy businessman from New York, she moved north, soon became pregnant, and gave birth to a daughter. But, along with the new demands of maternity, Mittie's health began to fail. She soon departed from her family and traveled to the womb of the South and the comfort of her sister Anna, "who has rubbed me with camphor every night since I have been unwell . . . my hair has not stopped dropping in the least and is painfully thin but Anna thinks she sees some fine hair coming."[129] Although, in 1859, Theodore Roosevelt the younger enjoyed a secured birth and several months of healthy existence, because of his mother's fragility he soon found himself in the hands of his grandmother and a succession of nurses. A bottle soon replaced the breast, and the competition of a younger brother came in February of 1860. By this time, even the initial stages of motherhood were too difficult for Mittie. The birth was difficult and painful and she was unable to nurse at the breast.[130]

Mittie continued to have difficulty with life's stresses. Before her mother made a trip to the South to visit her son who had been wounded fighting for the Confederacy, Mittie was stricken with many intense pains. She felt similar pains when her husband left for his wartime administrative post in Washington. She wrote to her husband: "I wish you were not so good. It makes me feel so sad. I am not so strong-minded as you know, and feel so dependent."[131] G. Wallace Chessman summarizes Mittie's intensified anxieties as follows:

> As the family's activities broadened and intensified, Mittie retreated more often to her room. It was said that her health was delicate, and likely she welcomed an excuse to get away. Somehow she had kept up before, but the case was getting too much for one accustomed to more leisurely Southern ways. Increasingly she showed a passion for cleanliness, an incompetence at money matters and housekeeping, a disposition to be late for appointments. When she appeared at parties, so immaculately groomed in her beautiful gown, she impressed all with her charm, but she just couldn't manage life efficiently.[132]

The biographer of Mittie's eldest daughter describes how Mittie's headaches allowed her to find retreat in her room for several hours until her excitement abated. Some time later, somatic symptoms took a compulsive turn, and she was not able to leave the house until she had taken two baths, one for washing and one for rinsing. Another writer relates that "she had a sheet spread on the floor each night next to her bed so that she might say her prayers in comfort and not be conscious of the possibility of dirt when addressing the Lord. When ill and the doctor came, a sheet would be spread over the seat where he was to sit."[133]

A letter of Mittie's, written soon before a reunion with her husband, illustrates some of the dynamics of the passive-dependent wife:

> I love you and I wish to please you more than anything else in the whole world and will do everything I can to please you that is not unreasonable. I think that you have been perfectly lovely to me in your care of me always and so good and indulgent and thoughtful and I am so proud of you and honor and respect you so *don't be too hard upon me.*[134]

Theodore (Teedie) developed a constellation of traits built around the dynamics of oral rage—caused by the fragile personality of his mother, her withdrawal from his intimate care, her somatization of feelings, her compulsive fear of dirt, her fear of abandonment by her husband, the the confusing shifts of Teedie from one guardian to another. Besides a wealth of literature describing his aggressive orality—the anger in his oratory, his characteristic use of his teeth, and his general aggressiveness—we must also consider his childhood asthma. Due to meticulous notes taken by his grandmother, Martha Stewart Bullock, it is possible to date Teedie's asthma to 1863. Of the few other records concerning Teedie's fourth year of life, it is possible to examine one incident of significance: the only time Roosevelt remembered his father physically punishing him. The incident's significance in Roosevelt's own eyes is illustrated by the fact that he described the event in his autobiography:

> I bit my elder sister's arm. I do not remember biting her arm, but I do remember running down to the yard, and perfectly conscious that I had committed a crime. From the yard I went into the kitchen, got some dough from the cook and crawled under the kitchen table. In a minute or two my father entered from the yard and asked where I was. The warm-hearted Irish cook had a characteristic contempt for "informers," but although she said nothing she compromised between informing and her conscience by a look under the table.[135]

The wrath of Theodore Roosevelt, Sr., must have been great, indeed, for his son Teedie had touched a soft spot. Roosevelt, like many men of his time, had a protectionist feeling towards women in general and had centered much of his existence around organizations helping little children in need. It is now possible to propose a mechanism for the asthma which soon followed. There was no way to get closer to his mother and Teedie was not satisfied to take his brother Ellie's strategy of extreme attachment to the surrogate represented by his grandmother. Teedie felt some of the intense devotion and increased affection his father felt towards children in need. His aggressive orality had to be under severe control and he was taught not to harm others. As a result the aggression was turned inward. The difficulty in breathing was an eloquent cry for closeness and care, and during his attacks he found that his father's love intensified.

The asthma created attention. He wrote in his autobiography that "I was a sickly, delicate boy, suffered much from asthma, and frequently had to be taken away on trips to find a place where I could breathe. One of my earliest memories is of my father walking up and down the room with me in his arms at night when I was a very small person, and of sitting up in bed gasping, with my mother and father trying to help me." He did not go to school but instead was privately instructed at home. His father wrote his wife: "Omit no effort to relieve him." Lincoln Steffens would later be told by TR: "I remember, I think I remember—him carrying me in my distress, in my battle for breath, up and down the room all night . . . . My father—he got me lungs, strength—life."[136]

But, as is true of the dynamics of psychic control, closeness through physical infirmity holds limited benefits. By age ten, Theodore was viewed less as a suffering child and more as a youth whose convalescence was very much in his own power. Theodore must get into shape. During this time the boy's interest in hunting intensified, and in Europe with his father in 1868 he climbed a mountain and hiked thirteen miles in one day. Later, in 1869, after an attack of asthma, he was forced by his father to smoke a cigar in bed. The day after Theodore's first smoke he was left behind while the family went on a sightseeing tour. It is not surprising that one of the only dreams Theodore recorded is a nightmare which occurred that very evening: "The Devil was carrying me away and I have cholera morbus." The young man is being punished for his physical disability; yet his stringent conscience forbids realization of his hostility except in symbolic form, as in the drawing below, which dates from 1869:[137]

Fig. 8. Theodore Roosevelt's childhood self-portrait

Theodore led the archetypal controlled existence—trained physically at the gym, trained intellectually by tutors, watched prudently by parents bent on his intellectual, moral, and physical development. As Mittie's health decayed further and she depended on her strong husband more and more, Theodore grew in strength, retaining an intense pool of aggression, now directed into fierce athletic competitions and hunting.

The Roosevelt family presents two resolutions to the childhood of psychic control, one successful, the other failure-ridden. As Theodore grew in strength, his brother Elliott grew weaker and more riddled with anxiety and doubts over his self-worth; he even wrote a short story about a man who killed his children and injured his wife when she attempted to stop the slaughter. During this period, Theodore made the following drawings, expressions of the aggressive, forward-reaching youth defending himself against castrating females:[138]

Fig. 9. Theodore Roosevelt's Drawings of Himself in Relation to Women

Elliott's resolution involved coping with rage and anxiety inwardly, and the psychic costs were often steep. Soon after his return from Europe, his father wrote of Elliott's strange illness: "Its foothold conquers the brain with all its attendant horrors of delirium etc. The doctor says that there is no cause for anxiety as it is only necessary to avoid all excitements for two or three years and he will entirely outgrow it. . . . Anything like a dispute seems worse for him than any other excitement."[139] A letter from Elliott sent from a rest on a dude ranch in the West indicates the cost of failure in psychic control: "Oh, Father, will you ever think *me* a 'noble boy,' you are right about Tede—he is one and no mistake a boy I would give a good deal to be like in many respects."[140] A later entry in his personal diary exhibits an extensive idealization of woman, built on a primal repression of initial maternal deprivation: "When my worship for women began I cannot tell . . . perhaps when the poor little mother . . . called me her loving son and only comfort . . . She [his wife] seems so pure and high and ideal that in my roughness and unworthiness I do not know how I can be happy."[141] Elliott failed eventually to meet his wife's expectations, becoming an alcoholic and dying after living anonymously with a mistress for some time after the death of his wife.

Theodore continued the successful resolution of aggressive drives through boundless action, self-discipline, and control, entering Harvard and gaining a reputation for his harsh schedule of work and lofty moral standards. His reaction to the death of Roosevelt, Sr., when he was still at Harvard, shows the dynamic of paternal idealization and relative feelings of worthlessness.

> I often feel badly that such a wonderful man as Father should have a son of so little worth as I am . . . during services today I could not help recollecting sadly of how little use I am, or shall ever be in this world, not through lack of perseance [perseverance] and good intentions but through sheer inability. I realize more and more every day that I am as much inferior to Father mentally as physically.[142]

Yet Theodore reacted to the loss with an immediate involvement in activity and continued to censor hostile thoughts—thoughts that ultimately found oblique expressions, one suspects, in his bizarre excursions to Africa and the American West, and the resulting orgiastic slaughter of wild animals.[143]

Woodrow Wilson likewise illustrates a childhood filled with the realities of psychic control. He was born in 1856, about three years before Roosevelt, in Staunton, Virginia. Both his parents were steeped in morality. His mother, Jessie Woodrow Wilson, came from a religious Scotch background, and his father, Joseph Ruggles Wilson, was a Presbyterian minister. Wilson would later write of his yearnings for his mother: "I remember how I clung to her till I was a great big fellow." Precisely as was the case with Roosevelt, Wilson enjoyed a relatively healthy infancy, yet later suffered an unhealthy boyhood, with digestive problems so severe as to necessitate his staying home from school.[144] Like Mittie, Mrs. Wilson had little vitality, and soon after Woodrow's infancy it was Mr. Wilson who took the domineering role in the household.

Likewise, all expression of hostility and aggression was unacceptable. When Woodrow, nicknamed Tommy, was tricked into believing he hurt a girl during play, he ran into the house crying "I am a murderer. It wasn't an accident. I killed her."[145]

Likewise, the development of his conscience—a conscience identified with the wishes of his father—was thoroughgoing and complete. Wilson would later remember that his father "would not permit me to blurt things out or stammer a half-way job of telling whatever I had to tell. If I became excited . . . he always said, 'steady now, Thomas. . . . Think! Think what it is you wish to say, and then choose your words and say it' "[146] Such language is reflective of psychic control, in which the ability to master one's tongue is essential and is seen as the external indication of successful focus and discipline. Wilson identified completely with the pursuit of a disciplined tongue, becoming consciously infatuated with language. Actually, the reverend's control of the boy's tongue was even more severe than Wilson later remembered it. After speaking on a subject, his father would question him, and then often ask him to write out a paraphrase so that the boy would be on record. If any section was slightly ambiguous, the reverend would caustically demand revision.

Instead of losing his interest in self-expression as a result of such discipline, Wilson overcompensated by attempting to master it. He became president of his baseball club, organizing meetings and practicing a crude parliamentary procedure, eventually idolizing Gladstone, the great "Christian statesman."

Wilson's father continued to preach the gospel of psychic control: "In short, dearest boy, do not allow yourself to dwell upon *yourself*—concentrate your thoughts upon *thoughts* and *things* and *events*."[147] The advice Wilson received from his mother was gentler, characteristically coming during times of trouble and bodily infirmity. The passive woman expressed a wish for stability: "You seem depressed—but that is because you are not well. You need not imagine that you are not a favorite. *Everybody* here likes and admires you. I could not begin to tell you the kind and flattering things that are said about you, everybody that knows you. . . . Why my darling, nobody could *help* loving you, if they were to try!"[148]

Tommy would later write of his need to "overcome evil desires, those powerful and ever present enemies, by constant watchfulness and with the strong weapon of prayer, and by cultivating those heavenly desires which are sure to root out the evil ones."[149] That the student Wilson was thoroughly instilled with the ideology of disciplined control is clear in his own writings:

> No man, whatever may have been his natural endowments of mind, has ever accomplished anything . . . except by untiring work and hard, though silent, and, perhaps, unseen *work*. . . . Genius without discipline is a ship without rudder or sails—a mere inert mass. . . . And let me again remind you that only by working with an energy which is almost superhuman . . . can we accomplish anything worth the achievement. Work is the keystone of a perfect life.[150]

Wilson, like Roosevelt, had reason for hostility. The absence of a reliable mother, who initially attempted intimate care but removed herself later, followed by a domineering, socializing father, represented a trying start in life. Examples abound of his father's sarcastic tongue. In an awkward puberty ritual similar to Roosevelt's having to smoke a cigar after an asthma attack, Wilson explained to a dinner guest when Tommy was late that his son was too busy discovering another hair in his mustache. The guest later testified: "I remember very distinctly the painful flush that came over the boy's face."[151] In addition, the didactic onslaught came from more than one generation. When he was president, Wilson visited a church his grandfather had preached in and recalled: "I remember my grandfather very well. . . . I remember how much he required. I remember the stern lessons of duty he gave me. I remember also, painfully, the things which he expected me to know which I do not know. . . . But I am reluctant because the feelings that have been excited in me are too intimate and too deep to permit public expression."[152]

One can search the man's entire life, as with Roosevelt, and find no sign of openly felt hostility toward either parent. His fragile mother he described as a "quiet character," with "a sense of duty, and dislike of ostentation," whose positive influence had shown "increasing force as these years of duty have accumulated."[153] Wilson also displayed an idealization of women in general.[154] He invariably hugged his father when they met and wrote him under epistolary greetings like "beloved" and "incomparable." Ray Stannard Baker stated: "His father was the greatest figure in his youth—perhaps the greatest of his whole life. . . . The letters between the two can be called nothing but love letters."[155] One writer calls Wilson's love for his father a "dominant passion." Wilson continued to associate his positive side with his father, remarking to Dudley Field Malone: "When I feel badly, sour and gloomy and everything seems wrong, then I know that my mother's character is uppermost in me. But when life seems gay and fine and splendid, then I know that the part of my father which is in me is in ascendance." Like Roosevelt an oldest son, Wilson, identified with the delegated task of becoming a moral leader, once indicating to his father that he felt he would one day hold a lofty position.[156]

Wilson also felt inferior to his father: "If I had my father's face anf figure, it wouldn't make any difference what I said." Biographer Alexander George indicates: "He once said the most difficult speech he ever had to make was one during which he suddenly spied his father in the audience; he felt exactly like a boy again, as though he would have to answer to his father afterward for what he said."[157] On another occasion, when a friend of his late father's visited him in the White House, Wilson wept at the thought of his father. As a graduate student at Princeton he wrote his father: "It seems to be that the older I get the more I need you; for the older I get the more I appreciate the debt I owe you. . . . my separation from you, instead of becoming a thing of want, becomes more and more undesirable."[158]

To many, Roosevelt and Wilson are distinct personality types. Yet on deeper analysis, their means of coping, their resolutions, are only slightly different modes of defense against similar pains. While Roosevelt expressed his rebellion and frustration through aggression, in a visceral confrontation with the world, Wilson used his intellect as an instrument of defense. As a boy, he reacted to parental pressures to learn by blocking out knowledge, becoming a mediocre student, until he found that little was gained by such a strategy. In later years, Wilson became increasingly moralistic and rigid in his alliances and associations. The constant is an intense feeling of mission which may be conceptualized as a result of a high degree of parental superego delegation. Wilson claimed he felt like a volcano; Roosevelt was described as a dynamo. An ethic of the necessity of constant work permeated their entire existences, lives of strenuous self-discipline and activity, lives dedicated to imposing new organizational structures upon their environments. In chapter six we shall see how their psychic control personalities were perfect instruments for the expression of the historical emotions of the entire control generation.

REFERENCES

1. Charles Stickland, "A Transcendentalist Father: The Child Rearing Practices of Bronson Alcott," *History of Childhood Quarterly*, Summer 1973, p. 15.
2. *ibid.*, p. 31.
3. "Extract from a Mother's Journal," *Mother's Magazine*, 1934, pp. 40-43.
4. William McLoughlin, "Evangelical Child-Rearing in the Age of Jackson: Francis Wayland's Views on When and How to Subdue the Willfulness of Children," *Journal of Social History*, Fall 1975, pp. 20-39.
5. Ibid., p. 22.
6. Ibid., p. 23.
7. Ibid., p. 27.
8. *Mother's Magazine*, December 1862, p. 374.
9. E. M. Olcott, diary, July 1856. New York Historical Society.
10. *Days at Muirhead* (New York: Robert Carter, 1861), p. 296.
11. E. M. Olcott, diary, December 1856. Loc. cit.
12. Ibid.
13. James Janeway, *A Token for Children* (New York, 1850).
14. Louis Gratalap, diary, 1863. New York Historical Society.
15. James Black, *Taking a Stand* (Boston: Henry Hoyt, [c. 1861]), p. 38.
16. *Broken Idols: A Story for Girls* (Boston: Sabbath-School Society, 1868).
17. Rebecca Read, *Above and Below; or, Why the Baby Died* (Boston: Congregational Publishing Society, 1872), p. 35.
18. Lydia H. Sigourney, *Sayings of the Little Ones, and Poems for Their Mothers* (Buffalo: Phinney & Co., 1855), p. 24.
19. Ibid., p. 28.
20. E. M. Olcott, journal, 1854. Loc. cit.
21. Catherine Elizabeth Havens, *Diary of a Little Girl in Old New York* (New York: Henry Collins Brown, 1920), p. 112.
22. L. M. Kuhns, "The Religious Training of the Children of the Church," *Lutheran Quarterly* 1:4 (1871); Jacob Burns, *Mothers of the Wise and Good* (Boston: Gould, 1850), p. 246; B. F. Barrett, *Beauty for Ashes: The Old and the New Doctrine Concerning the State of Infants After Death* (New York: D. Appleton & Co., 1855); A. J. W. Myers, *Horace Bushnell and Religious Education* (Boston: Manthorne & Burack, 1937).
23. Horace Bushnell, *Christian Nurture*, 1847.
24. *Southern Literary Messenger*, April 1854, p. 214.

25. Cornelia Meigs, et al., *A Critical History of Children's Literature* (New York: Macmillan, 1953); Richard Darling, *The Rise of Children's Book Reviewing in America, 1865-1881* (New York: R. R. Bowker, 1968).

26. *The Son Unguided and His Mother's Shame* (New York: John Gray, 1848).

27. John Habberton, *Budge and Loddie: Their Haps and Mishaps* (New York: G. P. Putnam's Sons, 1878), p. 6.

28. *What Changed Guy Dennis* (Philadelphia: American Sunday School Union, 1874), pp. 23-24.

29. *Memoirs of a Doll: A New-Year's Gift* (Philadelphia: American Sunday School Union, 1854), p. 31.

30. William . Thayer, *The Bobbins Boy; or, How Nat Got His Learning* (Boston: J. E. Tilton, 1860), p. 27.

31. *The Mischief Maker: Ralph Rattler* (Boston: G. C. Rand, 1854), pp. 63-64.

32. Glance Gaylord, *The Boys at Dr. Murray's: A Story of School Life* (Boston: Graves and Young, 1866).

33. *The Brother and Sister; or, The Way of Peace* (New York: Robert Carter and Brothers, 1855), p. 239.

34. Habberton, *Budge and Loddie*, p. 6.

35. T. S. Arthur, *The Poor Woodcutter and Other Stories* (Philadelphia: Lippincott, 1875), p. 152.

36. Bernard Wishy, *The Child and the Republic: The Dawn of American Child Nurture* (Philadelphia: University of Pennsylvania Press, 1968).

37. Samuel Osgood, "Books for Our Children," *Atlantic Monthly*, 1865, p. 724.

38. Meigs, *A Critical History*, p. 257.

39. Ibid.

40. Horatio Algier, Jr., *Strive and Succeed* (Chicago: M. A. Donohue, 1872).

41. Sigourney, *Sayings of the Little Ones*, pp. 20-21. Other literary sources include: Horace Scudder, *Childhood in Literature and Art* (New York: Houghton Mifflin, 1894); Edward Salmon, "Literature for the Little Ones," *Nineteenth Century*, October 1887; "Children: Their Blunders, Their Books, Their Humor, and Their Wit," *Southern Magazine*, April 1874; Henrietta Christian Wright, *Children's Stories in American Literature, 1861 - 1896* (New York: Charles Scribner's Sons, 1899); "Books for Children," *Quarterly Review* (London), December, 1842; "Books for Our Children," *Atlantic Monthly*, December 1865; "Children's Books of the Year," *North American Review*,

January 1866; "Children's Literature," *National Magazine*, January 1898; "Literature for Children," *North American Review*, April 1884; "The Children of Fiction," *Littell's Living Age*, Octomer 1892.

42. *Mother's Magazine*, 1833, p. 41.
43. Rev. B. Stowe, "Thoughts for the Thoughtless," *Mother's Assistant*, May 1850, p. 116.
44. Rev. C. Beckwith, "The Fate of Nations Dependent on Mothers," *Mother's Assistant and Young Lady's Friend*, January 1850, p. 4.
45. Charles Enfield, "Early Culture," *Mother's Assistant*, February 1849, p. 3.
46. Elizabeth Hull, "A Mother's Influence," *Mother's Assistant*, February 1849, p. 3.
47. "Obedience Is Its Own Reward," *Mother's Magazine*, August 1867, p. 245.
48. *Mother's Journal*, May 1851, p. 171.
49. *Mother's Journal*, March 1853, p. 79.
50. *Mother's Journal*, April 1852, p. 111.
51. Agnes Sinclair Holbrook, "Fear in Childhood," in *Studies in Education*, ed. Earl Barnes (1896).
52. G. Stanley Hall, *Life and Confessions of a Psychologist* (New York: Appleton, 1923), p. 41.
53. *Mother's Magazine*, November 1861, p. 334.
54. *Mother's Magazine*, January 1873; August 1866, p. 244.
55. Ibid.
56. Mrs. L. C. Tuthill, *Joy and Care: A Family Book for Young Mothers* (New York: Charles Scribner, 1855), p. 42.
57. "A Mother's Confession," *Harper's New Monthly Magazine*, January 1858, pp. 85-95.
58. Thomas Bull, *On the Maternal Management of Children in Health and Disease* (Philadelphia: Linday & Blakiston, 1849), p. 50.
59. Henry C. Wright, *Marriage and Parentage: The Reproductive Element in Man* (Boston: Bela Marsh, 1866); John Eberle, *Treatise on the Diseases and Physical Education of Women* (Philadelphia: Grigg & Elliott, 1844), p. 12; Edward H. Clarke, *Sex in Education* (Boston: 1875); R. L. Trall, *Sexual Diseases* (New York: Fowler & Wells, 1858); George H. Napheys, *The Physical Life of Women* (Philadelphia: J. G. Fergus, 1874).
60. Heywood Smith, *A Handbook of the Diseases of Women* (Philadelphia: Lindsay & Blakiston, 1878), p. 2; *The Young Husband's Book* (Philadelphia: Lea and Blanchard, 1843),

pp. 15, 38.

61. Elizabeth M. Sewell, *Home Life: A Journal* (New York: D. Appleton, 1867), p. 291.

62. Murray Nicholas, *The Happy Home* (New York: Harper & Bros., 1858), pp. 47-48.

63. Ibid., p. 48.

64. *Child at Home*, January 1862, p. 6.

65. *Mother's Journal*, December 1848, p. 365; January 1851, p. 10; *Mother's Magazine*, April 1870, p. 110.

66. Theodore Roosevelt, *An Autobiography* (New York: Charles Scribner's Sons, 1926); Clarence S. Darrow, *The Story of My Life* (New York: Charles Scribner's Sons, 1932); Richard T. Ely, *Ground Under our Feet* (New York: Macmillan, 1938); Frederic C. Howe, *Confessions of a Reformer* (Chicago: Quadrangle, 1967); William Allen White, *The Autobiography of William Allen White* (New York: Macmillan, 1946); Samuel Gompers, *Seventy Years of Life and Labor: An Autobiography*, 2 vols. (New York: E. P. Dutton, 1948); Tarence Powderly, *The Path I Trod: The Autobiography of Tarence V. Powderly* (New York: Columbia University Press, 1940).

67. Hall, *Confessions*, p. 80.

68. Martin Duberman, *Charles Francis Adams, 1807-1886* (Stanford, 1960); C. F. Adams, *Charles Francis Adams* (Boston, 1900).

69. Gerhart S. Schwarz, "Devices to Prevent Masturbation," *Medical Aspects of Sexuality*, May 1973.

70. O. S. Fowler, *Amativeness; or, the Evils and Remedies of Excessive and Perverted Sexuality* (Edinburgh: H. Robinson, [c. 1850] ).

71. R. L. Trall, *Sexual Diseases* (New York: Fowler and Wells, 1858), pp. v, 40.

72. R. P. Neuman, "Masturbation and the Development of the Modern Concepts of Childhood and Adolescence" (unpublished paper).

72. Charles West, *Lectures on the Diseases of Children* (Philadelphia: Henry C. Lea, 1874), p. 219.

73. Charles D. Meigs, *A Treatise on Acute and Chronic Diseases of the Neck of the Uterus* (Philadelphia: Blanchard & Lea, 1854), p. 22.

74. Edward Dixon, *Woman and Her Diseases from Cradle to the Grave* (New York: Charles H. Ring, 1847), p. 59.

75. Smith, *A Handbook of the Diseases of Women*, p. 2.

76. *Mother's Magazine*, March 1859, p. 111.

77. Ibid.
78. Clara Barton, *The Story of My Childhood* (Meriden: The Journal, 1907), p. 83.
79. William Lyon Phelps, *Autobiography with Letters* (New York: Oxford University Press, 1939), p. 13.
80. James P. Walker, *Character* (Boston: American Unitarian Society, 1863), p. 8.
81. Robert Nelson Corwin, *The Plain Unpolished Tale of the Workaday Doings of Modest Folks* (privately printed), p. 51.
82. Henry Kiddle, *Common-School Teaching* (New York: E. Steiger, 1877), pp. 8, 23, 33, 34.
83. Donald R. Raichle, "The Abolition of Corporal Punishment in New Jersey Schools," *History of Childhood Quarterly* 2 (Summer 1974); Lyman Cobb, *The Evil Tendencies of Corporal Punishment* (New York: Mark Newman, 1847), p. 82.
84. *Mother's Magazine*, April 1879.
85. Barbara Finkelstein, "Pedagogy as Intrusion: Teaching Values in Popular Primary Schools in Nineteenth-Century America," *HIstory of Childhood Quarterly* 2 (Winter 1975).
86. Raymond Callahan, *Education and the Cult of Efficiency* (Chicago: University of Chicago Press, 1962); Lawrence A. Cremin, *The Transformation of the School* (New York: Random House, 1961); Ruth Miller Elson, "The Child of the Nineteenth Century and His Schoolbooks," in *The Cult of Youth in Middle-Class America* (Lexington: D. C. Heath, 1971).
87. *Mother's Journal* December 1848.
88. Henry A. Shute, *The Real Diary of a Real Boy* (Boston: The Everett Press, 1902), p. 4.
89. Mark deWolfe Howe, *Justice Oliver Wendell Holmes: The Shaping Years, 1841-70* (Cambridge: Harvard University Press, 1957), p. 4.
90. *The Mischief Maker: Ralph Rattler* (Boston: G. C. Rand, 1854), pp. 63-64.
91. Ellen Glasgow, *The Woman Within* (New York: Harcourt, Brace & Co., 1954), pp. 47-48.
92. Thayer, *The Bobbins Boy*, p. 27.
93. William A. Alcott, *Young Mothers* (Boston: Light & Stearns, 1836), p. 111.
94. Ibid.; Robert Sunley, ' Early Nineteenth-Century American Literature on Child Rearing," in *Childhood in Contemporary Cultures*, ed. Margaret Mead and Martha Wolfenstein (Chicago: University of Chicago Press, 1955); Al Donné,

*Mothers and Infants, Nurses and Nursing* (Boston: Phillips, Sampson, 1859).

95. Caleb Ticknor, *A Guide for Mothers and Nurses in the Management of Young Children* (New York: Taylor and Dodd, 1839).

96. Ibid., p. 135.

97. *Mortality Statistics of the Seventh Census of the United States* (Washington: A. D. P. Nicolson Printer, 1855); Edward Shorter, *The Making of the Modern Family* (New York: Basic Books, 1975); Harriet Martineau, "Herod in the Nineteenth Century," *Once a Week 1 (1859): 196; "Forty Per Cent,"* Temple Bar *8 (1863): 513;* Oscar L. Dudley, *Saving the Children* (Boston, 1893).

98. Daniel R. Miller & Guy Swanson, *The Changing American Parent: A Study in the Detroit Area* (New York: John Wiley & Sons, 1958).

99. Shorter, *The Making of the Modern Family.*

100. Tuthill, *Joy and Care;* Caleb Ticknor, *A Guide for Mothers and Nurses;* Katherine Morris McClinton, *Antiques of American Childhood* (New York: Clarkson N. Potter, 1970), p. 153; C. LeFavre, *Mother's Helper and Child's Friend* (New York: Brentano's, 1840), p. 142; Jacob Hartmann, *The Modern Baby: The Art of Nursing* (New York: E. H. Blinn, 1881).

101. McClinton, *Antiques.*

102. *Mother's Magazine,* April 1860, p. 140; Lydia Child, *The Mother's Book* (Boston: Carter, 1831); Wishy, *The Child and the Republic,* p. 42.

103. Cobb, *The Evil Tendencies of Corporal Punishment.*

104. Richard Rapson, "The American Child as Seen by British Travelers," *American Quarterly* 17 (1971); H. H., *Bits of Talk About Home Matters* (Boston: Roberts Bros., 1877); Augusta Larned, *Talks with Girls* (New York: Nelson and Phillips, 1874); *Mother's Magazine,* September 1867; *Mother's Magazine,* May 1859, p. 134.

105. *Mother's Magazine,* August 1867, p. 241; Tuthill, *Joy and Care,* p. 103; *Mother's Journal,* April 1851, p. 103; Murray Nicholas, *The Happy Home* (New York: Harper and Bros., 1858), p. 21; *Mother's Magazine,* March 1859.

106. "The Relation of the Child to the Home," *The Unitarian Review,* June 1874, p. 321.

107. L. A. Kuhn, *The Mother's Role in Childhood Education: New England Concepts, 1830-60* (New Haven: Yale University Press, 1847).

108. Elizabeth Charlotte Ingersoll, *Libbie C's Memoir* (Rochester: Strong, 1858).
109. For an analysis of the psychosomatic dynamics of the Roosevelt household, see Glenn Davis, "The Early Years of Theodore Roosevelt," *History of Childhood Quarterly* (Spring 1975).
110. Catherine Elizabeth Havens, *Diary of a Little Girl in Old New York* (New York: Henry Brown, 1920), p. 16.
111. Sigourney, *Sayings of the Little Ones.*
112. Howe, p. 28; Hall, *Confessions.*
113. Howe, *Confessions of a Reformer.*
114. Adams, *The Education of Henry Adams*, p. 13.
115. Frank Lewis, *Edison: His Life and Inventions* (New York: Harper and Bros., 1910); Allen Davis, *American Heroine: The Life and Legend of Jane Addams* (New York: Oxford Universtiy Press, 1973), p. 5.
116. Ray Stannard Baker, *Native American: The Book of My Youth* (New York: Charles Scribner's Sons, 1941), p. 31.
117. Glasgow, *The Woman Within*, p. 63.
118. John Cody, *After Great Pain: The Inner Life of Emily Dickenson* (Cambridge: Harvard University Press, 1971).
119. William Lyon Phelps, *Autobiography with Letters* (New York: Oxford University, 1939).
120. Hutchkins Hapgood, *A Victorian in the Modern World* (New York: Harcourt, Brace, 1939), p. 17.
121. Leon Edel, *Henry James: 1843-1870: The Untried Years* (New York: J.B. Lippincott, 1953), p. 74.
122. Lucy Larcom, *A New England Girlhood: Outlined from Memory* (New York: Houghton Mifflin, 1889, p. 78.
123. Havens, *Diary of a Little Girl in Old New York*, p. 57.
124. Louis Gratalap, diary, 1863. loc. cit.
125. Sarah Jane Bradley, diary, 1848. New York Historical Society.
126. *Broken Idols: A Story for Girls* (Boston: Massachusetts Sabbath-School Society, 1868).
127. Helen Lansing Grinnell, diary, 1850-1867. New York Historical Society.
128. Glenn Davis, "Theodore Roosevelt and the Progressive Era: A Study in Individual and Group Psychohistory," in *The New Psychohistory*, ed. Lloyd deMause (New York: Psychohistory Press, 1975), p. 291.
129. Letter, Martha (Bulloch) Roosevelt to Theodore Roosevelt, May 15, 1855. All Roosevelt manuscripts cited are in Houghton Library, Harvard University.

130. Letter, Martha (Stewart) Bulloch to Susan (Elliott) West, May 7, 1860.
131. Letter, Martha (Bulloch Roosevelt to Theodore Roosevelt, June 2, 1873.
132. G. Wallace Chessman, *Theodore Roosevelt and the Politics of Power* (Boston: Little, Brown and Co.), p. 14.
133. Carleton Putnam, *Theodore Roosevelt: The Formative Years, 1858-1886* (New York: Charles Scribner's Sons, 1921), p. 53.
134. Letter, Martha (Bulloch) Roosevelt, to Theodore Roosevelt, n.d.
135. Roosevelt, *Autobiography*, pp. 8-9.
136. Lincoln Steffens, *The Autobiography of Lincoln Steffens*, (New York: Harcourt, Brace and World, 1931), 1:350.
137. Theodore Roosevelt, diary, 1869.
138. Theodore Roosevelt, letter home from Dresden, Germany, 1873.
139. Letter, Theodore Roosevelt to Martha (Bulloch) Roosevelt, November 27, 1873.
140. Joseph P. Lash, *Eleanor and Franklin* (New York: W. W. Norton, 1973).
141. Diary, Elliott Roosevelt, February 1883; Howard Umansky, "Theodore Roosevelt Family: A Case of Sibling Rivalry" (paper presented at the American Historical Association, San Francisco, December 29, 1973).
142. Putnam, *Theodore Roosevelt*, p. 151.
143. Lincoln Lang, *Ranching With Roosevelt* (Philadelphia: Lippincott, 1926).
144. Alexander L. and Juliette L. George, *Woodrow Wilson and Colonel House* (New York: John Day, 1956).
145. Sigmund Freud and William C. Bullitt, *Thomas Woodrow Wilson: A Psychological Study* (Boston: Houghton Mifflin, 1927), p. 11.
146. Alexander and Juliette George, *Woodrow Wilson;* George Osborn, "The Influence of Joseph Ruggles Wilson on His Son Woodrow Wilson," *North Carolina Historical Review* (October 1955), p. 337.
147. Ibid.
148. Arthur S. Link, *The Papers of Woodrow Wilson* (Princeton: Princeton University Press, 1966), 1:50.
149. James David Barber, *The Presidential Character: Predicting Performance in the White House* (Englewood Cliffs: Prentice-Hall, 1972), p. 104.
150. Link, *Papers*, Vol. I, pp. 244-45.

151. George and George, *Woodrow Wilson*, p. 8.
152. Rear Admiral Cary T. Grayson, *Woodrow Wilson: An Intimate Memoir* (New York: Holt, Rinehart and Winston, 1959), p. 17.
153. Link, *Papers*, 2:536.
154. *Ibid.*
155. Freud and Bullitt, *Thomas Woodrow Wilson*, p. 6.
156. George and George, *Woodrow Wilson*, p. 8.
157. "Wilson's Boyhood," in the Georges' *Woodrow Wilson*.
158. Ibid.

# CHAPTER THREE

## AGGRESSIVE TRAINING, 1880-1910

During the latter part of the nineteenth century, a progressive segment of the population, raised under the innovations of psychic control and now parents in their own right, was able to regress successfully to old, unsolved conflicts in the process of rearing its children and thereby forge new child-rearing methods. In the period from 1880 to 1910, we witness a decrease in authority bonds, a move in the direction of more empathy, a relaxation of authoritarianism, a reduced fear of children's instincts, and a resulting release of energy and expansive vitality.

An excellent statement of the essentials of aggressive training is the following remark, made in 1896: "Each child can be trained in the way *he* should go, but not every child can be trained to the exercise of powers which are not his."[1] Again, each parameter of the childhood experience—fiction, questions of religion and a u t h o r i t y , maternity-paternity, medical issues, sexuality, education, child-rearing practices, and the tangible impact of all of these on children—helps us to understand these evolutionary dynamics.

The concept of aggressive training is made most tangible in diaries and letters. For example, the diary of a young school teacher, Miss A. M. Libby, indicates the emerging intensification of warmth toward the child: "I feel as if I have learned a great deal about children in this year, but why couldn't I have learned it years ago. People don't give them chances. Those who teach them to obey generally do it with such a hard way."[2]

One trend of note in the documents of direct experience is the fact that individuals writing of their childhoods in the 1880s are—from the vantage point of the early twentieth century—more willing than their predecessors to articulate their most intimate and passionate feelings on paper, rather than drive them from consciousness. Mabel Dodge Luhan writes of being persuaded to sleep with a new servant, Elsa: "With a great firmness, I leaned over and seized her big warm breast in both hands. . . . I felt my blood. . . . as my sudden new, delicious pleasure increased, I grew rougher. I longed now to hurt it and bring something from it. I wanted to pound and burst it. . . . I wanted to force from this one the same steely stream of milk that I felt within, resisting me." She goes on to describe her innermost feelings concerning childbirth, her joyous pregnancy, her extremely healthy baby, and her subsequent rejection of it following her inability to nurse.[3]

Further evidence of this lessened repression and increased ability to bring feelings to consciousness is the memoir of Eleanor Abbott, *Being Little In Cambridge When Everyone Else Was Big.* She writes: "I can remember the day of my birth . . . not a memory of the event but a purely sensory imprint as it were on soul or flesh of the distinct shock coincidental with the experience of being born." Intergenerational strife is recalled with similar vividness. Abbott—whose grandfather Jacob Abbott wrote extensively on child rearing—recalls being squelched at the dinner table, first by her sister, then by her mother and father, all of them humiliated in front of their guests by her voicing an opinion. A subsequent incident with the girl's nurse draws our attention; she was being put into her nightgown by the nurse when the string went into a knot: "In an impulse of unprecedented panic I hurled myself from her lap to the floor and ripped the gown in two . . . 'Naughty, naughty nursie,' I cried out, 'don't tie anything around that hasn't any breath in it. And if you ever shut me up in anything that's locked, I'll kill you!' I screamed." Now, frantic, she tried to relate her memories of being born but was thrust out of the nurse's lap and called a horrid little girl. The implications of such painful memories are profound; but of more immediate concern is the novel ability to bring such pain to consciousness rather than keeping it suppressed or articulated only in oblique and symbolic forms. And although Abbott, like children of the previous generation, describes her attendance at funerals, she states that they were of limited fascination and interest. Not being psychologically bound, she would leave on the earliest opportunity.[4]

## AGGRESSIVE TRAINING LITERATURE

Whereas, in earlier years, literature concerned with children was very involved with authority and the dangers of trespassing upon it, the newer literature focused instead on a milder form of influence. *The Hoosier School-Boy* presents an interesting juxtaposition of physical (intrusive mode), psychic, and training (socializing mode) orientations. A school master is addressing his charges:

"When I am talking to you, I want to hear," he went on very quietly. "I am paid to teach you. One of the things I have to teach you is good manners. You," pointing to Riley, "are old enough to know better than to take your seat when your teacher is speaking, but perhaps you never have been taught what are good manners. I'll excuse you this time. Now, you all see those switches hanging behind me. I did not put them there. I do not say that I shall not use them. Some boys have been whipped, I suppose—like mules—and when I have tried, I may find that I cannot get on without switches, but I hope not to have to use them."[5]

The above passage lacks the bite of an earlier period, the spontaneity of the belief in the rightness of physical manipulation and control. This wielder of an aggressive instrument explains himself too thoroughly and lacks the inscrutability to truly be controlling his students by the pure use of physical force. His speech lacks the subtler shades of guilt-inducement, the abstract threats of damnation, the emotional intimacy of psychic control. Though couched in terms of an artifact (the whip) stemming from an earlier period, the teacher is really pointing his students toward a new and more desirable path.

A journalist notes in *The Atlantic Monthly Magazine* (1885) that contemporary popular children's books often present themes in which boys and girls are "seeking their fortune, working out their own schemes, driving railroad trains and steamboats . . . managing farms, or engaged in adventures which elicit all their uncommon heroism."[6] This indicates a sanctioned level of autonomy rarely present in the earlier submode.

The writer of *Childhood in Literature and Art* states that it is a novelty for the child in literature to possess a distinct personality; it "was the child as possessed of consciousness . . . a nature capable of independent action, thought and feeling, that now came forward. . . . the discovery seems to have been made . . . that the child is not merely a person, but a very free and independent person indeed."[7]

A piece in *Littell's Living Age* (1892) used a language and shows an attitude toward children which is not present in the writing of the previous generation (especially in the relaxation of its impetus to control):

> If children are happier, for the most part, in this age than they have ever been before; if their training is, though less severe, more likely on the whole to bring out the best in them; if both in study and in play they are both treated more wisely than was once . . . the case . . . it is largely due to the fact that their joys and sorrows, their fears, anxieties, hopes and aspirations . . . have been so admirably depicted by writers, who command our attention, that we have learned how to treat them more gently, more sympathetically.[8]

Such changes were the results of the progressive relaxation of control which grew out of earlier forms of manipulation, not sudden appearances at the dawn of the 1880s; fossilization was as common as in other periods. For example, in Martha Finley's popular "Elsie" series, we see such stories as *Grandmother Elsie*, in which a young boy is filled with self-loathing over his misbehaving. His father states in classic control mode: "What I want you to consider is your sinfulness toward God, and your need of forgiveness from Him."[9]

Still, the major writers of the period show a heightened concern with childhood while shunning the didactic axe. In the earlier period, it is difficult to compile a list of writers who dealt with the child in personalized and psychological depth; now, writers like Clemens and Howells create major novels revolving around children. Howell's *A Boy's Town*, though set in the 1860s, reflects the views of the period in which Howells wrote. The author does speak of the child as a savage—a view which was central to aggressive training—living under the dominion of fear rather than justice, lacking morality, often resorting to violence. But the other side of the picture is an exuberant freedom and a precious energy. His boys value each other for "character and perseverance, and it did not matter in the least that he was ragged and dirty." Howells admires their ambitions and sense of boundlessness.[10] Clemens demonstrates support of the novel notion that the younger generation may come in a visceral way to a grasp of societal morals (which we might describe as the societal artifacts created in an earlier psychogenic stage). Clemens carries forward the concept of a distinct child subculture, depicting interrelations of young people in which adults are not the central guiding forces—or in which adults exercise only a corrupting impact. Clemens's novels, often narrated by a child, depict vividly the conflicts and the spectrum of emotions involved in childhood life.[11]

The 1880s have been considered by some a golden age in children's literature. Writers like Mary Wells Smith depicted the freedom of farm life; Sidney Lanier wrote heroic tales for children; Howard Pyle's Robin Hood gained wide readership; and characters like Brer Rabbit, Brer Fox and Uncle Remus (with their lighthearted moral teachings) replaced the heavy-handed do-or-die mentality of earlier family stories. Writers on child-rearing continued to use botanical metaphors but with different implications in terms of the nature-nurture issue. The following poem appeared in *A Mother's Ideals: A Kindergarten Mother's Conception of Family Life* (1897):

A fresh little bud in the garden,
   With pistils close folded from view,
Brightly nods on a cherry "good morning"
   Through the drops of a fresh bath of dew
I must patiently wait its unfolding,
   Tho' I long its full beauty to see;
Leave soft breezes and warm, tender sunshine
   To perform the sweet office for me.[12]

The message is reiterated in prose: "Not for any single moment can we add anything into the child; one can only help to a more perfect unfoldment of what is within." Margaret Sangster's *Miss Dewberry's Scholars and What they did* (1882) likewise illustrates the emerging dynamics of autonomy: "If I had a girl or a boy to bring up, about the first thing I should try to do would be to teach them self-reliance. I'd begin when they were babies."[13]

## THE RELIGIOUS SECTOR

The progressive segment of the religious sector had likewise evolved; but even more telling is the general secularization of life and the waning of the use of religion for purposes of control. The movement from infant-damnation to weeding-out of bad tendencies to nurture now evolved into a tacit acceptance of inherent goodness or of the child as a tabula rasa. A spokesman for the World's Sunday School Executive Council stated in 1907 that "I believe that the true method of dealing with children is to tell them they belong to Christ from earliest children. I am not positive that every child needs conversion."[14] On occasion, there was more confidence in the child's powers of religious feeling, as in this sketch of St. Paul's Sunday School in New Haven: "Teachers often in weariness and discouragement, feel their instruction falls on barren soil [or is] spoken in vain. Not so, God's word faithfully taught will not fail. . . . good seed will bear good fruit."[15] A sermon entitled "Fathers and Sons," presented at St. James Church in October 1903, likewise illustrates the newer optimistic spirit. The plot of the story resembles the earlier didactic tales; it concerns two sons of a respectable lawyer, one steady and dependable, the other reckless. The latter, in a true return of the prodigal son, determines to reform himself and is immediately greeted with confidence and without retribution for his wrongs.[16] *The Child Study Monthly*, in 1898, has a four-year-old child stating: "God is everybody's papa. Papa ain't my real papa, is he. God is my real papa." The ability here to differentiate and therefore demystify parental authority speaks for increased autonomy.

Previous modes do persist in the religious sphere. Rev. William Worcester's *Duty to the Children* (1897) retains the environmental perspective, the precondition of psychic control: "The period of childhood, of growth and formation, gives us our best opportunity to exert an influence which will be effective. When we realize how great the results of our influence may be for happiness or misery through all of life, and not in this world but to eternity, we feel the sacredness of our duty to the children, and the importance of doing it wisely." He displays the traditional awe of the powers of parenthood as well as feelings of anxiety that the task could be too momentous.[17] An example of older views of the evolutionary process in reference to children is evident in a publication printed in London in 1888 by the Salvation Army and distributed in this country. The text expounds the view that the mother is of supreme, eternal importance, standing in God's place and acting directly from his authority: "You see, parents are *everything* to their children." One cannot begin too soon in the inculcation of obedience, for "children, like true soldiers, must always be prepared to run, fetch, and carry, or do whatever is required."

Self-denial is a cardinal virtue, and whipping may have a positive impact.[18]

On the progressive side, one Mrs. Henry observes that "It is through the things by which the child is surrounded" that good or evil is created in him. And she goes so far as to stand the earlier religious emphasis on its head, declaring that much of the beauty "of the divine plan has been lost: because the child has been *trained* instead of developed."[19] Another writer, in *Hints on Child Training* (1896), remarks upon the fact that the practice of breaking the will crushes out the "child's privilege of free choice."[20] Increasing secularization, along with the persistence of the control aspects of religion, is evident in an 1899 issue of the respected and widely read magazine *Outlook*. Here the Bible is described as containing fiction as well as philosophy. James Sully, an individual involved with the discipline of "child study," states further that children are simply confused by the accounts of God presented to them. Referring to many of the ideas as incongruities "half mythological-poetical, half theoretical," he emphasizes the cognitive dissonance involved in such conflicting messages. Sully accepts the child's questioning, puzzled attempts to bring the world into congruence with his own order. And Florence Winterburn refers to the fact that children naturally have a faith in God, and includes the following couplet:

> God hath His small interpreter—
> The Child must teach the Man.[21]

Luther Burbank writes: "There is no such thing in the world . . . as a predestined child—predestined for heaven or hell." Another work, published by the Religious Publishing Company of Chicago in 1907, indicates that the environment cultivates but does not implant tendencies. An even stronger emphasis on innate rather than parentally cultivatable tendencies occurs in *The Mother's Magazine* for November 1881: "Fortunately for mankind, human morality and religion have a much more solid foundation than this; they are based on feelings implanted in the nature of man, which intellectual cultivation or neglect can neither generate nor destroy."[22]

## PARENTS OF AGGRESSIVE TRAINING

In the realm of the social structuring of the role of motherhood, one may observe fairly precisely the movement from psychic control to the concept of aggressive training—the view that the parent is not generally defined as authoritative, or as imparting some greater authority, but that the parent may *influence* the child. For example, a title appearing in 1889 is *Conscious Motherhood: The Earliest Unfolding of the Child in the Cradle, Nursery and Kindergarten*. The concept of unfolding implies less a controlling maternal stance than a nurturing one.[23] The evolution of motherhood is evident in *The Outlook*. One writer urges mothers to become more educated in their tasks, but whereas in earlier years the enlightenment would come from the area of religion and morality, it is now to come from the area of psychology. The writer applauds the child's imagination, encouraging mothers to develop the faculty rather than condemn and suppress it; also present is a new relaxation concerning the mother-child bond, a slackening in the nature of authority. Mothers have fine instincts and are asked to use them to indulge a child's illusions, share them, and at times use them as vehicles of communication.[24]

M. J. Savage tells his readers that the mother, rather than being simply a molder of character, is also an agent of heredity. This role is articulated in terms of a sedate being of charm, gentleness, and patience. Gone is the moral immediacy of the imposition of bonds when he states: "You have a right to lead your own life, to develop yourself in your own way, to be free, to see your own happiness. . . . The child has these rights, all of them. . . ." He adds that it is of utmost necessity for the child to be trained in independence, concluding that the Virgin Mary is a negative example to mothers, presenting an impossible ideal, making mothers feel lowly in comparison.[25]

Another piece of advice simply not present in the earlier literature is that the mother should recognize that the child's temper is not something strictly to be feared, to be subdued and controlled, of potential danger to family, society, and the child's status in the hereafter, but that it contains energy of a potentially positive nature. The parent is viewed as an influence who, while avoiding corporal punishment and intensive psychological controls, may go one logical step further and influence through teaching. True, "a child's environment should include regularity, punctuality, cleanliness, and order," but "as far as possible we should let children be themselves; we should encourage simplicity and frankness in them by that best of all teachers, example." Whereas the ethics of psychic control implied the necessity of aiding the child in rising above his helpless state through rigorous discipline and training, the emphasis is now on the gentler means of guidance, such as sympathy, which "affords the best condition under which the child may create its highest ideals."[26]

*The Child Study Monthly*, a publication whose significance will be discussed later, tells the mother that it is time to *study* children: "Few mothers at this time have undertaken anything like a systematic study of children, though they may have devoted the best years of their lives to teaching and training their own."[27] A recurring theme in the literature is a degree of embryonic empathy on the part of mothers concerning the discipline of children—from Eugene Field's *Poems of Childhood* (1896), in which the narrator tells of how a mother feels the whippings with greater pain than her children, to a mother who, remembering the indignities of corporal punishment, has difficulties administering them to her own child.[28]

One has the impression that the father in this period is being given greater functions in the daily life of the child, with more immediate emotional consequences. Fatherhood has become a subject of interest among writers on and observers of American homelife in all classes. In *Conscious Motherhood* it is stated that "masculine influence alone, feminine influence alone, can never produce the broadest and completest human culture." Savage, in reference to more practical matters, says that both parents should be considered eligible to work if the necessity arises. After emphasizing the importance of "leaving children to their own inventions" as much as possible, *The Mother's Magazine*, in 1885, warns the parent to exercise self-vigilance in controlling the exercise of parental authority, so that it does not degenerate into a love of power. Significantly, the masculine pronoun is used in reference to "the parent": the first care of the parent "should be to subdue himself." In addition to a growing volume of literature addressed to "the parent" rather than simply "the mother," there is often an explicit expression of greater paternal involvement. Whereas the most common didactic story concerned motherhood, the reunification of mother and child as a means of expiating guilt, a sermon given in 1903 entitled "Fathers and Sons" involves a reckless boy who returns home and is immediately accepted by a loving father.[29]

## TRAINED SEXUALITY

Views of child sexuality move in a synchronous manner with other developments in the childhood experience—some progressive concepts evolving from traditional notions, many of the latter surviving intact, many falling into extinction. One major development is the virtual end of the theory of masturbatory insanity, as the theory finally succumbs to the lack of physiological or psychological evidence. Here is concrete evidence that an adult generation was finally able to regress to childhood levels and to work through sexual repressions. This is not to say that a feared, mysterious function was suddenly viewed as a rational aspect of biological life without moral and physiological ramifications. G. Stanley Hall, author of the celebrated and innovative *Adolescence*, does not take a positive stand toward masturbation; but his argument against it is not based on the old insanity theory but is put in terms of controlling energy: masturbation requires more excitement than coitus and therefore taxes the nervous system while wasting sperm. He further de-sexualizes the child as follows: "The adolescent interests seem to depend on the size and quality of the brain in direct ratio, and are inversely proportional to the growth and vitality of the reproductive organs."[30] L. Emmett Holt writes that masturbation "is not uncommon even in infancy. Many cases have been observed during the first year," but concludes that the habit leads to symptoms of morbidity, lack of energy, and epilepsy.[31]

Writers of the period still express such thoughts as: "The child should be taught by his mother that it is the office of the sexual organ more than anything else, to bring him to copartnership with God . . . and for this reason is especially sacred, and should be under the mother's care until the child is old enough to understand and care for himself." The same writer endorses circumcision as an aid in the control of lust and approves the use of the rod.[32] In 1897 a device was patented in the United States which used spikes on a fitted belt to make erection painful and discourage masturbation. A more complex device was patented by a psychiatric nurse in 1908. It was not until after World War I that interest in such devices waned sufficiently to preclude their manufacture.[33] Books repeatedly argued for the necessity of controlling the impulses; one warns parents not to allow children to spend the night with friends, invoking unstated but "grave reasons." Food and drink likely to stimulate—even tea or coffee—were stigmatized; strict adolescent chaperonage for the middle and upper classes continued; and a typical caution went: "Teach them from the first self-reverence in touch, as in mind and deed, and watch even their attitude in sleep, that the little arms are folded lightly upwards. . . . Be vigilant . . . that the childlike modesty is never relaxed."[34] Ellice Hopkins wrote that parents can never be too particular about little girls' underclothing, that girls must be taught that their bodies "are the temple of the Holy Ghost"; and Grace Dodge told young girls that in caring for themselves they must bathe all "sacred and hidden organs" but in "no other way should the girl touch or think of them."[3][5]

The views of Joseph Howe (1907) stand on the edge of progressive change. He speaks of masturbation as a vice and an addiction, "though less injurious to the female." Symptoms such as heart palpitation, some insanity, glandular disorders, as well as digestive problems and deformation of the genitals, are related to the practice. But there are some positive indications. First, Howe recognizes that child sexuality is more widespread than was formerly supposed, that it is not unheard of for nurses to stimulate children at the breast in order to keep them quiet, and that most children masturbate. He is more aware of a continuity between masturbation and coitus but still declares that intercourse may be indulged in three to four times a week without injury, while the same rate of masturbation is highly deleterious. (In intercourse the loss of energy is compensated for by "the magnetism of the partner.") Still, where intercourse is openly recognized as going beyond the functions of procreation, an inroad has been made concerning the potential harm of experiencing orgasm in the form of masturbation.[3][6]

William Bryon Forbush likewise illustrates the transformation of attitudes with regard to child sexuality. This "temptation" is best dealt with, he insists, "by revealing frankly and simply, as curiosity arises, the facts of sex." Masturbation is a nasty habit, but not a damning one; and in a remarkable breakthrough Forbush comments: "I think we may as well face the fact that the practice is, for at least a short period in life, well-nigh universal."[3][7] Child psychologist Earl Barnes, active in the "child study" movement, published an article in 1892 entitled "Feelings and Ideas of Sex in Children" in which he stressed that studies of normal sexual development in children need to be made. He clearly acknowledged that children have a sexual nature which should not be entirely repressed. Kirkpatrick writes of sexuality: "The instinct may be the basis of all manly and womanly virtues, stimulating to love, tenderness, emotion, courage, and high aspiration in social, aesthetic, moral and religious life"; on the other hand it may be the "force source" of certain negative qualities. The author denounces the prevalence of guilt over sexuality and the example of a particular advertising firm which had in its possession thousands of letters from guilty adolescents who were convinced that they were socially and morally ruined for having masturbated.[3][8]

## THE CHILD STUDY MOVEMENT

One area which reflects the development of the aggressive training mode is a development known as the "child study" movement, an approach largely centering around *The Pedagogical Seminary*, and later *The Child Study Monthly*, under the leadership of G. Stanley Hall of Clark University. Crucial in reference to the thesis of a relaxation of psychic control during this period is the fact that the movement—a cohesive group of scientists, psychologists, writers, and scholars—based its methodology on *observation* rather than active manipulation. An article in the *Seminary* in 1896 summarizes as well as any what the movement was about:

Among the opinions most strongly expressed and heartily approved were the following: that children are often almost criminally misunderstood; that one of the strongest desires of children . . . is to be sympathetically known; that the misunderstanding of children on the part of adults is lamentable and is beginning to be inexcusable since the search light of scientific child study shows so conclusively that the time has come when children must not only be loved as animals love their offspring, but parental love must no longer be blind if it is to be complete and efficient.[39]

For the first time children are considered to be misunderstood, rather than placing the emphasis on the adult as forming and molding the child. The writer speaks of two contrary possibilities: that parental action may *dwarf* development and that the child may act solely out of his own needs.

The child study movement sought to reach a keener understanding of the cognitive and, secondarily, the emotional realities of the child. One of the major issues was, of course, the nature-nurture controversy—the degree to which personality is a product of inherited or of learned characteristics. Central to the reality of psychic control is a belief system, embedded in mass consciousness, that the child is in essence as malleable as soft clay, to which forces may be applied with visible and lasting effect. A precondition of empathy is the contrary idea that the child possesses, to a large extent, a nature unto himself; that he is profoundly affected by the environment, yet possesses an individualized consciousness during each stage of development. The child can now be seen as exerting an *active* influence on its own behalf.

An association between childhood modes and nature-nurture issues may be helpful at this juncture: (1) innate nature (largely evil): intrusive mode and earlier; (2) tabula rasa (molding): psychic control; (3) inherited characteristics: aggressive training; (4) innate potentialities: vigorous guidance. In the first case, which represents a resignation to grim predetermined reality, the child is best kept under control through crude but effective means of discipline—the bad parts of the parents are projected upon and then beaten down in the child. In the second, the learning organism may be the delegate forged with the emotional binding and guilt of control. In the third case there is a move toward the belief in the child's individual capacities and ability to direct himself, which in turn preconditions a move toward empathy—the *emotional* realization of this self-directing being. Each stage is more sophisticated than its predecessor, as the feeling for the dynamics of personality formation expands through greater empathy: The belief in *innate nature* rests ultimately on inscrutable philosophical-religious systems, the invocation of supernatural powers, and reliance on absolute law. *Tabula rasa* involves some scientific thought, but of a vague sort (it is this phenomenon which created "maternal impressions," the notion that a passing thought of the mother influences the creation of the embryo in the womb), in which parents are afraid of their own powers. *Inherited characteristics* draws upon the new science of genetics, recognizing physical laws, but goes too far when it tries to draw conclusions about racial purity and oversimplifies genetics in looking for one-to-one inherited traits of personality and functioning. *Innate potentialities* draws upon psychoanalysis, a more sophisticated science of genetics, and other empirical studies of modern psychology. It allows for a realization of the *capacities* of the infant, whether in diet selection, social cooperation, or social interaction.

There is a certain vagueness associated with aggressive training, a feeling that "it is impossible to say where the influence of heredity ends and that of social suggestion begins." The mass circulation magazine *The Arena* chose to emphasize the power of heredity. Heredity is seen as the ultimate determiner of identity and the foundation of the home. Yet environment comes into play in determining the quality or shades of contour of the personality, determining the equilibrium which is the predominant thrust of the new aggressive influence:

> Heredity and environment act and react upon each other . . . with the regularity and inevitability of night and day. Neither

tells the whole story; together they make up the sum of life; and yet it is true that the first half—the part or foundation upon which all else must depend—has been taken into account so little in the scheme of human affairs that total ignorance of its very principle has been looked upon as a changing attribute of the young mother upon whose weak and underdeveloped shoulder rests the responsibility, the welfare, the shame or the glory . . . of generations that are to come![40]

"Heredity finds its limitation in environment, and the powers which use it as a medium of influence." A popular writer on home life articulates the essence of aggressive influence when she comments that achievement of progress may lie more in nurture in that the child has been too much "trained" and too little *developed.*[41]

Such directions of thought gave a new flavor to what in earlier times might have been termed predestination.[42] *The Pedagogical Seminary* expressed the idea that the degree of plasticity of the child is not as great as previously assumed, that "a child cannot be molded to our will." Views of innate qualities developed to the point where writers postulated periods of readiness—a schedule of the unfolding of inner qualities. One writer went so far as to attribute the emergence of the will to the thirty-fourth day of life, and joy to the thirty-second day. Child studies discussed the *awakening* of the moral sense, the *emergence* of the self-directing will, the child's *instincts.*[43]

It was not a broad leap for some in the child study movement to connect new views of individual development to the development of the race. Darwinism stressed that one of the outstanding characteristics of man's progress on the phylogenetic scale is his ability to learn, to survive a highly plastic, elongated, and malleable infancy. This capacity to be formed in part by the parental generation allows for progress and change, with the period of childhood becoming more extended as civilization progresses. John Fisk's work during the early 1870s considered the helplessness, duration, and plasticity of infancy the foremost development in human evolution. Yet, during the period from 1880 to 1910, writers stress the innateness of the child's personality in reference to broader questions of evolution. *The Educational Review* states that "every child is the product of all preceding generations." True, some continue to hold that cultural assimilation occurs during infancy, that "race acquisitions" could be relayed through the learning process and therefore modify inheritance, but at the basis of most theorizing is the grand scheme of a great unfolding, the idea that the child develops in accordance with the plan of evolution.[44]

A concrete expression of the movement toward the innate is a theory credited to G. Stanley Hall, a theory which eventually would fade from predominance along with the submode which created it. Most simply, the "recapitulation" theory states that the child naturally displays all the stages of civilization—from savagery upward—in his own development, for reasons inherent in genetic-biological-psychological realities. William B. Forbush articulates the theory in *The Pedagogical Seminary:*

> The birth of a boy is not his beginning. The prenatal child passes up through every grade of animal life from the simplest and lowest to the most complex. After birth he continues his evolution, in which he has already repeated the history of the animal world, by repeating the history of his own race-life from savagery into civilization.[45]

Sully speaks of the child's "primitive, savage" outbursts, and insists that separate standards, entirely apart from adult culture, must be applied to the child's mind—that good and bad are not necessarily relevant to the child's value system. Such a theory, resting on fixed sequences of development, is at its basis less controlling as an ideology of childhood than psychic control—for this theory attempts to extend embryology directly into sociology: the child's mental modes of functioning must move sequentially, in patterns as clear and as inevitable as Darwinian evolution.

Working in the same direction is the genetic movement, the belief that reform ultimately lies in the intelligent merging of genetic pools which would predetermine the quality of human beings. An article entitled "Practical Genetics"—taken from an address presented before a conference on child welfare at Clark University—states the child's stock must be good, for "if the foundation of his being is distorted and confused in heredity before his unfoldment begins, then the problem of healthy moral development is rendered insoluble before it is presented." The notion that "the actual is only a realized copy of the potential" is the doctrine of evolutionism, the insistence that progressive change is in essence preprogrammed.

Besides the theory of recapitulation, the new science of eugenics (the actual tracing of ancestral lines, and the racial concern with breeding) stresses "race instincts." As one writer puts it: "Every child is the product of all preceding generations."[46] One of the seminal works on child study in this period is James Sully's *Studies of Childhood* (1903). Sully speaks of "germs" of tenderness, the *instinct* of companionship, natural *propensities* for helping, freedom, and impulsivity.[47] Edgar James Swift's study of mental development illustrates the preconceptions of aggressive training: Swift believes the innate may take years in unfolding, even for a quality as basic as intelligence. So great is the possibility of deferred development that "every child must be regarded as a possible genius." Swift's point, still far from real empathy, is that adults should be patient in awaiting desired characteristics.[48] The belief in unfoldment, in precise periods of readiness, grew to such a point that Luther Burbank actually spoke of the problem of overeducation. Birney speaks of temperaments and Mumford entitles his study of child life *The Dawn of Character*. He stresses that mortality may be developed "through the strengthening of the higher and a weakening of the lower impulses of nature," entailing "deliberate repression of the undesirable tendencies, deliberate and conscious cultivation of the desirable tendencies"; if there are molding influences, they are largely unconscious. Habits are crucial but they are built on the foundation of instinct.[49]

The move from control is integral to almost all the materials of the movement: "Again, both teacher and parent must be able to share the feelings of the child, to understand his motives and impulses. They must be able to put themselves in his place, to look upon the child's interests with the child's eyes." The adult's role is candidly questioned: "Self observation is necessary, either to introduce certain definite conditions into the experiment, or to observe the results of the experiment, or to make an analysis of the mental process. . . . Child study . . . must go hand-in-hand with self-observational psychology of the adult mind."[50] Another writes: "Not for any single moment can we add anything into the child; we can only help to a more perfect unfoldment of what is within."[51] The concept of child self-discipline follows naturally: "Children will often discipline themselves if allowed to, especially if we calmly talk the matter over with them.' As in earlier years, the dominant theme in advice to mothers is calmness, sureness, and gentleness, as well as an all-seeing eye. The quality of sympathy rises on the parental scale: "Sympathy affords the best conditions under which the child may create its highest ideals."[52]

The writings of G. Stanley Hall do much to elucidate the positions of the child study movement. Fascinated with the work of Freud, whom he invited to Clark University, Hall nevertheless did not embrace psychoanalytic insight with its emphasis on the unconscious and its explicit acknowledgment of child sexuality. Although his *Adolescence* divided life into stages, his views of child sexuality were not far removed from repressive notions. What Hall did contribute was a focus on detached and objective observation and a clear statement of the purposes and limits of parental intervention. Hall declared that "the complexity of the child's nature even during the first three years is amazing, and only a . . . paintstaking observation can yield results of value." At the same time, Hall could make such fossilized pronouncements as: "The only duty of small children is habitual and prompt obedience . . . The more absolute such authority the more the will is saved from caprice and feels the power of steadiness. . . . Dermal pain is not the worst thing in the world, and by a judicious knowledge of how it feels at both ends of the rod, by flogging and being flogged, far deeper pains may be forfeited. . . . The severe process of breaking the will is needful."[53]

Tracing an evolutionary thread—a stepwise movement of continual alteration through time by the process of creative regression—means that one must focus upon the progressive. One central aspect of the creation of the new childhood is the emerging faith in the natural impulses. Whereas in the earlier period a faith emerged in the ability to manipulate the child's impulses, to mold them, to make them socially useful, these impulses are now brought a step closer to the adult mind; by relaxing the authority bond, adults allow these drives to find greater expression, and, to a more successful degree than in earlier periods, they "ride" with them. We see an emphasis on nature, associated with the freer aspects of existence, the pure and exhilarating health of the biological world. Edgar James Swift sees truancy not as evidence of youthful depravity, as it might have been seen in earlier years, but rather as a temporary reenactment of latent ancestral patterns: "It is the awakening in the boy of the *natural* life of the race" (italics added).[54] In *The Training of the Human Plant* (1907), Luther Burbank gives his endorsement to the benefits of exposing children to nature and warns against cramming a child's mind with too much education during the first ten years of life.[55] The well-known developer of the standardized psychological test, Edward Lee Thorndike, includes similar thoughts in one of his published notes on child study, remarking upon the value of making use of the child's primitive traits and stressing the importance of the "out-of-door" life, working and playing with animals and plants.[56]

Yet along with nature comes play; and, in the minds of many, play was no casual matter—it was the harder side of aggressive training. *The Kindergarten Magazine* warns that play characteristics relate to racial and national character and that the vigor of play is a measure of the vigor of adult life, teaching endurance, will, and morality. This 1899 publication includes the information that Boston pledged $200,000 a year for the purpose of building additional playgrounds and fields.[57] Stuart H. Rowe's *The Physical Nature of the Child and How to Study It* (1903) observes that action is "the first law of growth," giving credence to the notion that because of genetic endowment children vary enormously in mental and physical action.[58] Edward A. Kirkpatrick's *Fundamentals of Child Study* (1904) states that "nothing can be more unwise than to tell a child he must never fight. . . . Fighting is a crude form of social action adapted to the early stage of human development and usually results in valuable lessons."[59] Edgar James Swift's *Mind in the Making: A Study in Mental Development* (1908) includes a description of truancy in terms of a "reversion to the migratory habits of our ancestors. It is the awakening in the boy of the natural life of the race, and a revolt against the gloom of the schoolroom."[60] One senses in these comments an element of fear as well as a positive valuation of the primitiveness of children. If children are not naturally in possession of moral obligations, their "criminal" instincts must receive appropriate training.

One indication of the hard side of training is present in *Littell's Living Age* (1893). The writer indicates that each generation has the obligation to advance upon the preceding one and that parents should strive to leave their children "morally, mentally and physically superior to themselves" and should feel satisfaction in knowing they have not lived in vain.[61] Thorndike adds in 1901: "A better way to make use of primitive traits in children might be to provide them systematically with a chance to lead a really primitive and out-of-doors life, to work and play with animals and plants, to get their own . . . and learn some of the simple ways to overcome nature's obstacles."[62]

But the child study movement as a coherent self-conscious body was not long-lived; it was more a passing manifestation of progressive developments. Frederick Bolton notes in the *Journal of Pedagogy* that, as early as 1902, there was a decreased interest in child study, that its benefits and values were not coming forth as hoped, that the child study societies had little to say which was not already manifest to observant parents.[63] It is with an eye on the movement as a manifestation rather than a cause of what is here called aggressive training that its writings have been traced.

## THE PEDAGOGY OF TRAINING

The first cousin of child study is the progressive movement in education, which also placed a new emphasis on the innate. For example, "Heredity and Education," in *The Educational Review* (1891), states that "every child is the product of all preceding generations. ... The problem of education is by means of environment to modify, and as far as possible ... bring the good into expression and power."[64] The sources also illustrate the continuity between the control and the aggressive submodes, and the gray area of schooling in which the two are sometimes indistinguishable.

Institutional manifestations occurred in various spheres in 1897 when a group of mothers, educators, clergymen, and politicians organized "The National Congress of Mothers," whose purpose was to carry mother-love "into all that concerns or touches childhood in home, school, church or state." In 1904, the Congress organized a campaign for the organization of parent-teacher associations whose membership soon reached a hundred thousand.[65] Success here marked a decrease in the emotional-distancing function of the schools.

Writers on child-rearing were now less concerned with molding, with the permanence and gravity of adult actions toward the child, and more concerned with *reaching* the child. George Allen Hubbell wrote: "How can you reach the will of a child? You can storm the will, you may even break it, but the wisest course is to win the will, and that end is reached through feelings. ... Feeling is to man what steam is to the engine, electricity to the electric car—it is the motive power which energizes him for the activities of life."[66]

Coming to terms with the child's emotional realities to a greater degree, progressive adults nevertheless held dynamic ideas for the younger generation and still wished to infuse energy into it, a sense of discipline, a knowledge of the proper path to take. John Dewey, whose ideas grew throughout this period and who would later be a leader of the progressive education movement, was a spokesman for the softer side of aggressivity when he spoke of a "child nature," a natural and real nature which should not be suppressed. Although he did not abandon the aim for the vigorous life, he did call for an abandonment of what he termed the "theory of effort," the belief that maturation is a difficult process calling for control and self-discipline at each stage of growth:

> While the theory of effort is always holding up to us a
> strong vigorous character as the outcome of its method of

education, practically we do not get this character. We get either the narrow, bigoted man who is obstinate and irresponsible save in the line of his preconceived views and beliefs; or else we get a character dull, mechanical ... because the principle of spontaneous interest has been squeezed out of him. ... While we are congratulating ourselves upon the well disciplined habits which the pupil is acquiring, judged by his ability to reproduce a lesson when called upon, we forget that true effort must be the result of interest, stemming from the child himself.[6][7]

Others were also concerned with the problem of overdoing the vigorous intellectual aspects of child development. Dr. William A. Hammond, for example, objected to "Brain-Forcing in Childhood" in an 1887 issue of *Popular Science Monthly*.[6][8]

At this point we have come to a paradoxical stage in the evolution of childhood, an expression of seemingly conflicting psychological typologies. On the one hand we witness the movement of America into the obsession with "vigor" and "forward movement" that is often called the "virility impulse." At the same time we see a relatively gentler movement by the same individuals in reference to their children. As we have seen, the parent-child relation is a very special one, the embryo of all progress. The unique aspect of the relation is that regression is inevitable and necessary for progress, while in other social actions it appears only intermittently and in slower rhythms. In thinking and writing about and relating to its children, a generation only moves beyond itself through its reworking of the most formative primal dynamics—and paradox in opinions is therefore the rule rather than the exception.

Moving from the softer to the harder side of aggressive training, one may observe a cult of vigor and efficiency. William James, respected for his liberal credentials, is careful to retain aggressive elements in his view of education. His *Talks to Teachers* (1899) includes endorsement of memory training, the necessity for hard work in the learning process, and competition:

To veto and taboo all possible rivalry of one youth with another, because such rivalry may degenerate ... does seem to savor somewhat of sentimentality, or even fanaticism. The feeling of rivalry lies at the very basis of our being, all social improvement being largely due to it.

He directly responds to the "softer" arguments of the period:

We have of late been hearing much of the philosophy of tenderness in education; "interest" must be assiduously awakened in everything, difficulties must be soothed away. "Soft" pedagogics have taken the place of the old steep and rocky path to learning. But from this lukewarm air the bracing oxygen of effort is left out. It is nonsense to suppose that every step in education can be interesting; the fighting impulse must often be appealed to . . . rouse his pugnacity and pride, and he will rush at the difficult places with a sort of inner wrath at himself that is one of his best moral faculties.[69]

The aggressivity of training heralds a decrease in the intensity of the emotional bonding of psychic control. The reflections of a kindergarten mother illustrate this desire to distance the child's training while continuing the intensive and schedulized development of the child:

> This question of punishment will forever exercise parents, and there will never be discovered a just and equitable set of punishments if we search forever. My experience has been that right here the kindergarten comes to our rescue. If it were possible for each child to be daily separated for a certain number of hours from the mother, even at the age of two, and put in a little world of children his own age, he would learn the sharing, the obedience and yielding to 'must' that come from living together with many of our own age, instead of fighting out each little point in a hand-to-hand combat with his mother, who has often paved the way to disobedience through harassing him.[70]

This is a complex mixture, indeed, in which separation from a partly culpable mother represents the benevolent imposition of a peer-group discipline that is "kinder" because it is more effective.

An article in *The School Journal* (1905) entitled "Education and the Cult of Efficiency" stresses the necessity for creating a vigorous generation (strong males, fertile robust females) that will associate righteousness with strength. The author writes: "No nation is truly prosperous until every man has become not merely a consumer but a producer." He asks: "How shall we make it possible for the student to get that culture, efficiency, and power out of his studies which his development requires?"[71] In the words of another exponent: "The special aim is the constant increase of social efficiency at such a rate as will produce the

maximum development possible during the school period."
Whereas the control child achieves progress through morality, the
aggressive child achieves it through vigor and forward-reaching
social orientation. Intelligence is now a force:

> He who has sailed in a modern steamship through an ocean
> storm has seen the mighty vessel cleave the bellows and
> scarcely slacken her speed in the teeth of the hurricane.
> Down in the depth of the ship men are piling coal in the
> furnace and releasing a force—the imprisoned sun-power of
> uncounted ages—that baffles the waves and defies the
> whirlwind. And so it is with our ship of state . . . the force of
> intelligence . . . will lead our nation in the straight course of
> progress.[72]

And so it is with the child, within whom lives a force which can be
released through discipline, a force that will bring the nation-state
to virile glory. This energistic release is manifested in the scientific
observation of the child, in the rise of educational administration,
and in the efficiency ethic. It will later be argued that this is the
source for the entire fabric and pattern of a major part of
twentieth-century American society.

For all the imagery of energistic release, the ambivalence
concerning instinct remained. *The Journal of Pedagogy* proposes
that young children are all, by nature, almost completely selfish.
From six to twelve, a few are unselfish, but it is usually not until
adolescence that some sense of social concern emerges. "The child
is, and ought to be, an egoist." The important aspect of this
statement is the persistence of the demand that the child take all
cues from adults. Though the author states that a child lacks
powers of self-criticism and introspection, he adds that "a
heightened self-consciousness in childhood is morbid." Observing
that heredity is important ("Blood does count for something, with
a vengeance"), the author states in another article that moral
action in early life can only stem from imitation and suggestion
rather than intellect.[73] Another writer comments in *The Children
of the Future* (1898): "We must entirely rely upon the parental
instinct in this matter, be it ever so strong and pure . . . the rearing
of children in our complex civilization is so delicate and difficult a
matter as to necessitate the development of 'child reason' into a
higher faculty."[74] The air is still filled with discussions of will
training, one study stating that the will should be trained rather
than broken.[75] A comment printed in 1908 is similar: "The fact
is, that the process of education consists largely in transforming

the instincts ... which in their original state are wild and unmanageable, into domesticated and useful habits."[76] And a pamphlet, "The Relation of School Discipline to Moral Education," resolves that self-control is the essence of proper education.[77]

More needs to be said about the move toward empathy in order to accurately portray the dynamic fluctuations between aggressive and creative development. "Rationalism in the Nursery," appearing in *Open Court* (1899), states that children should be given the chance to form their own opinions: "There is no better system of education than that which springs from the conflict of innermost interest, that originates within the sphere of the child's own experiences." One should not deny the child's imagination, even if it causes him fear: "Place yourself in the child's position, and thence start further operations."[78] For the first time adults are able to perceive the disadvantages of overregulation in the schoolroom. *Popular Science Monthly* ran an article in 1896 which reflects a real degree of confidence in the child's native educability: "Very early, even before they begin to talk, they manifest a desire to know the causes of things; and they continue to show natural curiosity until they go to school, which they seem to recognize as a place where curiosity is very much out of place."[79] The article observes that school *produces* boredom, through overregulation. Herbert Spencer is quoted as stating that the goal of education is the development of self-governing (autonomous) human beings rather than those compliant to others. The author disapproves of the institutionalized discouragement of spontaneity and endorses education through play.[80]

H. Clay Trumbull, in *Hints on Child Training*, insists that breaking a child's will is tantamount to destroying his powers of free choice; he states clearly the ethic of aggressive training, with its reliance on the innate: "A little babe is not a mere bit of child-material, to be worked up by outside efforts and influences to a child reality; but he is already a living organism, with all the possibilities." He adds that it is improper and wrong to try to curtail a child's actions when he is learning.[81] Florence Hull Winterburn, a popular writer on childhood, in her book *From the Child's Standpoint: Views of Child Life and Nature* (1899), argues that childhood is naturally an honest time. She states that children naturally have faith in God, deplores the practice of imposing professions upon sons, disapproves of the practice of having children show off talents—musical or otherwise—and pleads for child autonomy and a break away from the mere representation of

parental desires: "The vanity of a parent which sees in a child
nothing but a miniature of self is the more reprehensible when it
compels him to engage for this youthful representation an
attention he could not gracefully ask in his own person."
Winterburn burns through the fallacy that childhood is the
"lighthearted" period of life: "That children do not feel deeply,"
is simply wrong; "those who have entered into the feelings of
these little ones and tried to understand them, know they are not
superficial." Winterburn is emotionally ready to loosen the
authority bonds and to try to relate to the emotional realities of
the child, with a lessened degree of projection from the parent.
"Children are not only happier when they are trusted, but better
than when constantly watched."[82] A study in *Popular Science
Monthly* concerned with "The Nervous System and its Relation to
Education" assumes that when a student is not learning it is not so
much the fault of the child as the teacher.[83] All of this is novel, a
revolution in submodal progress.

   *The Mother's Magazine,* whose contents so well reflected the
developing ethic of psychic control in the 1850s and 1860s, now
indicates it has moved with the tide of evolution. In 1885 the
view is expressed that children are best left to "their own little
devices and inventions." Their parents should be vigilant, but
vigilant over *themselves* in order to guard against love of power.[84]
Motives behind childhood lying are explored in a new way. Nora
Archibald Smith's *The Children of the Future* (1898) rejects
earlier views of innate evil, or wild basic impulses, and examines
new possibilities: the child might be imitating adult behavior, or
he might be lying out of fear, a desire for attention, or simply
because his imagination makes it difficult at times to discern
reality.[85]

   The kindergarten movement was an outgrowth of aggressive
training. A study published by the Chicago Kindergarten Training
School in 1891 argues that the natural activity of the body
manifested in instincts must be *guided*, that nervous energy must
not be suppressed, that obedience without force is an ideal for
which to strive. The aggressive side of the kindergarten movement
is present in its adherence to the ideals of Froebel, which stress the
importance of occupation, play, and vigorous social interaction.
The Springfield Conference on Physical Training, published in *The
Kindergarten Magazine,* comes to these conclusions concerning the
necessity for vigor: (1) play characteristics have a relationship to
"racial character"; (2) "the vigor of the play life is a measure of the
vigor of adult or national life"; (3) "the complexity of play is an
index of the capacity for civilization"; (4) child traditions are

forces of stability; and (5) the play of infants is uniform while the play of older children reflects particular cultures.[86]

## THE PRACTICES OF AGGRESSIVE TRAINING

Finally, we must examine the realm of actual child-rearing practices. Analyses of respected practices indicate a new consensus concerning scheduled feeding, a slightly older age for weaning, a distinct drop in approval of cold baths to "harden" the child, a marked decrease in the number of those who believe teething to be a disease, and an increase in discussions of childhood sex-play. There is a general endorsement of breast feeding on the grounds of heightened emotional security for the infant and the mother.[87] A book concerned with the modern baby (1881) advises the mother to manipulate the breasts in order to encourage the flow of milk. *A Home Book for Mothers and Daughters* (1897) states that the new scheduled feeding is beneficial to both the mother and the child but adds that "rules and principles, no matter how admirable in themselves, should not be converted into a Procrustean bed upon which to stretch and rack the tender form." Holt sees a moral question associated with breast feeding, stating that it is "no small thing to deprive an infant of its mother's breast when, as statistics show to be true of children of wet nurses, this fact reduces its chances of survival to one in ten." Another urges breast feeding as soon as possible after birth, indicating that no artificial food approaches mother's milk for nutrition.[88] Periods of readiness are stressed for various functions (according to one source, 7-1/8 months for crawling and one year for beginning to walk; also, twenty hours of sleep is said to be required daily in the first month of life). Cries of anger are stopped by stroking the head, but the child is not to be fondled every time it cries. The same writer speaks out against shaping the head of the newborn and manipulating the umbilical cord to make it fall off. Circumcision continues to be seen as healthy.[89]

## THE CHILDHOOD OF FRANKLIN DELANO ROOSEVELT

As Theodore Roosevelt displays a childhood which falls well within the control period, so does Franklin Roosevelt exhibit a *trained* childhood. His mother, Sara Delano Roosevelt, had an easy pregnancy and, except for a shortening of her daily horseback ride, was able to continue most of her daily activities. But

Franklin's birth in 1882 was prolonged and painful. Sara received an overdose of chloroform and the baby appeared blue and limp from the anesthesia. But the infant was quickly roused and weighed a strapping ten pounds at birth. The baby made a quick recovery, and—also a positive sign—thrived on his mother's milk.

Sara's diary is a relatively even and delighted report of Franklin's progress. Sara breast-fed him until he was over one year of age and weaned him in May 1883. According to Sara, the boy was proud of his new accomplishment. However, a series of nurses indicates that access to his mother could not have been entirely consistent, one nurse being dismissed as unsatisfactory. Five or six additional servants made it unnecessary for Franklin's parents to "curtail in the slightest their social life or travels, once the baby was weaned."[90] Thus, distancing proves crucial in placing Franklin within the training rather than more advanced submodes.

Though distancing measures continue, the mother is no longer the entirely fragile being of psychic control. Sara's behavior during a transatlantic voyage illustrates her stamina. In a fierce storm during which the captain was knocked unconscious and water began to rush into the Roosevelts' cabin, Sara had the presence of mind to hold the boy up toward the ceiling. Franklin's assertions of will were not violently reprimanded with the withdrawal of affection characteristic of psychic control. When he put a piece of glass in his mouth, he was requested to put it down and asked, "Where is your obedience?" Franklin responded, "My 'bedience gone upstairs for a walk."[91] The most thorough biography of the early years comes to the conclusion that Franklin was seldom if ever physically punished and rarely humiliated, though he was carefully watched to make certain he would assume the carriage and habits of a gentleman. Control was also evident in the schedule of studies and recreational activities entirely planned by his parents, including drawing, dancing, music, and academics. He enjoyed ornithology, a hobby which also interested his cousin Theodore, but did not share the latter's taste for shooting and personally stuffing the animals. Theodore collected guns; Franklin's collecting instincts settled on postage stamps.

The general tone of Franklin's childhood, and of the ego delegations aimed at assuring his place in society, lacked the intensity of Theodore's early years. One writer observed that the emphasis was on performance rather than on controlling his precise feelings—a basic difference between the psychic control and the aggressive training submodes. Franklin's mother remembered that he laughed a lot as a child, although in early adolescence he went through a shy period. The paternal relation is less remote and idealized, Franklin calling his father "Popsey" and engaging in activities with less competitive spirit and more team feeling.

One biographer, summing up Roosevelt's early years, presents an accurate portrayal of trained qualities:

> Serene and secure it was, not serene in the sense of passivity, not secure in the sense of unchallenging. Like other children, Franklin Roosevelt had to adapt to the environment he progressively discovered. His parents set a framework within which he could develop. . . . He was expected to get along; he spent much of his time with adults, met many strangers.[92]

One might add to this summary that Roosevelt was presented with a relatively rigid set of acceptable behaviors. He had to vigorously sift out rebellious urges in favor of a specified code of behavior, often tacit but always operative.

By the time Franklin left for school at the age of fourteen he was described by many as sensitive, introspective, shy—perhaps a little delicate—a touch vain, but nevertheless aware, energetic, and possessing many interests. He was known for his stoicism during accidents, once hiding from his mother the extent of a serious mouth injury in order not to shock her, another time requesting that his father not be awakened.

Roosevelt would go on to demonstrate sufficient autonomy from his parents to make decisions over which they were not enthusiastic—from his decision to marry Eleanor Roosevelt just after college to his decision to enter politics. On the other hand, his mother's influence was often a domineering and demanding one. She remained at his side through much of his career, controlling his finances during his early married life and all but running the household. At times a moralistic and strident force, her presence no doubt exacerbated feelings of guilt with regard to Roosevelt's ill-fated affair with Lucy Mercer. In chapter six we shall see how his aggressively trained personality was a perfect instrument for the expression of the historical emotions related to the New Deal.

REFERENCES

1. H. Clay Trumbull, *Hints on Child Training* (Philadelphia: John D. Wattlers, 1896).
2. A. M. Libby, diary. New York Historical Society.
3. Mabel Dodge Luhan, *Intimate Memories* (New York: Harcourt, Brace, 1933), pp. 31, 208-9.
4. Eleanor H. Abbott, *Being Little in Cambridge When Everyone Else was Big* (New York: D. Appleton, 1936), pp. 84-90.
5. Edward Eggleston, *The Hoosier School-Boy* (New York: Charles Scribner's Sons, 1890), p. 102.
6. "Childhood in Modern Literature and Art," *Atlantic Monthly Magazine*, December 1885, p. 766.
7. Horace E. Scudder, *Children in Literature and Art* (New York: Houghton Mifflin, 1894), p. 235.
8. H. Sutton, "The Children of Fiction," *Littell's Living Age*, October 1892, pp. 268-9.
9. Martha Finley, *Grandmother Elsie* (New York: Dodd, Mead, 1882), p. 293.
10. William Dean Howells, *A Boy's Town* (New York: Harper and Bros., 1898).
11. Albert E. Stone, Jr., *The Innocent Eye: Childhood in Mark Twain's Imagination* (New Haven: Yale University Press, 1961).
12. Andrea Hoffer Proudfoot, *A Mother's Ideals: A Kindergarten Mother's Conception of Family Life* (New York: A. Flanagan, 1897).
13. Mrs. Margaret Sangster, *Miss Dewberry's Scholars and What They Did* (New York: Thomas Whittaker, 1882), p. 99.
14. "Sunday Schools the World Round," (official report of the World's Fifth Sunday School Convention in Rome, May 18-23, 1907).
15. John C. Hollister, St. Paul's Sunday School, 1852-1882 (New Haven: 1882).
16. "Fathers and Sons," (sermon read at St. James Church, October 11, 1903).
17. Rev. William L. Worcester, *Our Duty to the Children* (Philadelphia: American New Church Tract and Publication Society, 1897), p. 4.
18. The General of the Salvation Army, *The Training of Children* (London: The Salvation Army Book Department, 1888), pp. 36, 83.
19. Mrs. Serepta Nyrenda Irish Henry, Studies in Home and Child Life (Battle Creek: Good Health Publishing Co., 1897), p. 54.

20. Trumbull, *Hints on Child Training.*
21. Stuart H. Rowe, "Fear in the Discipline of Children," *Outlook*, September 1898, p. 236; James Sully, "Studies of Childhood," *Popular Science Monthly*, January 1895, p. 363; Florence Hull Winterburn, *From the Child's Standpoint: Views of Child Life and Nature* (New York: The Baker and Taylor Co., 1899).
22. Luther Burbank, *The Training of the Human Plant* (New York: The Century Company, 1907), p. 67; Antoinette A. Lamoreaux, *The Unfolding Life: A Study of Development with Reference to Religious Training* (Chicago: Religious Publishing Co., 1907); *Mother's Magazine*, January 1881, p. 322.
23. Emma Marwedal, *Conscious Motherhood: The Earliest Unfolding of the Child in the Cradle, Nursery, and Kindergarten* (Boston: D. C. Heath and Co., 1889).
24. "Child Training," *Outlook*, November 1899, p. 673.
25. M. J. Savage, *Man, Woman and Child* (Boston: Geo. H. Ellis, 1884), p. 82.
26. Mrs. Theodore Birney, *Childhood* (New York: Frederick A. Stokes Co., 1905), pp. 61-8, 98.
27. *Child Study Monthly*, June 1896, p. 66.
28. Eugene Field, *Poems of Childhood* (New York: Charles Scribner's Sons, 1896).
29. Marwedal, *Conscious Motherhood;* Savage, *Man, Woman, and Child*, p. 82; *Mother's Magazine*, March 1885, p. 66; "Fathers and Sons."
30. G. Stanley Hall, *Adolescence: Its Psychology*, 2 vols. (New York: D. Appleton, 1905).
31. L. Emmett Holt, *The Diseases of Infancy and Childhood* (New York: D. Appleton, 1897).
32. Henry, *Studies in Home and Child Life*, pp. 54-68.
33. Schwarz, "Devices to Prevent Masturbation."
34. Ellice Hopkins, *On the Early Training of Boys and Girls: An Appeal to Working Women* (New York: B. Mason Mannett, 1884), p. 17; Ellice Hopkins, *The Power of Motherhood; or, Mothers and Sons* (New York: E. P. Dutton, 1901), p. 59.
35. Grace H. Dodge, *A Bundle of Letters to Busy Girls on Practical Matters* (New York: Funk and Wagnalls, 1887), p. 100.
36. Joseph Howe, *Excessive Venery, Masturbation and Continence* (New York: E. B. Treat, 1907).
37. William Byron Forbush, *The Boy Problem* (Boston: The Pilgrim Press, 1901).

38. E. A. Kirkpatrick, *Fundamentals of Child Study* (New York: Macmillan, 1904).

39. "A Preliminary Sketch of the History of the Child Study Movement for the Year Ending September, 1896," *Pedagogical Seminary* 4 (1896): 115-6.

40. Helen H. Gardener, "Environment: Can Heredity be Modified?" *Arena* (July, 1894): 152.

41. Henry, *Studies in Home and Child Life*, p. 54.

42. Gardener, "Environment"; Edgar James Swift, "Some Criminal Tendencies of Boyhood," *Pedagogical Seminary*, (March 1901): 89.

43. "Practical Eugenetics," *Pedagogical Seminary* (September 1909): 386-87; T. S. Lowden, "The First Year of an Infant's Life," *Post Graduate Wooster Quarterly* (July 1895); James Sully, "Studies of Childhood," *Popular Science Monthly* (1894): 734; "Springfield Conference on Physical Training," *Kindergarten Magazine* 12, (1899): 57-58.

44. John Fisk, *Excursions of an Evolutionist* (Boston: Houghton Mifflin, 1891); Amory H. Bradford, "Heredity and Education," *Educational Review* 1 (February 1891): 149.

45. William Byron Forbush, "The Social Pedagogy of Boyhood," *Pedagogical Seminary* 8 (October 1900): 307.

46. Bradford, "Heredity and Education," p. 149.

47. James Sully, "Studies of Childhood," serialized in *Popular Science Monthly* 45 (1894).

48. Edgar James Swift, *Mind in the Making: A Study in Mental Development* (New York: Charles Scribner's Sons, 1908), pp. 31-32.

49. Burbank, *Training of the Human Plant*, p. 17; Birney, *Childhood*; Edith R. Mumford, *The Dawn of Character: A Study of Child Life* (New York: Longmans, Green, 1910), p. 8.

50. George M. Stratton, "Child Study and Psychology," *Educational Review* 14 (September 1897): 138.

51. Proudfoot, *A Mother's Ideals*, p. 107.

52. *Child Study Monthly* 5 (November 1899): 221.

53. Hall, *Adolescence*; G. Stanley Hall, "Notes on the Study of Infants," *Pedagogical Seminary* 1 (1891): 138; G. Stanley Hall, "Moral Education and Will Training," *Pedagogical Seminary* 2 (1892): 82.

54. Swift, *Mind in the Making*, p. 37.

55. Burbank, *Training of the Human Plant*, p. 17.

56. Edward Lee Thorndike, "Notes on Child Study," *Columbia*

*University Contributions to Philosophy, Psychology, and Education* 8 (1901): 153.

57. "Springfield Conference on Physical Training," p. 37.
58. Stuart H. Rowe, *The Physical Nature of the Child and How to Study It* (New York: Macmillan, 1903), p. v.
59. For the cultural values associated with education, see Lawrence A. Cremin and R. F. Butts, *A History of Education in American Culture* (New York: Holt, Rinehart & Winston, 1953).
60. Swift, *Mind in the Making*, p. 37.
61. Frederic Adye, "Old-Fashioned Children," *Littell's Living Age* (September 1893): 824.
62. Thorndike, "Notes on Child Study," p. 153.
63. Frederick E. Bolton, "New Lines of Attack in Child Study," *The Journal of Pedagogy* 15 (September 1902): 29-45.
64. Bradford, p. 149.
65. Kirkpatrick, *Fundamentals of Child Study*, p. 105.
66. George Allen Hubbell, *Up Through Childhood: A Study of Some Principles of Education in Relation to Faith and Conduct* (New York: G. P. Putnam's Sons, 1904), pp. 253-4.
67. John Dewey, "Interest in Relation to Training of the Will," supplement to the *Herbart Year Book* for 1895, pp. 213-4.
68. William A. Hammond, "Brain Forcing in Childhood," *Popular Science Monthly*, 1887.
69. Bernard Wishy, *The Child and the Republic* (Philadelphia: University of Pennsylvania Press, 1968), p. 157.
70. Proudfoot, *A Mother's Ideals*, p. 122.
71. William H. Maxwell, "Education for Efficiency," *School Journal* (July 1905): 115-7; see also Raymond E. Callahan, *Education and the Cult of Efficiency*.
72. I. W. Howerth, "The Social Aim in Education," *The Fifth Yearbook of the National Herbart Society* (Chicago: University of Chicago Press, 1899), p. 69; Maxwell, "Education for Efficiency," p. 117.
73. "A Study in Precocity and Prematuration," *Journal of Pedagogy* 16 (April 1905): 165.
74. Nora Archibald Smith, *The Children of the Future* (New York: Houghton Mifflin, 1898), pp. 21-22.
75. Trumbull, *Hints on Child Training*, p. 38.
76. Ernest Hamlin Abbott, *On the Training of Parents* (New York: Houghton Mifflin, 1908), p. 44.
77. W. T. Harris, "The Relation of School Discipline to Moral Education," *Third Yearbook of the National Herbart Society* (Chicago: University of Chicago Press, 1897).

78. "Rationalism in the Nursery," *Open Court* 13 (February 1899): 102-5.
79. Henry L. Clapp, "The Educative Value of Children's Questioning," *Popular Science Monthly* (October 1896): 803.
80. Ibid.
81. Trumbull, *Hints on Child Training*, p. 92.
82. Winterburn, *From the Child's Standpoint*, pp. 96, 125.
83. John Ferguson, "The Nervous System and Its Relation to Education," *Popular Science Monthly* (August 1895).
84. *Mother's Magazine* (March 1885): 65.
85. Smith, *The Children of the Future*.
86. Elizabeth Harrison, *A Study on Child-Nature: From the Kindergarten Standpoint* (Chicago: Chicago Kindergarten Training School, 1891); "Springfield Conference on Physical Training," pp. 50-57. Additional sources on education drawn upon are: Lewis W. Parker, "Compulsory Education: The Solution of the Child Labor Problem," supplement to *Annals of the American Academy of Political and Social Science*, July 1908; "Suggestions for a Philosophy of Education," *Pedagogical Seminary* 5 (1891); Bradford, "Heredity and Education"; Forbush, "The Social Pedagogy of Boyhood"; Charles H. Sears, "Home and School Punishments," *Pedagogical Seminary* 6 (1898); G. Stanley Hall, "Child-Study and its Relation to Education," *Forum* (August 1900).
87. Celia B. Stendler, "Sixty Years of Child Training Practices: Revolution in the Nursery," *Journal of Pediatrics* 36 (1950); Clark E. Vincent, "Trend in Infant Care Ideas," *Child Development* 22 (1951); John E. Anderson, "Child Development: An Historical Perspective," *Child Development* 27 (1956); Alice Ryerson, "Medical Advice on Child Rearing, 1550-1900," *Harvard Educational Review* 31 (Summer 1961).
88. Holt, *The Diseases of Infancy and Childhood*, p. 159; Louis Starrs, *Diseases of the Digestive Organs in Infancy and Childhood* (Philadelphia: P. Blakiston's Son & Co., 1901).
89. Christine Herrick, *A Home Book for Mothers and Daughters* (New York: The Christian Herald, [c. 1897]).
90. Rudolph Marx, *The Health of the Presidents* (New York, 1960), p. 353; Mrs. James Roosevelt, as told to Isabelle Leighton and Gabrielle Forbush, *My Boy Franklin* (New York: 1933), p. 12.
91. Gerald D. Nash, *Franklin Delano Roosevelt* (Englewood Cliffs: Prentice-Hall, 1967), p. 73.
92. James David Barber, *The Presidential Character*, p. 215; see

also Kenneth S. Davis, *FDR: The Beckoning of Destiny, 1882-1928* (New York: G. P. Putnam's Sons, 1971).

CHAPTER FOUR

VIGOROUS GUIDANCE, 1910-1940

More relaxed authority bonds and an increased capacity for empathetic relations allow for a new childhood experience in the vigorous guidance period. The realities of guidance are best spelled out by the new science of psychoanalysis. The basic drives of the child are acknowledged as well as the complexity of its psychology. The child's energy is now a positive force, and its emotions are less threatening. Because these drives are less a threat, the parental generation is better able to accommodate the child's needs. The parent is better able to become aware of projections and parental dynamics thrust upon the child so that they may be diminished as empathetic relations develop.

The new accommodation of the child's needs is visible in all parameters of culture. Progressive education becomes institutionalized and child-protection laws are enacted. For the first time, masturbation is not thought of as necessarily harmful but as one of many natural behaviors; the child now has a "sexual life." Throwbacks within the mode such as Watson's behaviorism are mercurial and quickly rejected under the impetus to accommodate and not manipulate the child's needs.

Yet the guidance is still vigorous and very much a part of the socializing mode. A premium is placed on the child's achievement, and the relaxation of environmental manipulation is always in reference to the axiom that the child must absorb the surrounding culture, must be taught and socialized. Thus instincts must be guided into the proper paths (sublimation) so that the inevitable processes of repression may be as painless as possible. Play, school, social interaction, and exercise all have the express purpose of growth. Guidance, as training, still has the adult in the lead; the push is simply less aggressive now.

## GUIDANCE FICTION

The area of fiction indicates a relaxation of many ambivalences toward the child, especially in the degree of aggressive attitude and in the preoccupation with vigor. Surveying the Newberry Medals awarded in the twenties and thirties for children's writing, one observes a slackening off not only of didactic themes but also of the degree of parent-child conflict present in the literature of the aggressive period. *Dr. Doolittle*, award winner of 1923, is about a man known for qualities of "patience, reliability, mixed and delightful humor, energy and gaiety." An award-winning children's author in the 1930s stated that "A child sees everything sharp and radiant . . . sorrow in childhood is a monstrous, alive thing, and one has not yet learned any philosophy that can dull the corners of it."[1] This is a step ahead of the more embryonic empathetic observations recorded during the aggressive submode. As early as 1912, *Harper's Magazine* published an article, "Children in Fiction," in which the author remarks upon the contemporary awareness of the pathos of childhood.[2] There are still books like *Swatty: A Story of Real Boys* —a watered-down Huck Finn— and the one-dimensional *Father's Gone A-Whaling*, which appeal to the less developed imagination, but at the same time there appears a genre of literature better able to resonate with many children's imaginations. *Raggedy Ann in the Deep Woods* (1930), in the tradition of *Alice in Wonderland*, includes personified objects and animals. In addition, one writer has pointed out the relative decline in the number of what can be termed juvenile-delinquency novels during this period, suggesting a reduction in the degree of child-society conflict.[3]

## THE NEW PSYCHOLOGY

A more striking indication of a new submode is in the area of guides to parenthood. A rash of new books made the connection between psychology and parenthood explicit: *Psychology and Child Training* (1925), *The New Psychology and the Parent* (1923), *The Psychology of Childhood* (1930), *Child Upbringing and the New Psychology* (1933), *Parenthood and the Newer Psychology* (1926), *The Normal Child*.[4]

A major accomplishment of the new psychology is the acknowledgment of the importance of the early environment. Psychic control necessitates this as a condition for its expression, aggressive training relegates environment somewhat, but vigorous guidance presents an entirely new perspective. First, the nature of parental influence was inscrutable in the control period. Processes of interaction with all-important implications were almost impossible to comprehend; they were never explained but were instead dictated as lying in the nature of things—from the potency of the maternal expression and tone of voice to the vagaries of maternal impressions. The genetics of the aggressive submode attempted to ascribe, in more specific ways, characteristics which are innate, and some headway was made in at least pinning down a specific area of matter (genetics) which contained such influence. With the new primacy of environment, parental power was not as fearful nor inscrutable because of the realization of the nature of behavior and a greater feeling for the processes of personality formation.

For the first time, a conscious recognition of the phenomenon of projection was committed to print: "Parents are prone to project on the child their own unfulfilled wishes and desires, regardless of whether they are in keeping with the instinctive needs of the child or not," says *Parents' Magazine* in 1929.[5] One writer speaks of the possible functions of love: as an expression of power ("power love"), as a means of gaining rejuvenation, as a means of compensating or sacrificing. All involve aspects of projection in parent-child dynamics, the adult bringing to the relationship, and playing out, problems which were formulated well before the child's conception.[6] (It is of note that the direct effect of psychoanalysis on the popular literature was not great, one estimate is that from 1915 to 1928 there were only three or four truly psychoanalytically oriented articles a year.)

Margaret Ribble writes at the same time of the "new" psychological needs—emotional needs which, if not met, inflict pains on the child that may mark it for life: "The art of mothering is to discover and satisfy the particular need of the individual child . . . not every woman should be a mother."[7] Arland Weeks moves a step beyond the recapitulation theory of aggressive training: "As the living generation summarizes its ancestors, so our final personality recapitulates the series of selves reaching back to childhood. And the final individual which we are is the consistent outcome of our selves back to babyhood."[8] This is the kind of insight attained by means of creative regression to one's own infancy.

H. Crichton Miller's *The New Psychology and the Parent* includes the observation that "the destiny of the child is social efficacy; the problem of the child is psychological freedom; the obstacle to the child is authority; and the test of every child's development is his fierce attitude towards racial experience."[9] Blanch Weill, in her *Through Children's Eyes: True Stories Out of the Practice of a Consulting Psychologist* (1940), crisply states: "One thing I can tell you definitely. A naughty child is an unhappy child." She continues: "A word of fairly recent coinage expresses this attempt to understand why people do what they do. Empathy: the experiencing *into* another person."[10]

With such insight, some adults were prepared to see how parental authority can arrest development through encouraging or necessitating massive defense structures. Miller speaks of the child's urge for self-realization and completeness, citing the spontaneity of the Montessori method and telling the parent to be conscious of his own patronage and urges for power. Frances G. Wicks, author of *The Inner World of Childhood: A Study in Analytical Psychology* (1927) urges that "we must be constantly investigating our own attitudes. We have no more right to a personal will-to-power attitude with our children than in any other human relation." Edgar J. Swift's *The Psychology of Childhood* (1939) includes parental self-discipline as an ideal in child-rearing.[11] *The Pedagogical Seminary* called for a more profound understanding of behavior: "For applied psychology and education nothing is of greater importance than studies which reveal, even though to small degree, the motivations of conduct, and which thus enable the teacher, employer, parent, or whoever has to deal with the individual in question, to foresee and guide conduct."[12]

Frank Howard Richardson's *Parenthood and the Newer Psychology* (1926) isolates love as the single most important aspect of the parent-child relationship. Reestablishing the primacy of the environment, he states that discipline must be an "affirmative" process in which a basic approval of the child must be present. The English publication *Child Upbringing and the New Psychology* (1933) presents American parents with the conceptualization that "mental and nervous" illnesses may be "traced to faulty upbringing, education and environment."[13]

Another writer declares: "To-day . . . the mother . . . has met with increasing attack. . . . Mothers tend too often to warp the lives of their children with their affection and to hinder rather than help in the struggle· for individual fulfillment." Fritz Wittels writes an article entitled "Sadistic Tendencies in Parents."[14] In a similar vein, Frances G. Wicks declares: "It becomes apparent therefore that when we are dealing with the neurotic difficulties of children it behooves us to examine the unconscious life of the parent for when his difficulties are cleared the troubles of the child often vanish of themselves." And William Pyle says that "In a very true sense a man is *made*. He is the product of all the forces that act upon him, particularly those that act upon him in his earlier years."[15] All of these texts stress that for all the potentially fearful implications of the new psychoanalysis, what might have been totally unacceptable to an earlier generation is now subject to conversation and study. One publication even comes forth with the then astonishing notion that appearing nude in front of the child may be a harmless way of satisfying his curiosity, with little or no negative result.

Of course there was a backlash from earlier submode authorities. Dr. Bernard Sachs's *The Normal Child*, for example, seeks to protect parents from an overemphasis on sexuality, warning that making the unconscious conscious might cause the child to lapse into anxiety and hypochondria. Nevertheless, Sachs writes in 1926 that environment is more important than heredity.[16]

A. S. Neill states in his introduction to Mannin's *Common-Sense and the Child: A Plea for Freedom* (1932) that "the children who become problems are nearly always the children of parents who hate themselves." The attitude you have to your child is always the attitude you have to yourself. Mannin insists that there is no such thing as a naughty child, only an unhappy one. Readers are told that the child does not create endearments but the kind of love which has at its basis sympathetic understanding—close to what has been termed, in this study, empathy.[17]

Many now call for a new intimacy on the part of parents; but, unlike what Stephen Kern has aptly termed the "explosive intimacy" of the Victorian years, it is an intimacy in which the parent seeks to learn about the child through its own behavior. *The Pedagogical Seminary* writes of the child's *individuality*, which must be respected, and there is a more conscious awareness and concern of children's fears. Dr. Douglas A. Thom writes: "Do not minimize [or] criticize the fears of childhood." A more profound understanding of delinquency is also consciously articulated by Thom, who insists that the jealous child is essentially a miserable child. It is significant that writers begin to stress the *autonomy* of the child, one quoting Kahlil Gibran's verse that the child is not a thing possessed by a parent but an expression of the life process ("life's longing for itself"). Much of the literature argues that the child is naturally normal and that abnormality or psychological neurosis is something done *to* the child. One parent describes the guidance of a child in this way: "I, his mother, can only show him the way and make his work easier by my experience . . . . All that the child really gains he must gain for and by himself." This writer has come to terms with the progressive ability to be gentle with the child: "Let us get forever away from the old conception of the word, and look upon discipline in its new and gentle guise, as the regulating of instinctive desires and the effort on our part, not to coerce or combat, but instead to clear away the obstacles in the child's path." She stresses letting the child make his own decisions, granting him responsibility, and accepting children's periods of depression as they come and as vital aspects of their interaction with the environment. There is, at the same time, a pull away from the aggressive submode when the writer remarks upon the danger of too much sympathy and the value of increasing a child's power by self-reliance, of letting do for the child what he can do for himself."[18]

## GUIDED SEXUALITY

The sexual remifications of vigorous guidance are not surprising. Summarizing the first three submodes, we may observe the following progression: first, the ideology of psychic control summarized by the spermatic economy, and the latent-incestuous ties to the mother; second, aggressive training's relaxation of the spermatic economy, de-emphasis of the moral necessity of sexual control, and relaxation of incestuous ties; finally, the guided period with its acceptance of child sexuality as natural.

In the years between 1910 and 1940, the child's sexual nature is often acknowledged, though amidst a larger body of work reflecting fossilized attitudes. Holt warns that a child's masturbation increases nervousness and exaggerates lack of self-control. Holt's 1929 edition of a work originally published in 1894 continues to cite masturbatory "diseases" such as lower moral sense and loss of endurance.[19] Dr. Bernard Sachs published a 1936 child care book which advises that sexual education should be limited so as not to overstimulate, that a little repression is beneficial, and that the best strategy concerning sexuality is to ignore it. Sachs concludes that the field of child study is "oversexed." He states that the sexuality of children two or three years of age is actually the *result* of parents who have been influenced by psychoanalysts who "insist on bringing sexual feelings into the limelight."[20] The sexual instinct, like all instincts, must be kept under control.[21]

Yet what is characteristic of the period of vigorous guidance is the progressive breakthrough of ideas that we now know to be empirically true, particularly the idea that the child is a sexual being who will naturally explore the sexual as well as the other parts of his or her body. *The Pedagogical Seminary*, the bastion of what is here termed aggressive training, came out with this statement of child sexuality in its seventeenth volume in 1920:

> The sex life of the child is a very different thing from that of adolescent years, but it is none the less strong. Its main characteristics are the relative independence of the different instincts which go to make it up, and the fact that sex-satisfaction is found on the body of the child. Sexual pleasure may be produced by thumb-sucking, by stimulation of the excretory regions through retention, by masturbation.[22]

Such was the progress in the discovery of self which took place in a period of less than fifty years. The introduction to Dr. Albert Moll's *The Sexual Life of the Child* (translated from the German) was written by none other than the pioneer of learning and testing, Edward Thorndike, who observes: "Conscientious and observant teachers realize, in a dim way, that they cannot do justice to even the purely intellectual needs of pupils without understanding the natural history of these instinctive impulses, which, concealed and falsified as they are under traditional taboos, nevertheless retain enormous potency." Moll follows with the point that masturbation is *not* a specifically harmful process as so often claimed. In a particularly bold statement he insists that masturbation is only dangerous if habitual and adds that almost all individuals have masturbated once or twice a week for some period of time.[23] Ernest R. Groves's *Sex in Childhood* (1933), also a vivid illustration of the newer empathy both in title and content, goes as far in the direction of casualness as to say that masturbation is analogous to daydreaming, not particularly productive, but essentially harmless. Another child-care book of the 1930s states that excretion is, for the child, during certain periods of its life, associated with sex.[24] It should also be noted that *Training the Girl* (1914) includes the older precautions but makes a reference to a young girl's sex life as a beautiful "talent" which, if properly channeled, may add beauty and service to her life.[25] Another writer remarks that "the child's attitude [toward sex] is curious and playful and innocent. The mischief is always contributed by the mystery . . .poses and pretenses of the elders."[26] Interest in masturbation-prevention devices waned as their therapeutic value was questioned. As late as 1917 an inventor patented a garment with genital shields, but the device lacked the severity of earlier gadgets.

Dr. Douglas Thom comes forth with the notion that "sex becomes a real problem only when it is a symptom of poor adjustment of the total individual and his 'total situation' in life."[27] This is the type of insight, so simple in its clarity and today almost axiomatic, that in its context reveals a new psychological openness founded on previous advances in the treatment of children, their feelings, and their bodies.

Jesse Taft, in the *Annals of the American Academy of Political and Social Science* (1930), makes the connection between sexuality and guilt, stressing that the child's sexuality is a part of the whole person, a manifestation of broader processes. Taking his general analysis a step further on the road toward empathy, he states: "More and more, we are aware that our usefulness to the child . . . depends upon our own emotional freedom and flexibility—our own capacity to separate our personal problems from those of the child and make identification a tool of greater understanding, and not an escape from ourselves."[28]

Likewise, the most progressive elements in pediatrics were moving beyond aggressive views of the child, though there is a continuation of the obsession with power and vigor. *Training the Boy* (1913) includes the observation that solid muscular tissue is essential in preventing fatigue in the male, often conditioned by hard knocks and "the other seasoning" experiences which include "a small amount of fighting."[29] One writer states in 1939: "When we remember how compactly the baby has been packed for nine months of ante-natal life, surrounded by a fluid exerting a comforting pressure and absorbing all the jar, we can understand that the sudden release from this must be terrifying. The sensation must be to a wild degree that of falling in every direction, i.e. great insecurity." Although this is followed by the notion that swaddling clothes hold some advantage by approximating the womb, it is a rare statement of the trauma of birth, paralleling the work of Rank, and itself reveals a forward movement in creative regression and empathy.[30] Gradually, too, progressive pediatrics departed from the earlier obsession with genetics.

## INSTITUTIONAL DEVELOPMENT

Institutional innovations characteristic of the guidance period include the Children's Bureau established under Theodore Roosevelt. It expanded its activities in 1919 with a conference on child welfare standards, the same year that saw the passing of a major child labor law. (This is an interesting example of TR's ambivalences: on the one hand teaching his eldest son Ted to swim by throwing him bodily into the water, on the other hand establishing the first federal agency dedicated to child welfare.) A vivid illustration of progress in the area of child welfare is the fact that between 1885 and 1915 the death rate among infants under one year of age dropped from 273.6 to 94.6 per thousand. Studies of child welfare became more probing, better able to face harsh realities. *Baby Farms in Chicago*, for example, describes the shocking incidence of "incestful family lines" and reports on doctors and others privately selling children for from twenty-five to one hundred dollars. The study concludes: "There is no law at the present in the state of Illinois which prohibits traffic in children or which requires registration of children, given away or placed out to board."[31] The *Pedagogical Seminary* in 1911 notes that all states except Nevada have passed legislation on child labor. The journal lists the basic rights of childhood, including: (1) the right to be well born; (2) the right to parental name, support, and protection; (3) play and recreation; (4) education; (5) exemption from work; (6) humane treatment; (7) protection of health and morals; (8) decent environment. Between 1911 and 1931 all but three states enacted aid-to-mothers laws.[32]

## THE BEHAVIORISM OF JOHN WATSON

A crucial phenomenon of the process of psychic evolution is that each advance toward empathy with the child must include new defenses against the fresh anxieties released by the new closeness. Psychologist John Watson first gained national recognition with the publication of his *Psychological Care of Infant and Child* (1928). Basing much of his advice on L. Emmett Holt's *The Care and Feeding of Children*, first published in 1894, he advocated conscious withdrawal of the expression of affection. (In fairness to Watson, he was advocating not the termination of affection per se but the withholding of the *expression* of it.) Watson took Holt a step further. For example, Holt opposed kissing because it could transmit disease, but Watson's objections were based on the creation of dependency and the arrest of psychological growth. He felt mother love could prevent the child from the necessary process of "conquering the world." Toilet training, in his opinion, should be effected by means of a special toilet seat to which the under-one-year-old is strapped; the infant should then be left alone with the door closed. Children should be taught to play alone from the beginning; when playing with other children, they should also be left alone. He deplored the lack of able mothers, the lack of expertise in the "profession" of parenthood. Watson was very much, in his own way, a part of the new environmentalism, writing: "Isn't it possible that nothing is given in heredity and that practically the whole course of development of the child is due to the way I raise it?" He added: "I believe that if a child has been badly managed up to the age of seven years, it is impossible to correct the difficulties in the emotional slants of the child completely. . . . Because of his lack of mental development the child is outside the realm of morals. He is neither moral nor immoral. He is non-moral. He is but a candidate for morality."[3 3] Watson insisted on viewing all developments according to the laws of learning, the passionless development of conditioning.[3 4]

Watson cannot be immediately dismissed; his goals were no different from those of the other innovative thinkers whose ideas proved to be part of an ongoing (progressive) thread. Watson wished for the "end result" of "a happy child free as air because he has mastered the stupidly simple demands society makes upon him." He wished for an "independent child," an "original child." And some people were listening. Holt's 1929 edition of *The Care and Feeding of Children* states that the less kissing the better; *Wholesome Parenthood* (1929) states briskly the need for conditioned habit and reflex; *Mothercraft* (1926) concludes that there is "a time for work and a time for play—a regularity in all he does"; William Forbush writes at the same time of stimulus and response, regularity and consistency, as a means of forming good habits; and a *Comparative Psychology Monograph* (1936) discusses the "repertoire of reactions" such as reflex and defensive responses.[35] Many writers make reference to the benefits of a system of rewards and punishment (termed in other instances positive and negative reinforcement). Many parents were willing to accept Watson's assumptions that the child harbors dangerous impulses which must be regulated scientifically and dispassionately at the earliest stages of development (passion was thought to fixate and prevent growth). One extensive study of the *Reader's Guide to Periodical Literature* for the years 1910 to 1935 revealed that of the 146 articles relating to the child, a major theme was the danger of too much love, and few indicated a danger in too much regulation. Some parents could subsequently remember attempting as consistently as possible to enact Watson's mechanistic decathected prescriptions.[36] Later, as the more progressive sectors gained wider appeal, swamping Watsonian notions, these parents regretted their faith in his system.

The refutation of Watson became thorough and eventually complete. *The Parents' Magazine* ran an article in 1930 stating: "Don't let Watson and Freud frighten you. It's perfectly safe to love your children if you want to."[37] William McDougall came forth with an even more forthright condemnation: "The strict behaviorists do not trouble themselves about the social life of man; they are sufficiently occupied with the self-imposed task of proving that animals and new-born babies are . . . machines." He entitled his article, appearing two years before Watson's major and most popular book, "Men or Robots?"[38]

One parent remembers Watson with no affection, although she did try to raise her children according to his teachings: "In those days, when my son cried, I inspected his simple, white flannel nightgown with the sleeves tied around his hands to prevent thumb-sucking, and examined his diaper for open safety pins or wetness; if he persisted, I was allowed to turn him on his side or his stomach, just once, but never, never, on pain of acquiring an everlasting guilt complex, could I pick him up or fondle him." She came to believe that this regimen could only cause damage to both parent and child, remembering some of Watson's more ludicrous ideas such as the possibility that a child might be better off if it never knew its real parents and the idea that toilet training might take place at the age of three to five weeks.[39]

Another example of the superficiality of the behaviorist fad is a piece published by Watson's wife Rosalie in *The Parents' Magazine* (1930): "I am the Mother of a Behaviorist's Sons." Her first topic is toilet training; she relates how she took her son to a physician, told the doctor that he was brought up behavioristically, and was relieved to hear that the boy was probably better off to be well adjusted, if a little constipated. Yet Mrs. Watson's reservations proved to be extensive. She explains how she missed being allowed to have the children in her sleeping quarters, and related that her family had so lost the habit of spending some time together after an evening meal that, on birthdays and holidays, "the whole family becomes emotionally exhausted and very grateful when bedtime arrives." She adds with a great deal of candor and good humor that she occasionally felt the urge to break a rule: "I love to help the children tie up their father's pajamas in knots and put hair brushes in people's beds . . . I like being merry and having giggles. The behaviorists think it is a sign of maladjustment, so when the children want to giggle I have to keep a straight face or brush them off to their rooms—but we get away with a lot!"[40]

## VIGOROUS GUIDANCE AND EDUCATION

Vigorous guidance is explicit in educational theory in this period, especially in the applications of Maria Montessori's ideas. Montessori, the Italian educator who emphasized the favorable manipulation of the environment to suit the creative needs of the child, presented ideas which moved beyond the education of the aggressive period and reached out toward the child on a yet deeper level. Montessori was not ready to speak in a broad sense of freedom in the classroom, nor was she willing to abandon discipline and standards of achievement and competition. But she did insist that the child's energy is a positive force, which makes it expedient for adults to create an appropriate environment which may harness it. Beyond manipulating the child's brain and mind, the adult must manipulate his environment. The parent still knows and is in control of the body of information the child may obtain, but the child—rather than being force-fed—is allowed to move about and find this information himself. Tied to the tradition of the positive value of "work," Montessori emphasized orderly action as a way of maximizing energy. Her emphasis on energy and vigor has a Rooseveltian tone: "His own self-development is his true and almost his only pleasure . . . . to exercise his intelligence in the reasoning connected with his undertaking, to stimulate his will power by deciding his own actions." She stressed the value of exercise (a popular word in her writings) and endorsed repetition as a facilitator of training. Thus, in 1912, the educator endorsed the work ethic, the vigor of aggressivity, the necessity of discipline, but strove to move beyond established authority bonds, to separate the child from these ties by the logical step of redirecting the adult involvement to the child's environment.

Montessori's work may be viewed as the transition point between aggressive training and vigorous guidance. On the one hand, she states (1932): "In order to begin the task of reconstructing man's psyche, we must make the child our point of departure. We must recognize that he is more than just our progeny, more than just a creature who is our greatest responsibility. We must study him not as a dependent creature, but as an independent person who must be considered in terms of his own individual self." On the other hand, she lauded an environment favoring the qualities of meticulousness, concentration, control of the body, and a love of silence, in addition to punctual obedience and a delight in obeying. Stanley Cobb, who felt the new freedom only confused children, supported Montessori without feeling the internal contradiction.[41] Montessori continued to make the distinction between man's savage past and the demands of civilization which makes control of the instincts and direction of them into the proper paths essential. In this aspect her thinking was already fossilized.[42]

An awareness of the child's emotional reality and the way it relates to his educative nature (his search for knowledge and creativity, his energy levels, his motivation, his fear or positive feeling concerning the unknown) was given theoretical voice. The reaction to the ideas of psychoanalysis was sometimes an explicit rejection. *The New Psychology and the Parent* (1923) brought out the obvious defense that there must be unknown things in genes which determine a child's educability, although the value of a knowledge of the unconscious was proclaimed.[43] One analysis discovered that few of the parenting manuals published during the 1930s concerned themselves with Freud; out of the long list of studies, only sixteen contained any reference to Freud, and the unconscious was mentioned in only six.[44] On the other hand, a study published in 1919, concerned with the child's unconscious mind and education, states the following: "If it is the duty of the individual to recognize and adapt himself to the greatest amount of unconscious life, it is surely that of the teacher not to ignore but to study the manifestations of the unconscious as they are developed in children."[45] One of the obvious breakthroughs is that the parent tended less and less to deny—and to punish—the more disturbing aspects of his child's nature. According to *The Child's Unconscious Mind* (1919), "a tendency to inflict pain and a pleasure in inflicting pain upon others is normally found in all healthy children at one stage of the development of their personality."[46] A fuller grasp of the realities of the child's mind is obvious, and as is the case with all early psychoanalytic thought, the child is seen to undergo frustrating processes of inevitable repression as the superego comes into conflict with the id. One English writer, whose work was available in America, phrased it in this way: "It will be observed that this *dynamic element of progressive control includes a progressive control of the lower phases of the self by the higher phases* of the self."[47] Another states: "Each of us has to contend with a profound resistance against the free and unimpeded development of those who are closest to us, unless that development harmonizes with our own unconscious wishes—which wishes are still partially infantile and primitive. . . . within our children the elements of conflict have been implanted from the past." Progress requires first analysis and then the act of disciplining "out of ourselves the primitive possessive tendencies."[48] Psychoanalysis allowed for the discovery during this period that most neuroses can be traced back to traumas before the age of six years which have produced arrested development.


## VIGOROUS GUIDED BEHAVIOR

The area of actual behavior also elucidates the implications of vigorous guidance. Indicative of guidance is the creation of a book of sufficiently intimate interest in children to be entitled *Dream Life for Children* (1918), which presents material of paradigmatic significance. The narrative of a middle-aged female adult presents a dream in which she sees an old woman in one corner of a room and in the other an infant in distress. Aware of the needs of both of these individuals, the narrator feels in possession of almost superhuman powers to satisfy their needs. After satisfying them (in ways not detailed), she looks up and sees a huge flying machine resembling a bow and arrow. The woman continues: "Immediately I took flight and rose out of the ceiling of the room." Soaring through the clear night sky and over the sea, she was overcome with a feeling of perfect simplicity and exhilaration. Eventually she could hear the sound of the water below, then the force of the wind, until "I fearlessly swung my machine right about into the teeth of the gale." She continues: "And with utmost joyous exultation, I swerved about and sailed right through the rushing currents of air beating vigorously on my face." She speaks of knowing some great power and of being one with it. Finally, she descends into "the basement of a distressingly unsavory tenement district." The old woman and the child seem to be present, but the latter is now a full-grown agile boy. He displays an awed interest in the flying machine which "stood conspicuously against the dingy background." At that moment the narrator realizes he is her child, Laurence. He pleads: "O Mama, will you give it to me?" The woman feels the difficulty of giving such a machine away, especially because it meant staying to take care of the old woman, staying in the basement of a tenement. But the woman thinks: "My machine would give me no joy if I knew this poor old creature was down there alone and no one to take care of her." A decision is made: the boy is shown the controls, he is lifted into the seat, and takes off. The woman feels joy at his departure. After the machine disappears, a still greater one appears and transforms the basement area into a chamber filled with light. It takes her, also, upward into the night.[4][9]

The symbols and images of the dream contain such clarity as to make extensive analysis and in-depth knowledge of the woman's personal psychic history and the circumstances surrounding the dream unnecessary. The old woman is an aspect of the narrator; the child is her child; and along with the vital connection of equating the child's needs with her own, she feels an exhilaration, a sense of transcending the past. After her flight, the child is imagined as healthy and grown, and he asks for the very basis of the woman's new happiness, the source of her energies. When the woman is able to grant him this, his means of autonomy, her own happiness remains and is intensified. Central to the theory of this study is the concept that such a dream could not have existed in earlier modes. This dream is the product of a mind which has moved sufficiently forward to decrease the degree of projection into the child, to achieve sufficient empathy through creative regression so that the child's growth and independence may be a source of pleasure.

Records of home life indicate a new capacity to tolerate the child's temper. One record describes a child of forty months who explodes in a temper tantrum, strikes a servant girl with a file, and then throws it down in anger. After being told to close the door, he first acts as he will not, then does it and immediately bursts into tears. His father tells him calmly to go out of the room and to return only after he has quieted down. The child kicks the door resentfully and is again calmly told to stop. Minutes later, the child returns calm and recovered, getting up into his father's lap.

At the beginning of the period (1910), older elements of aggressive training are still predominant. A boy was hiking with his father and asked to be carried, but was told: "If you are going to be my little 'mountain boy' you must learn to walk farther than this." The boy answered that he was always being told that, but soon declared "I will" and proceeded to walk the entire distance without complaint. When the boy was four, he said: "I am going to be brave and braver till I get as brave as papa!" Later, he hurt himself, but choked back his tears and said: "I pretty near didn't cry a bit." Upon going into a dark room of which he was afraid, he stated: "I am going to be brave."[50] Yet even though training themes predominate in this example, guidance dynamics are clear. The child's anger is no longer so threatening, and the parent may express disapproval without recourse to physicality and even without the open threat of guilt. Instead, resort is made to the withdrawal of love or the appeal to a highly developed conscience. There are none of the control lectures of godly wrath, or the later appeals to the potency of human aggression, but a patient assurance that what is troubling the child will pass, surely and evenly. The child's motions for reconciliation are accepted, and life smoothly continues. Yet the "aggressive" side of training and the "vigorous" side of guidance are evident when the child tires and must show his stamina by completing a hike, or is urged to exhibit qualities of stoicism when in pain from an injury or when entering a dark room.

Another characteristic of guidance is that although the child feels hemmed in by social demands—evolution has not yet transcended this dynamic—diaries indicate that he or she is able to perceive a way out of these constraints. A child relates a fantasy which is reflective of a new autonomy: "Darkness on all sides but one small hole. Low and jagged rock sticking out. A small dent in the rock, water has fallen here for years. A small hole . . . a passage then a small opening . . . no, no hole at all. The horror of being cased in forever . . . but the main cavern at the opening, and then light!"[51] English observers remarked upon the relaxed tone prevailing between Americans of different generations, the facility with which children asked, and were encouraged to ask, questions, the willingness on the part of child and adult to share reactions and feelings.[52] Besides the new facility of interaction between generations and the expansive feelings of freedom, comes a greater distance from authority, vividly illustrated by the following representative guidance view of religion: "I object to telling my thoughts about religion, because they are very delicate. . . . I will say this though. I do not believe in any established religion, and I do believe in something superior. But how I believe and feel about it, is inside my soap bubble."[53]

Parents begin to show a greater sensitivity concerning their true feelings toward children, as in the following:

Alma had. a hard time . . . if you want to put it in a nutshell, you could say it was like this: I was never home with Alma when she was little and helpless. I never felt she needed to be cuddled and protected. When I came home I felt she was big enough to do this . . . you're big enough to do as I tell you. . . . That's really it . . . I feel I don't give Alma the affection I give the other children. I try to, especially lately.[54]

## THE VIGOROUS SIDE OF GUIDANCE

Much needs to be said in reference to the "vigorous" side of guidance, to the elements which were the legacy of psychic control and aggressive training, now tempered and modified. Most evident is the concern with development: the child is expected to reach a particular minimal level of proficiency, achieved through vigorous effort, discipline (though not as stringent as in other submodes), and social interactions of a competitive nature. One educator states that "an education is bad which leads to the formation of habits of idleness, convalescence, failure, instead of habits of industry, thoroughness, and success."[55] Thus we see that one of the precepts of vigor is movement, constant development. And just as the anathema of psychic control was disobedience to authority, and the anathema of training was a slovenly attitude, so now lack of movement, change, and development is seen as the prime negative quality.

Even the play of children was conceptualized as a means of social reform. Books like Henry Curtis's *Education Through Play* (1915) and Joseph Lee's *Play in Education* (1916) gained wide readership.[56] Dewey conceptualized play as the means by which the child responds to the world, and thus an important aspect of development. He stressed that the play environment should be manipulated by the parent to insure maximal development, much as Montessori recommended manipulation of the classroom environment. One writer observed a warlike quality in play—his article was entitled "Play as the Moral Equivalent of War"—in which primitive instincts are expressed and molded by the child himself.[57] Whereas earlier submodes had the parent molding the child, now the child is to mold his own instincts, gradually repressing the antisocial, allowing the social to surface and develop. Team sports are likewise emphasized, and new playgrounds are designed to ensure social development—whether on the baseball diamond or the large climbing apparatus on which children would organize their territorialities.

Hall's credo of "physical vigor and juvenile idealism" found ample expression in the new conception of play, in which a considerable amount of aggressive expression was considered inevitable. One writer declared in 1929: "It is impossible to lay down rules for dealing with fighting instincts and tendencies—that are universally valid."[5 8] Rather than envision the fighting instinct as all but eliminated in the process of an enlightened maturation, it is possible to accept it and to redirect it into play and competitive sports.[5 9] The *Parents' Magazine's* answer to the question "Must Boys Fight?" is that fighting is "a natural and normal instinct." Moreover, it has the positive function of "cultivating strength and skill. . . . As our boys grow older they can be shown how the energy that might be spent in fighting can be utilized in wholesome sports or other worth-while activities."[6 0] Another source indicates: "While aggressive combativeness is to be discouraged, one should try to retain enough of the fighting instinct in each child to make sure that young people do not grow up with a soft indifference to injustice."[6 1]

Relying on the same paradigm used by early psychoanalysis—that the antisocial drives must be repressed in the child, or redirected in constructive ways—Katherine Glover writes of guiding a deep drive "toward perfection into its proper channel."[6 2] The properly *structured* environment allows the child to "become fearless, independent, full of initiative and develop quite early into maturity of thought and action."[6 3] Much as early psychoanalysis can be seen as a conflict theory—in which conflicting drives must be reconciled, even at the price of repression and frustration—so frustration is, in this period, conceived of as inevitable, whether on the losing side in a ball game or in another sphere of action: "It has been found that certain conflicts are a necessary accompaniment of mental growth."[6 4] The primacy of play in the process is overtly stated: "Growth is the secret of play, and play is the secret of growth. The man who has never played at all is non-existent. He could not have grown up if he never played."[6 5] Play is seen not only as a means of individual direction and refocusing of instinctual drives, but also as a means of development and of separating the wheat from the fiber. *The Pedagogical Seminary* relays the same concepts in reference to the cure of stammering: "Some say that the stammerer has a right to stammer if he wants to. But that is not so. Society's duty is to protect itself from contagion and against incompetents, and the stammerer is certainly in that class."[6 6]

Yet, by the same token, the restraints upon this push are more thoroughgoing (which in turn is the main difference between "aggressive" aspects of training and the "vigorous" side of guidance). There is a more sensitive concern with parental exploitation of the younger generation. What was earlier known as "brain forcing" in children[6][7] gains wider acknowledgment, writers warning against making the school learning experience too intensive.[68] *The Pedagogical Seminary* speaks about a balance or equilibrium among nourishment, rest, and energetic strivings.[69] A later issue of that magazine proclaims: "The study of the child has often been called a Copernican revolution since before it the child was adjusted to the school, whereas now everything in the entire educational system is conditioned by the nature and needs of the child." Dewey elaborates: "The specific adaptability of an immature creature for growth constitutes his *plasticity*. This is something quite different from the plasticity of putty or wax. It is not the capacity to take on change of form in accord with external pressure. It lies near the pliable elasticity by which some persons take on the color of their surroundings while retaining their own bent." The child is thus filled with "potentialities" which may be disturbed if manipulated by parental or adult hands.[70] Another writer articulates restraints on vigor in terms of individuality: "Children are separate entities, not merely offshoots from the family tree, necessarily like it. They are independent beings developing on individual lines, and they must be studied in this light, studied from babyhood to maturity, and each must be trained according to his or her own needs."[71] Another indicates the fallacy of transposing adult values upon the child: "We forget that life means change, growth, variation. Fixed, uncompromised conceptions" too often stifle, for "youth like childhood is eager, adaptable, creative. . . . Such qualities constitute the very essence of progress."[72]

## THE CHILD-REARING OF VIGOROUS GUIDANCE

Child-rearing suggestions display growth and movement beyond the distancing measures of the aggressive period—the concern with muscularity and vigor, the emphasis on organized and competitive play, the still relatively stringent controls over child activity. *The New Psychology and the Parent* (1923) summarizes the diminished authority bond: "We must realize that these children of ours are climbing: they must be allowed to choose their own paths to the peaks above; the trail which we blazed may be for them not the most direct ... the problem of the child is psychological freedom."[73] *The Management of Young Children* (1930) includes the statement that "the imaginative effort necessary to enter the child's world is made by few adults." "New Ideas About Obedience" (1929) includes the revelation of the phenomenon of projection: "Parents are prone to project on the child their own unfulfilled wishes and desires, regardless of whether they are in keeping with the instinctive needs of the child or not."[74] *Character Building in School* (1912) is mainly concerned with physical development, speaking of the boy as "a servant which must be trained."[75]

One characteristic of the guidance period is the desire, an aspect of the growing sophistication of empirical psychological research, to pin down temporal periods of development. Thus one study indicates ages to the nearest week for the mastery of locomotive functions.[76] Toilet training is more relaxed (with the exception of the throwback extremism of Watson); one source indicates that training by the age of six months is sufficient.[77] An article in *Child Development* indicates three months as the age for the emotion of delight, six months for angry distress and disgust, twelve months for elation, eighteen months for true jealousy.[78] Another source speaks of the possibility of discipline without punishment and says that the child should never by chastised in anger.[79] Existing tabulations and charts of practices allow us to say that those practices most associated with repression of the child have decreased and that those allowing for less authoritarian parenting and for greater empathy and less projection onto the child have increased. There is, for example, a further increase in support for breast feeding on the grounds of an improved emotional nurturance between mother and child and a decrease in infant mortality. Raymond Fuller, associate director of the National Child Labor Committee, summarizes this psychic evolution in the realization that "out of the nature of children arise their needs; out of children's needs, children's rights."[80]

## THE CHILDHOOD OF LYNDON JOHNSON

Lyndon Johnson's childhood vividly illustrates a mixture of submodal influence. His mother was advanced late-guidance while his father adhered to aggressive training and occasional early guidance. The effects of these two sides of Johnson's upbringing will be illustrated in their historical significance in chapter seven.

Rebekah Baines Johnson, Lyndon's mother, was frustrated by her husband's modest success in local politics, her own lack of opportunity in pursuing a writer's career, and her father's defeat for a congressional seat. Yet she remained close to her son regardless of such frustration, teaching him the alphabet by age two and spelling and reading by age four. Lyndon did receive "freeze-outs" or was ignored when he misbehaved, but such episodes were infrequent and of short duration. Rebekah communicated her concern for her son's education, showing a consistency that represented a progressive innovation in the maternal role:

> Many times I would not catch up with the fact that he was not prepared on a lesson until after breakfast time of a school day. . . . Then I would get the book and put it on the table . . . and devote the whole breakfast period to a discussion. . . . By following him to the front gate nearly every morning and telling him tales of history and geography and algebra, I could see that he was prepared for the work of the day.

Indeed, Johnson's advanced mother contributed to his discomfort in the *less* advanced public school. He was teased as a mama's boy and was eventually forced to leave school for an extended period of time due to whooping cough. Rebekah paid for dancing and violin lessons for Lyndon, and the boy was guided by his mother with diligence and insistence upon his performance, yet with none of the psychic control use of guilt and depression, and with less of the training demands for perfection or adherence to rigid standards of behavior.

Lyndon's sense of responsibility illustrates the existence of ego strength. He watched after the women of the household when his father was away on business, and he was the unquestioned leader of his siblings. When Sam Johnson was away at the legislature for extended periods, Lyndon practiced executive skills by delegating work to his younger brother and three sisters. A letter demonstrates the boy's sense of duty to his mother: "The end of another busy day brought me a letter from you. Your letters always give me more strength, renewed courage and that bulldog tenacity so essential to the success of any man. There is no force that exacts the power over me that your letters do. . . . I hope the years to come will place me in a position where I can relieve you of the hardships that it has fallen to your lot to suffer."

Johnson's father's influences included training and guidance elements. More on the guidance side is evidence of the boy's autonomy. When the eleven-year-old Lyndon went campaigning with his father, he was interested in the man's oratory; but there is no evidence of the incessant, almost desperate kind of identification that Woodrow Wilson felt with his father, compelling perfect emulation. Rather, he was fascinated but soon moved on to other interests. He sometimes challenged his father. At fifteen, when he smashed up the family car, his father humiliated him by ordering him to drive the car repeatedly around the courthouse. Even in this crisis, however, there was a sense of emotions being instantaneously vented rather than repressed.

Yet Johnson's father instilled the masculine ethic central to aggressive training. Here lie the origins of Lyndon's desire to prove his manliness, his forceful and domineering character, and his desire to be firm. Such influence would one day emerge in reference to Vietnam policy, just as the maternal influence is evident in the Great Society programs. Johnson had to be a man among men and prove mettle of body and mind. The boy had little taste for hunting, but he tried to to please his father, and he would later seek to prove his ability to succeed in politics, war and other "manly" pursuits.[8][1]

REFERENCES

1. Bertha Mahony Miller and E. W. Field, *Newberry Medal Books* (Boston: Hour Book, 1955), p. 174.
2. Richard Le Gallienne, "Children in Fiction," *Harper's Magazine*, December 1912.
3. Ellis Parker Butler, *Swatty: A Story of Real Boys* (New York: Houghton Mifflin, 1920); Alice Cushing Gardiner and Marcy Osborne, *Father's Gone A-Whaling* (New York: Doubleday and Page, 1926); Johnny Gruelle, *Raggedy Ann in the Deep Woods* (New York: P. F. Volland, 1930).
4. Arland D. Weeks, *Psychology and Child Training* (New York: D. Appleton, 1925); H. Crichton Miller, *The New Psychology and the Parent* (New York: Thomas Seltzer, 1923); Edgar James Swift, *The Psychology of Childhood* (New York: D. Appleton, 1930); Richard A. Howden, *Child Upbringing and the New Psychology* (London: Humphrey, Milford, 1933); Frank Howard Richardson, *Parenthood and the Newer Psychology* (New York: G. P. Putnam's Sons, 1926); Bernard Sachs, *The Normal Child* (New York: Paul B. Hoebber, 1926).
5. Douglas Thom, "New Ideas About Obedience," *Parents' Magazine*, 1929, p. 95.
6. Arthur Frank Payne, *My Parents: Friends or Enemies* (New

York: Brewster, Warren & Putnam, 1932).

7. Margaret A. Ribble, *The Rights of Infants: Early Psychological Needs and Their Satisfaction* (New York: Columbia University Press, 1943).

8. Weeks, *Psychology and Child Training*, p. 2.

9. Miller, *The New Psychology and the Parent*, p. 37.

10. Blanche C. Weill, *Through Children's Eyes: True Stories out of the Practice of a Consulting Psychologist* (New York: Island Workshop Press, 1940).

11. Frances G. Wicks, *The Inner World of Childhood* (New York: Appleton-Century, 1927), p. 90.

12. A. Tanner, "Adler's Theory of Minderweitigkeit," *Pedagogical Seminary* (June 1915), p. 204.

13. Richardson, *Parenthood and the Newer Psychology;* Howden, *Child Upbringing and the New Psychology*, p. 4.

14. V.F. Calverton and Samuel D. Schmalhausen, eds., *The New Generation* (New York: Macaulay Co., 1930).

15. Frances Wicks, *The Inner World of Childhood*, p. 90; William H. Pyle, *The Psychology of Learning* (Baltimore: Warwick & York, 1928), p. 13.

16. Sachs, *The Normal Child*.

17. Edith E. Mannin, *Common-Sense and the Child: A Plea for Freedom* (Philadelphia: J. B. Lippincott, 1932), p. 10.

18. Mrs. Burton Chance, *Self Training for Mothers* (Philadelphia: J. B. Lippincott, 1914), p. 66.

19. L. Emmett Holt, *The Care and Feeding of Infants* (New York: D. Appleton, 1929).

20. Sachs, *The Normal Child*, pp. 9, 51, 99; *Keeping Your Child Normal* (New York: Paul Hoebber, 1936), p. v.

21. Ibid.

22. *Pedagogical Seminary* 17 (1920).

23. Dr. Albert Moll, *The Sexual Life of the Child* (New York: Macmillan, 1913), p. vi.

24. Ernest R. Groves, *Sex in Childhood* (New York: Macaulay Co., 1933).

25. William A. McKeever, *Training the Girl* (New York: Macmillan, 1914).

26. Calverton and Schmalhausen, eds., *The New Generation*, p. 284.

27. Douglas A. Thom, *Normal Youth*, p. 46.

28. Jessie Taft, "A Changing Psychology of Child Welfare," *Annals of the American Academy of Political and Social Science* 151 (1930): 128.

29. W. A. McKeever, *Training the Boy* (1913).

30. Winifred de Kok, *Guiding Your Child Through the Formative Years: From Birth to the Age of Five* (New York: Emerson Books, Inc., 1935), pp. 9-10; Emily Harris McIntosh, *Do Love Other Children* (Washington: Clarence E. Davis, 1912); Len Chaloner, "Must Babies Cry," *Parents' Magazine*, 1935, p. 27; C. Anderson Aldrich, *Babies are Human Beings: The Interpretation of Growth* (New York: Macmillan, 1938), p. 4.

31. Arthur Gueld, *Baby Farms in Chicago* (1917), p. 25; Ernest C. Meyer, *Infant Mortality in New York City* (New York: Rockefeller International Health Board, 1921); "American Child Hygiene Association," (New Haven: Lyon, 1922).

32. Thomas C. Carrigan, "The Law and the American Child," *Pedagogical Seminary* 18 (June 1911): 168.

33. John B. Watson, *Psychological Care of Infant and Child* (New York: Norton, 1928); B. Cunningham and B. Littlejohn, *Parents' Magazine*, December 1926, p. 8; Herbert Martin, *Formative Factors in Character: A Psychological Study in the Moral Development of Childhood* (New York: Longmans, Green & Co., 1925), p. 4.

34. Watson, *Psychological Care.*

35. L. Emmett Holt, *The Care and Feeding of Infants;* Mary C. Whitaker, *Mothercraft: A Primer for Parents* (Cleveland: Jordan Co., 1926).

36. Miller and Swanson, *The Changing American Parent;* Sylvia S. Seaman, "Did Our Children Survive Our Upbringing?" (unpublished paper, cited by permission of the author).

37. "Are Parents Bad for Children?" *Parents' Magazine*, May 1930.

38. William McDougall, "Men or Robots?" *Pedagogical Seminary*, March 1926, p. 91.

39. Seaman, "Did Our Children Survive our Upbringing?"

40. Rosalie Rayner Watson, "I Am the Mother of a Behaviorist's Sons," *Parents' Magazine*, December 1930, pp. 16-18.

41. Maria Montessori, *Education and Peace* (Chicago: Henry Regnery Co., 1949); Maria Montessori, "Blazing New Trails in Education," *Parents' Magazine*, April 1924; Stanley Cobb, *New Horizons for the Child* (Washington: Avalon, 1934).

42. Dorothy Canfield Fisher, *A Montessori Mother* (New York: Henry Holt, 1912).

43. Miller, *The New Psychology and the Parent.*

44. Geoffrey H. Steere, "Freudianism and Child-Rearing in the Twenties," *American Quarterly* 20 (Winter 1968); Nathan Hale, Jr., *Freud and the Americans: The Beginning of Psychoanalysis in America* (New York: Oxford University Press, 1971).

45. Winifrid Lay, *The Child's Unconscious Mind: The Relations of Psychoanalysis to Education* (New York: Dodd, Mead, 1919), pp. 63-64.
46. Ibid., p. 90.
47. Percy Griffith, *A Synthetic Psychology; or, Evolution as a Psychological Phenomenon* (London: John Bale, 1927), p. 176.
48. Frederick Pierce, *Understanding Our Children* (New York: E. P. Dutton, 1926), p. 198.
49. Mattie K. Foster, *Dream Life for Children* (Boston: Four Seas Co., 1918).
50. E. A. Kirkpatrick, *The Individual in the Making* (New York: Houghton Mifflin Co., 1911), p. 122.
51. Agnes De Lima, *The Enemy the Child* (New York: New Republic, Inc., 1930), pp. 219-20.
52. Elizabeth McCracken, *The American Child* (New York: Riverside Press, 1913).
53. De Lima, *The Enemy*, p. 219.
54. Lois Meek Stolz, *Father Relations of War-Born Children* (New York: Greenwood Press, 1954).
55. Edwin Grant Conklin, *Heredity and Environment in the Development of Men* (Princeton: Princeton University Press, 1916), p. 365.
56. Dom Cavallo, "Social Reform and the Movement to Organize Children's Play During the Progressive Era," *History of Childhood Quarterly* (Spring 1976).
57. Ibid.
58. William Henry Pyle, *Training the Children: Principals and Practice* (or, *The Child*) (New York: Century, 1916, 1929), p. 51.
59. Ibid.
60. Beatrice Gesell, "A Child Faces Our World," *Parents' Magazine* (March 1930).
61. Caroline Benedict Burrell, *Our Girls and Our Times* (Boston: W. A. Wilde Co., 1927), p. 34.
62. Katherine Glover and Evelyn Dewey, *Children of the New Day* (New York: D. Appleton-Century, 1934).
63. Cobb, *New Horizons for the Child*, p. 39.
64. Mandel Sherman, "Character in the Making," *Parents' Magazine*, January, 1932, p. 11.
65. Raymond G. Fuller, "Child Labor and Child Nature," *Pedagogical Seminary*, March 1922, p. 49.
66. "Stammering and Its Extirpation," *Pedagogical Seminary*, June 1916, p. 169.

67. William A. Hammond, "Brain-Forcing in Childhood," *Popular Science Monthly*, April 1887.

68. Henry Dwight Chapin, *Heredity and Child Culture* (New York: E. P. Dutton, 1922), p. 137.

69. George N. Dearborn, "The Sthenic Index in Education," *Pedagogical Seminary*, June 1912, p. 180.

70. John Dewey, "The Conditions of Growth," (1916); William A. White, *The Mental Hygiene of Childhood* (Boston: Little, Brown, & Co., 1919).

71. Burrell, *Our Girls and Our Times*, p. 34.

72. Gesell, "A Child Faces Our World," p. 11.

73. Miller, *The New Psychology and the Parent.*

74. William E. Blatz, *The Management of Young Children* (New York: William Morrow & Co., 1930).

75. Brownlee, *Character Building in School*, p. 27.

76. Mary M. Shirley, *The First Two Years: A Study of Twenty-Five Babies* (Minneapolis: University of Minnesota Press, 1931).

77. Helen C. Goodspead and Emma Johnson, *Care and Training of Children* (Philadelphia: J. B. Lippincott, 1929), p. 90.

78. Katherine M. Bridges, "Emotional Development in Early Infancy," *Child Development*, December 1932, p. 340.

79. Grace Langdon and Irving W. Stout, *The Discipline of Well-Adjusted Children* (New York: John Day, 1952.)

80. Other sources used in drawing the thesis of vigorous guidance include: A series of articles in *Pedagogical Seminary:* "Eugenetics," March 1914; "Men or Robots?" March 1926; "What the Nursery Has to Say About Instincts," June 1925; "Mood in Monologue," June 1913; "Child Labor and Child Nature," March 1922; "A General Survey of Child Study," September 1918; "Nursery and Savagery," June 1915. Also Paul Popenoe, *The Child's Heredity* (Baltimore: Williams & Wilkins, 1929); "How Much Are Parents to Blame?" *Parents' Magazine* January 1927; Helen Goodspead, *Care and Training of Children* (Philadelphia: J. P. Lippincott, 1929); Ella Lyman Cabot, *Seven Ages of Childhood* (New York: Houghton Mifflin, 1921); Francis Brown, *The Sociology of Childhood* (New York: Prentice-Hall, 1939); Ada Hart Arlitt, *The Child from One to Six* (New York: McGraw-Hill Co., 1930); Herbert Martin, *Formative Factors in Character* (New York: Longmans, Green & Co., 1925); Frederick Pierce, *Understanding Our Children* (New York: E. P. Dutton, 1926); William Henry Pyle, *Training Children* (New York: Century, 1929); Sidonie Gruenberg, *We, the Parents* (New York:

Harper and Bros., 1939); Kathleen Norris, *Mother and Son* (New York: E. P. Dutton, 1928).

81. The only psychological research conducted on Johnson's childhood is Doris Kearns, *Lyndon Johnson and the American Dream* (New York: Harper and Row, 1976). Because Kearns relied extensively on Johnson's own recollection, more detailed knowledge must await further research.

CHAPTER FIVE

DELEGATED RELEASE, 1940-1965

The final trend present in modern culture which is of sufficient statistical frequency to be labeled a submode may be called delegated release. The reasoning behind this nomenclature will be apparent when the basic changes it embodies are examined.

Evolutionary development may be considered from two sides. On the one side are the more positive aspects, with major inroads made in freedom, empathy, emotional closeness, and encouragement of the child's autonomy. These innovations involve the transcending not only of stringent discipline but also of the concern with vigor and the proper direction of energy which so dominated the period of vigorous guidance. Decreased parental projections onto the child and decreased anxiety about approaching its intimate feelings have produced previously unprecedented levels of freedom and autonomy. The child is no longer thought of as being filled with energies in need of control, or even antisocial impulses, but rather as containing potentialities which could be distorted through improper child care.

On the negative side are the delegation aspects of the family dynamics, qualities which place delegated release still very much within the socializing mode of child rearing. The concept of delegation is central to the analysis of the entire socializing mode. Helm Stierlin, in *Separating Parents and Adolescents*, describes the dynamic of the transmission from parent to child of specific delegated roles to be played out by the child in order to satisfy particular parental needs.[1] In this sense, all socialization involves delegation, for the parent predetermines necessary missions for the child in reference to his or her own emotional needs and capacities.

Delegations may be usefully divided into three classes: ego, superego, and id. The control period's delegations come primarily in reference to the superego; these are missions which enact dynamics based on guilt, right and wrong, and especially control of the instincts. The aggressive and guidance submodes involve delegated missions primarily of the ego—missions centering around personal development, powers of coordination, scientific thought, and proper social interaction.

With the introduction in the forties and fifties of the release submode, parental psychology is also infused with id delegations. The delegation of id missions is not a conflict-free process, but rather one which involves the acting out by the child of the frustrated, repressed, infantile wishes of the parent. The delegation of the id seems to involve a gap between the generations—as the older generation vicariously experiences impulses which they have kept buried under the training and guidance experience—but in fact the "generation gap" turns out to be an unconscious defense designed to hide the delegation process.


MOTHERHOOD

The delegated release missions of the id are complicated processes, but a clear means of comprehension lies in centering the analysis on the mother, who remains the key agent of delegation. The initial step in delegating id missions is a growing new consciousness of the whole area of women's rights and frustrations. These frustrations came to be experienced in many areas, primarily in reference to motherhood itself. Mothers felt more and more stifled by the assumption of exclusive maternal responsibility for infant and child care. A series of books grew from the resulting feelings of resentment toward husbands and men in general, culminating in books with titles like *The Case Against Having Children*, *Mother's Day is Over*, and *The Baby Trap*. One study begins with the statistic of 750,000 unwanted children born each year in the United States and goes on to state that every child deserves to be wanted.[2] Many parents bring hostile feelings out into the open, one woman admitting that

although she likes children, she detests motherhood.[3] Some
parents attribute their lack of marital happiness to the presence of
children, and some individuals admit being tempted to put their
children up for adoption: "I feel that my wonderful daughter
deserved a better mother. I don't deny my dear love for her, but I
have denied my resentment and my unhappiness with
motherhood. The result has been frequent bouts of rage and loss of
control. . . . Yet most of the advice I get from my . . . friends has
been: 'Get pregnant again—you'll be so busy with the children you
won't have time for those unnatural feelings of yours.' "[4] An
ability to admit long-buried feelings is clear in the following:
"Scores of mothers, and a few fathers, have confessed to coming
very close to battering a child, to momentarily feeling such anger,
hating a child so much, that maiming or killing him would be a
pleasure." Another study explores the possible motivations for
having children other than the joy of creation—from the child as
status symbol, to affirmation of one's own maturity and
sexuality.[5] Individuals who do not find fulfillment in parenthood,
whose feelings of being hemmed in by a child recapitulate their
own infancy, are quoted: "I had anticipated that the baby would
sleep and eat, sleep and eat. Instead, the experience was
overwhelming. I really had not thought particularly about what
motherhood would mean in a realistic sense."[6] One mother's
recollections capture the feelings of isolation which may
accompany being literally alone with the child: "I got so down
that I just sat around the apartment crying and thinking, my God,
I'm going to live here and die here and nobody's going to ever
know that I exist."[7]

The reality and immediacy of the maternal delegation of id
frustrations, and the persistence of the father who is still not an
intimate part of the child-rearing experience, are best illustrated
by the documents of actual experience. The recollections and
writings of Pearl Buck illustrate some of the key dynamics. The
author states in *To My Daughter With Love:* "For surely sex is an
area as wide as life itself, permeating as it does every part of the
life of man and woman." Buck tells a one-year-old: "Keep up your
normal and justified methods of protest. Spit out of your mouth
what you wish not to eat, or set your teeth and refuse to open
your mouth at all. If extreme measures are necessary, scream and
throw the dish on the floor. . . . Feel no duty toward keeping your
diapers dry." Sensual attitudes and behaviors are urged which the
woman would not have dared herself, yet which she can envision
as having positive influence. At the same time, the daughter is the
special recipient of delegated desires: "As a woman, you are free

today as you have never been free. Old tradition, binding you for
centuries, are breaking now. . . . Indeed, so long has (woman) been
told that she is inferior to man that she herself has come to think
that she must be his inferior, and so, like a slave, to accept,
humbly or angrily, the narrow space allotted her. . . . Mozart's
sister was known to be more talented than he was, but her father
would not allow her to continue her musical education, lest it take
her beyond her 'sphere.' "[8]

Mothers during this period speak openly of their conscious
delegations. One states frankly: "I want Carol to be
straightforward, and to be able to stand up for herself. I want her
to be direct; I don't want her to rely on submission to get by. Not
only is that something we've been forced into, but it's a cop-out.
. . . My mother never had a career. . . . I just grew up assuming that
I was going to be a secretary."[9] The mother-daughter relationship
is defined as holding the unique potential of allowing the mother
the vicarious means of allowing her personal fulfillment and
transcendence of the limited role of woman. Another mother
remarks: "My son is seven, and already it's as if I'm not really part
of his life anymore. But with Ann I feel like, here's a chance! She
was born before I got involved with feminism, but even then I
thought, 'She's going to be more, she's going to be able to make
choices.' "[10] Another says that "no relationship has ever reduced
me absolutely to primitive emotions the way my relationship with
my daughter has."[11] And another remarks: "Perhaps the very
helplessness and dependency of the infant increases our rage
because we long to change places with him for the moment."[12]


SEXUALITY

Of all the primary instinctual processes of the id, sexuality is
most central to the new delegated release in reference to
mother-daughter relations. Mothers of the forties and fifties began
to recognize that their sexual upbringings were not all they could
be. The following is illustrative of these feelings:

> I don't remember when I started masturbating, but I
> remember when she [mother] found out about it, and how
> upset she was. I was about six; she was giving me a bath, and
> I was rubbing myself, and she asked me why I was doing that.
> I didn't know how to tell her I was doing it because it felt
> good, so I said, 'It itches.' She told me it was very bad if I
> itched there. It might mean that there is something wrong

with me. She really scared me. I grew up thinking that if I masturbated it meant there was something wrong with me. I was afraid of my own body.[13]

This same mother not only does not chide her daughter for masturbation, but lets her indulge in the practice, feeling that it is only a problem if it interferes with other activities. Some mothers openly advocate the virtues of sexuality: "We talk about sex very freely, and she asks me lots of very sophisticated questions, about things that never occurred to me until after I was married. We had a discussion about oral sex the other night. She touches on it and then goes off on something else. I don't push it."[14]

The sexual elements of the mother-daughter relationship are not smoothly enacted but rather filled with the ambivalence which marks the mother's own attitude toward sexuality. A clinician notes the contradictory attitudes of one mother:

Yet, Yvonne put Vicki in an uncomfortable situation even as I was talking to them. She had told me that she didn't like Vicki to use 'gutter language,' such as 'doing pussy,' but while we were talking she asked Vicki if she could describe 'doing pussy.' Vicki clammed up. . . . There was obvious confusion between Yvonne's use of a phrase she condemned and her desire for her daughter to be able to discuss sex with a stranger.[15]

This mother continued to express her feelings that her own childhood had been "invaded by adult demands" (the socialization of vigorous guidance) and referred to her husband as limiting her "space" or invading her own autonomy. The writer who interviewed this couple rightly observes that a mother in some way frustrated in her identity as a woman may "live out her fantasies of rebellion or sexual freedom she never felt able to realize" through her daughter. Another writer conducted extensive interviews in the late 1950s and found that mothers consistently indicated that they found girls' bodies more cuddly than boys', that it was easier to be physically intimate with them. The study postulated that overly libidinal binding between mother and daughter may hinder the "gentle push" helpful when the infant initiates the first distancing from the mother in order to develop a sense of autonomy.[16]

Subtle ambivalences are in effect even in relationships of considerable psychogenic advancement. A study conducted in the mid-sixties found one particular mother to have the highest ratings in terms of empathy and loving mothering. Yet detailed analysis revealed that she never really took her daughter's cues asserting autonomy and in subtle ways expressed her sensual desires through the child.[17]


THE AMBIVALENCES OF DELEGATION

The ambivalences of motherhood have been stressed by many writes. Herbert Hendin says that "the cynicism of so many young women students has its source in the experience of mothers who had been embittered by their disappointment and had by pronouncement ... instilled in their daughters a hatred of motherhood and the wish that they be invulnerable to men."[18] Though this is an overstatement in relation to delegated release, and also makes reference to earlier submodes, it is a good description of the delegation of matenal frustration. Hans Sebald, whose study also focuses on earlier submode individuals, describes a maternal syndrome he calls "Momism": the modern mother, who has come to dominate within the home, regards her role almost as a profession, but a profession which she finds as unfulfilling as a dead-end job, without advancement, adequate cooperation, or retirement benefits. Sebald writes, "The halfway emancipated woman is therefore inclined to practice Momistic practices."[19]

The mother-daughter relationship is stressed because it is a more intense form of the general trend in delegated release to assign tasks of the unfulfilled id to the child. To a certain extent, id orientation is generalized to parenthood, though the father has extended his functions in the nursery little beyond the point reached in the guidance submode. A male writer indicates that "the sight of the aggressive primitive male animal" is likely to shock the mother more than the father but stresses that instinctual drive is part of the normal childhood experience.[20] Margaret S. Mahler writes that the "*libidinal* availability of the mother, because of the emotional dependence of the child, facilitates the optimal unfolding of innate potentialities."[21]

The reality of infancy as primarily a feeling, or id experience, is emphasized. A Teachers College bulletin of Columbia University says that "the essence of parent-child relations, it must be emphasized, lies in how a parent *feels* rather than in what a parent *does*."[22] A book entitled *Fathers are Parents, Too* (1951) indicates that "an infant does not think as much as feel sensations not only purely physiological, but sensations reacting in visceral fashion to acceptance or rejection, warmth or coldness."[2][3] The baby gains sensual satisfaction from excretion, eating, and even masturbation. The process of socialization must not stifle such necessary and positive id satisfactions. The author goes on to say that "the fact remains that no man has ever yet been able to love another woman unless he has first loved his own mother and wished, in his own childish way, that she were his own."[2][4] Play is seen as a positive release, especially as a mode of expressing basic, instinctive aggression.[2][5]

There are elements of paternity particular to delegated release. Because of the increased nurture on the part of both parents—along with the persistence of the physical distance of the father, which has now become conspicuous because of expressed maternal dissatisfactions with the situation—a certain splitting in perception of the father occurs in many of the release children. Kenneth Keniston, writing in reference to one of the most detailed studies of a homogeneous group of release youths, indicates: "On the one hand, the father was portrayed as highly ethical, intellectually strong, principled, honest, politically involved, and idealistic. But on the other hand, this same father in other contexts was seen as unsuccessful, acquiescent, weak or inadequate."[2][6] The split is related to the actual split in paternal availability in the earlier years, often warm and accepting when present, but suddenly gone, foraging a competitive existence in the hard, outside world. The child's eventual decision of minimal parental success in this world springs from a perception that the home, and the child along with it, is often abandoned in favor of these other pursuits, and the child's resentment is now for the first time openly expressed.

Another source of splitting stems from parental resentment of the child. Vicarious realization of parental id tasks is not the same thing as satisfying one's own wishes directly as one feels them while growing up. The child is seen to have those objects, the absence of which frustrated the parent. The youth of the thirties, the parent of the forties, often the product of depression years and relatively less comfortable standards of living, observes a middle-class child who is given greater opportunity for id expression. The child eats as no generation has, often setting the schedule during infancy himself, and is given more sexual freedom and a wider range of acceptable behaviors. As Keniston remarks, "Behavior that springs from values rather than experience is often forced, or artificial."[2][7]

Ambivalences stemming from the reduction in the distortion of the child's id development create a degree of anxiety which is expressed in a variety of forms (even this most advanced submode of socialization has not transcended chronic parental anxiety). Thus one often encounters in this submode the view that perhaps childhood has become too nurturing a period, too carefree for the good of society. One writer wonders if such autonomous, freedom-oriented children can be socialized into the institutions of culture when they come of age. Another indicates: "We have not only trapped our children, even tricked them, we have deluded ourselves that we could provide a happy childhood for our offspring while defending the truth about the way things really are. And many young people can't forgive us for the basic failure."[2 8] Along with the fear of the loss of a sense of reality is a fear that the loss of parental control will allow for a more insidious influence, that of the peer group, which will take on the powers of personality formation.[2 9]

A new parental self-consciousness is observed by many, combining the fear of being too totalitarian with an anxiety over the results of leniency. Doubts are expressed as to whether freedom and empathy are consonant with reaching the kinds of educational goals perceived to be necessary after the successful launching of the Sputnik by the Soviets in the late 1950s.[3 0] The *New York Times* reports of parents who may not be enjoying children as much as possible because of concern over warping them. A writer observes that the radical changes in childhood caused many to "expect too much too soon," to imagine that modern psychology would be a panacea and would release the child totally from neurosis.[3 1] Caution is prescribed: "And when we stop demanding perfection of ourselves, our children will be freer to discover their own strengths and weaknesses and will not be afraid of their difficulties, inadequacies and failures."[3 2]

## DR. SPOCK

The writings of Dr. Benjamin Spock are representative documents of delegated release. The significance of Spock is reflected in the fact that more than two million copies of his *Common Sense Book of Baby and Child Care* have been sold since the mid-forties. Spock begins by advising the mother to trust her instincts, and not to be overly concerned that she is not doing her job. Spock's message is that society has come to a point at which it deserves a confidence in itself, a belief that all will end well that is not aborted through anxiety. A product of aggressive parenting, raised by a mother who constantly observed her children, whose attempt at breast feeding eventually failed and who suffered a series of miscarriages, Spock seeks to release parents from those anxieties he observed in his own parents.[33]

Spock, of course, is still consciously a spokesman for socialization. Parents, whose job inevitably entails hard work, should *expect* things from their children. Spock admits to his own distance, and even a certain coldness, as a father.[34] As late as 1960 Spock retained a belief in the recapitulation theory: "We must remember that each child as he develops is retracing the whole history of mankind, physically and spiritually, step by step. Human beings are born sociable. . . . One of the principle reasons that young children worry about their parents' anger is that their own anger is more violently, more barbarically felt than is the adult's."[35] Although parents should not play judge over children's quarrels, the feeling of jealousy can be constructive in building competitive drive and a sense of achievement.[36] Another socializing prescription is his suggestion that the parent who observes his child masturbating should guide the child's hands away from its genitals.

Yet, as the author of the most widely circulated of all child-care manuals, Spock concentrates on the push of innovation rather than the pull of reaction. For him, a release from the anxieties of parenting is the foremost task of the educator; he wishes to show that parenting can be almost entirely a pleasurable and fulfilling experience. Although Spock endorses regularized feeding and schedules, the ideal is that the child is to set those schedules himself; for in a novel statement of the abilities of the child, Spock believes that the child best knows how to select the patterns as well as the content of its diet.[37] Rather than repeat earlier, Spartan views on conditioning the child to disturbances in the environment, Spock pleads for protecting the child from frightening sounds and sudden shocks. Aware that the oldest child is likely to be the recipient of the parents' "infantile emotional residue," he urges a sensitivity that seeks to minimize this through the reduction of parental anxiety. Spock identifies the various developmental difficulties of the child, including separation anxiety at age two, sibling rivalries, and the various difficulties associated with socialization processes. He has not gone beyond the socialization view that the child must be trained in various functions and not allowed to develop them on his own accord, but he seeks to mitigate the severity of the frustrations long associated with it. The child is naturally a helper who wants to accept responsibilities.

Spock is as much concerned with the welfare and feelings of

parents as he is with children, to the point where a major motif in his writings is to allow the child the kinds of freedoms (in true delegated release spirit) which the parent was most likely denied: the child is to experience new levels of sensual awareness. The net impact of all this is that Spock, in a manner representative of his period, is urging parents to delegate both ego functions *and* id functions to their children.


## THE DECLINE OF AUTHORITY BONDING

Having established the hard side of delegated release—the delegation of id tasks, the expression of maternal frustration through the child, the persistence of such aspects of socialization as achievement and proper courses of development—the remainder of this chapter will be devoted to the soft (release) side. Just as much of the material concerning delegation studies childhood in the late forties and fifties, the early and mid-sixties are especially fertile in providing evidence of inroads in the growth of empathy, the decrease of authority bonds and projections, and the growth of the developmental distortion view of personality formation.

Decrease of authority is central to delegated release. Whereas during earlier submodes the governmental analogies are almost always authoritarian, with the father as sovereign and the children as subjects (at best a limited monarchy), now studies appear referring to the home as a democracy. *Democracy in the Home* (1954) sees parental acceptance of childhood individuality as the precondition for true democracy in the home. Another study indicates that first father and then mother have resigned from dictatorial positions in favor of familial democracy.[38] Another writer, urging that the parent should define his or her role more as helper and friend than dictator or preacher, argues that "the more a child feels loved and appreciated for *himself*, the more readily will he accept reasonable hints."[39] Another uses the terminology of the legal process, calling for a more constitutional use of parental powers: "But correction should be correction and not vengeful employment of authority. There are two parties to punishment—the punisher and the punishee. Thus in the case of children, the first party is alone the complaintant, prosecutor, jury, judge, and hangman—executor of that penalty he himself decreed."[40]

Another writer[41] chose to list autocratic as opposed to democratic concepts in reference to child-rearing:[42]

| Autocratic Society | Democratic Society |
|---|---|
| Authority figure | Knowledgeable leader |
| Power | Influence |
| Pressure | Stimulation |
| Demanding | Winning co-operation |
| Punishment | Logical Consequences |
| Reward | Encouragement |
| Imposition | Permit self-determination |
| Direction | Guidance |
| Children are to be seen, not heard | Listen! Respect the child |
| You do it because I said to | We do it because it is necessary |
| Prestige-centered | Situation-centered |
| Personal involvement | Objective detachment |

Fig. 10. Democratic Versus Autocratic Society

Such a listing is of interest because it illustrates the nature of delegated release at the same time that it shows it to be still an active submode of socialization. Progress is present in the primacy of knowledge over authority, influence over power, and stimulation over pressure. Imperatives are abandoned in favor of cooperation, with confidence that a nondistorted child can appreciate logic if guided rather than directed. At the same time, some main elements of socialization are present: the concept of the parental leader, the focus on external stimulation for learning, the competitive quality of the parent "winning co-operation," as well as equations of authority with passion and of democracy with objectivity and emotional evenness.

The entire texture of delegated release material indicates a decrease in authoritarian parenting. A new dynamic is present for the first time—the dissociation of love from action. A true enactment of dissociating love from action involves the transcendence of socialization itself, after which the parent may truly take all cues from the child, entering the mode deMause terms the Helping Mode (see part one). As for delegated release, the most progressive segments of the submode are able to envision, or voice, the attitude of unconditional love as an ideal.

Dorothy Baruch's *New Ways in Discipline* (1949) includes a suggestion for a new dictum: "I love you for what you are, beyond any nasty thing you might do. I love you because you are you." Another writer uses nearly the same language: "The type of love a child needs is the kind that says, 'I love you . . . not for what you do or don't do, but because you're you.'"[4][3] And another puts it this way: "The essence of parent-child relations, it must be emphasized, is more in how a parent *feels* than in what a parent *does*."[4][4]

## EMPATHY

Another aspects of delegated release is an extended conception of empathy. The word now gains common usage and becomes a subject for discussion and analysis. Also present is a more sensitive understanding and overcoming of parental projection: "Your child is not you. It is not his job in life to reflect . . . your success, or even that you are a good parent. He cannot be used to ease your burdens by sharing your guilts. He cannot be used to live the battles you have lost. Your job is to guide him, to aid him, to encourage him, to see, respect and love him as an individual."[4 5] On such a basis empathy may progress and is sometimes informally encouraged in women's magazines: "Perhaps if you'd put yourself in *your* youngster's shoes," or "Recognize what children are really like and what they need."[4 6]

A deeper understanding of the nature of empathy emerges in the psychoanalytic and psychological texts. One study, "The Effects on Parents of the Child's Transition Into and Out of Latency," articulates the reality of parental regression and empathy during the process of child rearing: "The younger the child, the greater the parents' reliance on intuitive understanding, an understanding based on memory traces of similar childhood states, now revived through closeness of the child and identification with him. In this manner parents may regress and progress with their children."[4 7] A more catholic, ethological perspective, this view sees man as the first animal in the evolutionary hierarchy to transcend the purely reproductive role and see his offspring through to maturity. Because personality formation is such an intensively learned process, the parent has stored memories of his or her own childhood and may reexperience them in parental situations; this may apply even to the ultimate symbiotic pleasure of the nursing experience. A knowledge of the dynamics of what deMause calls "psychic fossilization" is articulated: "They are behaving toward their son as their parents behaved toward them. A habit of restraint, of stifling of empathetic potential, can run through a family from generation to generation as each new set of parents accords its young the treatment it received earlier." In context, an empathizer, or subject, accepts, for a brief period, the object's total emotional individuality, not only his simple emotions but his whole state of being—this history of his desires, feelings, and thoughts as well as other forces and experiences that are expressed in his behavior. The object senses the empathizer's response and realizes that for a brief point in time the two have fused. . . .

Empathy is different from sympathy. . . . In sympathy, the subject is principally absorbed in his own feelings. . . . Sympathy bypasses real understanding of the other person, and that other is denied his own sense of being."[4] [8]

The empathy of delegated release is still the empathy of socialization, albeit advanced socialization. One writer indicates, "If a parent can honestly face a confrontation with the child's inner feelings, the parent will have reached a state of mellowness and maturity that will allow him to really help the child *while still maintaining the parental role*" (italics added).[4] [9] Of importance is not only the desire to empathize but also the concern with remaining "parental," which hints at a danger of making the relationship overly symmetrical.

Another writer sums it up with a statement of empathy very advanced for the early 1940s:

> As adults, we tend to interpret a child's behavior in the light of our own adult feelings. Having forgotten many of our own childhood experiences and our emotional reactions to them, we see things no longer as through a child's eyes but only as through the eyes of an adult. . . . My personal experience has been that the best way to reach the child's own level so as to understand his point of view is to fit myself into his environment, instead of expecting him to fit into mine.[5] [0]

## THE DEVELOPMENTAL DISTORTION VIEW

On the softer side of delegation, the release side, in addition to increased empathy and decreased authority bonding, there is a detailed articulation of the developmental distortion view of personality formation. The roots of neurosis are now seen more in terms of the transmission of parental problems to the child than of ineffective functioning on the part of the child itself. The *New York Times Magazine* reminds readers that parents are the entirety of their children's universe, that their negative influence may be as profound as their positive influence.[5] [1] What may seem insignificant to the parents may be important or even traumatic to the child. A more thoroughgoing awareness of the layers of motivation behind the punishment of children recognizes its destructive impact, its cutting off of the child's creative energies. As one journalist records in *Redbook:* "Far from teaching children anything, I believe, our persistent and often nagging involvement in their responsibilities simply makes them blinder and blinder to what the responsibilities are."[5] [2]

The environmental distortion view allows for new insights, such as the fact that differing personalities within the same family do not necessarily argue for genetic determination, since decreased repressions on the part of investigators and parents allow for the discovery of the marked differences in the treatment accorded each child. This is now seen as holding true even for the earliest experiences of pregnancy, birth, and infancy. There is increased sensitivity to subtle means of abandonment, from the placing of the child in boarding schools, to the excessive use of baby-sitters and summer camps.[53] One observer makes an overt connection between physical well-being and receiving love, expanding upon Anna Freud's earlier observations of war-torn children.[54] At times, the developmental distortion view is concisely and cogently stated: "A misbehaving child is a discouraged child," or "Punishment only creates the power of resistance and defiance."[55]

Recent research continues to verify the position that the empathetic, loving care of the child maximizes human potential. *The First Year of Life*, published in this country in 1965, emphasizes that the first year of life is the most plastic, and that emotional deprivation in institutions is responsible for depression and has inevitably negative results: "The absence of mothering equals emotional starvation. We have seen that this leads to a progressive deterioration engulfing the child's whole person. Such deterioration is manifested first in an arrest of the child's psychological development; other psychological dysfunctions set in, paralleled by somatic changes. In the next stage this leads to increased infection liability and eventually, when the emotional deprivation continues into the second year of life, a spectacularly increased rate of mortality."[56] Besides the usual needs for existence, *Psychiatry and Pediatrics* (1948) includes the need for love from the time an infant is born; *Hygeia* (1942) notes a need to be cuddled and to belong; another work calls love a right and a need and lists it first on a tabulation of necessary conditions for health.[57]

## THE CHILD-REARING PRACTICES
## OF DELEGATED RELEASE

A final section is in order in this sketch of delegated release: evidence of actual practices. Practices prove to be extensions of the underlying emotional orientations of release, both the hard and the soft sides. The discussion of feeding is important, for feeding is direct nurturance in infancy as well as a symbolic forum for the expression of views of child nurture in general. The dominant theme of delegated release is that the parent may allow for relatively increased expression on the part of the child—not for the creation of anarchy, but for the child to construct its own individual logical system. Structure does remain, for delegated release is still a socializing mode and parents search for gentler ways to impose it; but now it is the child who theoretically establishes his own schedule, creating a new method of feeding: schedule according to demand. A fascinating expression of the harder side of id delegation is the situation regarding breast feeding. One study remarks on the unfortunate situation that in Great Britain almost every baby is breast-fed for a short time only. But whereas fifty percent of British babies are breast-fed for six months or more, in the United States fewer than twenty-five percent of children are breast-fed even during the initial stay at the hospital.[58] The only sensible explanation for this is its relation to maternal frustrations. The relative passivity of bottle feeding, the nurturance of the child while the mother is deprived of the pleasure of providing her own milk, expresses her own feelings of isolation in the home and detachment from the very id impulses she wishes her child to absorb. The child sucks the bottle and the mother warmly aids the child's enjoyment, but she stands back from *her own* body with the detachment of her own delegated ego.

The practice of toilet training illustrates the release or soft side of the submode in its decrease in control impetus. With insight into the importance of control of the bowels, writers procede cautiously but still retain the notion of the necessity of training: "Viewed psychologically, bowel training is more than bowel training. It is part of the child's training in his whole feeling about his body and its functions;—therefore, in a highly important sense, it also serves to train him in his later attitudes toward pleasure itself."[59] Although this writer suggests eight months to a year as a desirable time at which to have completed the task, the importance of eliminating shame or severe pressure is stressed. One study in 1960 actually discovered that a high degree of psychosomatic or psychogenic disorders are correlated with stringent toilet-training practices.[60] Another (1949) draws the insight that training of the bowels may be a projective means of expression on the part of the parents: "The trouble with the control of the child's bladder and bowel is that too often it becomes the control of the mother instead of the child. In other words, the mother too often feels the need for her to control the child's urination and defecation rather than to help the child to establish this for himself when he has developed physiologically and emotionally enough to do so."[6][1]

Delegated release parents believe that just as it is not necessary to force a baby to read, so it is also not necessary to force a child to stop sucking its thumb; the relief of anxiety is not to be confused with the cause.[6][2] A Gallup poll in 1962 found that sixty percent of parents questioned believed themselves to be less strict than their own parents.[6][3] Those who are a part of the delegated release outlook associate restrictiveness and authoritarianism with the creation of an aggressive, hostile individual.

With delegated release, this tracing of the evolution of American socialization reaches its conclusion. Following this chapter is a chart summarizing the four socialization submodes and basic defining themes. Yet regardless of the detail of description or even the direct quotation of actual individuals, the analysis must remain a partial sketch and an abstraction. Only when the products of the submodes, the individuals involved, are examined in an adult historical context can the distinct stages become truly concrete. As we shall see in the final chapters of this book, the submodes also define four stages of American history, and tracing these stages on the social or group level will serve to further clarify the childhood precursors.

| SOCIALIZING SUBMODE | DEFINITION | CENTRAL MECHANISMS | SEXUALITY | RELIGION | PARENTAL TASK | QUALITY MOST FEARED |
|---|---|---|---|---|---|---|
| Psychic Control | Intensive control of the child's mind and body through psychic rather than physical means centering about superego delegations | Guilt, affective binding within the family, severe repression | Spermatic economy (the body is a fixed quantity of energy), didactic condemnation | Authoritarian, inscrutable | Molding the child, creating an agent of social and moral progress, whose instincts are under control | Disobedience to authority |
| Aggressive Training | Intensive and aggressive training of traits (some inherited) centering about delegations of the ego | Activity scheduled by adults, competitive sense and rational self-discipline | Ambivalence, sense pleasure is hedonistic, of no social value outside of childbearing | Vast decrease in its use as control, less authoritarian and central to daily existence | Creation of a strong, competitive, achieving and rational human being who realizes potential | Idleness |
| Vigorous Guidance | Vigorous, goal-oriented guidance of the child to expected modes of behavior and achievement centering about ego delegations | Delegation of sense of achievement and goal-orientation, desire for recognition and excellence | Not necessarily harmful, at times releases tension, best de-emphasized | No longer an issue of socialization, rationalized and decathected | An accomplished, flexible, liberal individual, amiable to corporate culture | Lack of development and unsociability |
| Delegated Release | Infusion into the child of id qualities absent in guidance, stressing decrease in authority bonds, increase in empathy | Id delegation | A positive aspect of life, but consciously not emphasized | ------ | Creation of a feeling, integrated individual who continues to achieve as guided individual | Lack of feeling and sense of personal efficacy |

Fig. 11. Summary of the Submodes of Socialization

## REFERENCES

1. Helm Stierlin, *Separating Parents and Adolescents: A Perspective on Running Away, Schizophrenia and Waywardness* (New York: Quadrangle, 1972).
2. Anna and Arnold Silverman, *The Case Against Having Children* (New York: David McKay, 1971); Shirley Radl, *Mother's Day Is Over* (New York: Charterhouse, 1973); Ellen Peck, *The Baby Trap* (New York: Bernard Geis, 1971).
3. Silverman and Silverman, *The Case Against Having Children.*
4. Radl, *Mother's Day Is Over,* p. 24.
5. Peck, *The Baby Trap.*
6. Betty Rollin, "Motherhood: Who Needs It?" in *Family in Transition* ed. Arlene S. Skolnick and Jerome H. Skolnick (Boston: Little, Brown and Co., 1971), p. 351.
7. Virginia Barber and Merrill Maguire Skaggs, *The Mother Person* (New York: Bobbs-Merrill, 1975), pp. 46-47.
8. Pearl S. Buck, *To My Daughters With Love* (New York: John Day, 1949).
9. Signe Hammer, *Daughters and Mothers, Mothers and Daughters* (New York: Quadrangle, 1976), p. 32.
10. *Ibid.,* p. 33.
11. Barber and Skaggs, *The Mother Person,* p. 197.
12. *Ibid.,* p. 200.
13. Hammer, *Daughters and Mothers,* pp. 48-49.
14. *Ibid.,* p. 98.
15. *Ibid.,* p. 52.
16. Margaret S. Mahler et al., *The Psychological Birth of the Infant: Symbiosis and Individuation* (New York: Basic Books, 1975).
17. *Ibid.,* 151.
18. Herbert Hendin, *The Age of Sensation* (New York: Norton, 1975), p. 45.
19. Hans Sebald, *Momism: The Silent Disease of America* (Chicago: Nelson Hall, 1976).
20. Staff of the Child Study Association of America, *Children in Wartime* (New York: Child Study Association, 1942). p. 8.
21. Mahler, *Psychological Birth.*
22. Percival M. Symonds, *The Dynamics of Parent-Child Relationships* (New York: Bureau of Publications, Teachers College, 1949), p. xiii.
23. O. Spurgeon English and Constance J. Foster, *Fathers are Parents, Too* (New York: G. P. Putnam's Sons, 1951).
24. *Ibid.,* p. 70.

25. Benjamin Spock, *The Common Sense Book of Baby and Child Care* (New York: Duell, Sloan and Pearce, 1965).
26. Kenneth Keniston, *Young Radicals: Notes on Committed Youth* (New York: Harcourt, Brace & World, 1968), p. 55.
27. *Ibid.*, p. 236.
28. Henry Malcolm, *Generation of Narcissus* (New York: Little, Brown and Co., 1971), p. 154.
29. Sidney Callahan, *Parenting: Principles and Politics of Parenthood* (Garden City, N.J.: Doubleday, 1973).
30. Martha Lear, *The Child Worshippers* (New York: Crown, 1963), p. 224.
31. Eda LeShan, "When Parents Convict Themselves," *New York Times Magazine*, July 12, 1964.
32. *Ibid.*
33. Lynn Z. Bloom, *Doctor Spock: Biography of a Conservative Radical* (New York: Bobbs-Merrill Co., 1972).
34. Spock, *Baby and Child Care*; "A Child's View," *Ladies' Home Journal*, June 1960; *Dr. Spock Talks with Mothers: Growth and Guidance* (New York: Houghton Mifflin, 1961.
35. Spock, "A Child's View."
36. Spock, *Dr. Spock Talks.*
37. Spock, *Baby and Child Care.*
38. Christine Beasley, *Democracy in the Home* (New York: Association Press, 1954).
39. A. B. Auerbach, *The Why and How of Discipline* (New York: Child Study Association of America, n.d.), p. 11.
40. Dorothy Barclay, "Punishment: The Debate Goes On," *New York Times Magazine*, May 19, 1957, p. 48.
41. See also Lois Meek Stolz, *Influences on Parent Behavior* (California: Stanford University Press, 1967).
42. Rudolf Dreikurs and Vicki Soltz, *Children: The Challenge* (New York: Sloan and Pearce, 1964), p. 153.
43. Dorothy Baruch, *New Ways in Discipline: You and Your Child Today* (New York: Whittesey House, 1949); "How to be a Better Parent," *Readers Digest*, October 1969, p. 188.
44. Symonds, *The Dynamics*, p. xiii.
45. Sam Blum, "Will Your Children Grow Up to Be Like You?" *Redbook*, December 1962, p. 135.
46. "When Badness is Really Good," *Better Homes and Gardens*, January 1950, p. 19; Phillip Lopate, "Getting at Feelings," *New York Times Magazine*, August 31, 1975, p. 23.
47. Judith S. Kestenberg, "The Effects on Parents of the Child's Transition Into and Out of Latency," in *Parenthood: It's Psychology and Psychopathology,*, ed. E. James Anthony and

Therese Benedek (Boston: Little, Brown & Co., 1970), p. 291.

48. Norman L. Paul, "Parental Empathy," in *Parenthood: Its Psychology and Psychopathology*, p. 102.

49. Carole Klein, "Dream World, Real World," *New York Times Magazine*, October 16, 1966, p. 102.

50. Elizabeth B. Hurlick, *Modern Ways with Children* (New York: McGraw-Hill, 1966), p. 102.

51. Robert Lamborn, "Parents Are More Important Than Anybody," *New York Times Magazine*, October 16, 1966, p. 102.

52. "The Transformation of the Chronic Nag," *Redbook*, August 1965, p. 8.

53. H. L. Harris, *Doing Our Best for Our Children* (London: Angus and Robertson, 1946).

54. Stolz, *Influences.*

55. Dreikurs and Soltz, *Children*, p. 70.

56. Rene A. Spitz, *The First Year of Life: A Psychoanalytic Study of Normal and Deviant Development of Object Relations* (New York: International Universities Press, 1965), p. 281.

57. Hale F. Shirley, *Psychiatry for Pediatrics* (New York: The Commonwealth Fund, 1948); Ruth Becky, "Your Child's Personality," *Hygeia*, September 1942; David Abrahamsen, *The Emotional Care of Your Child* (New York: Trident Press, 1969).

58. Karen Pryor, *Nursing Your Baby* (New York: Harper & Row, 1963), p. 89; Harold Orlansky, "Infant Care and Personality," *Psychological Bulletin*, January 1949; Ann Usher, "Can Today's Mothers Nurse Their Babies?" *Better Homes and Gardens*, January 1950.

59. Anna M. Wolf, *The Parents' Manual* (New York: Simon & Schuster, 1941), pp. 157-58.

60. "Book Review: The Mother-Child Interaction in Psychosomatic Disorders," *Marriage and Family Living* (May 1960), p. 193.

61. Edith Bauxbaum, *Your Child Makes Sense: A Guidebook for Parents* (New York: International Universities Press, 1949), p. 22.

62. Arnold Gesell and Frances Ilg, *The Child from Five to Ten* (New York: Harper & Bros., 1946).

63. "The Problems of Raising Children," *Ladies' Home Journal*, May 1962.

PART III:  THE PERIODIZATION OF TWENTIETH-CENTURY
AMERICAN HISTORY

CHAPTER SIX

PROGRESSIVISM AND THE NEW DEAL

The following two chapters seek to illustrate the ways in which four major periods of twentieth-century American history are logical outgrowths of the four submodal childhood experiences detailed in the preceding chapters. Just as different species of seeds grow into distinct plants, so the four psychoclasses of individuals may be seen to create distinctive social conditions. Because psychogenic theory is still in its infancy, it would be premature to attempt a detailed analysis of America in the past century. These final chapters, then, are intended as an introduction to the psychogenic methods of broadly periodizing history.

DeMause's psychogenic theory presents a discernible pattern of the historical expression of psychoclasses. This pattern consists of three phases: rebellion, triumph, and reaction.[1] The first discernible mass expression of a psychoclass comes when its oldest individuals are in their twenties and thirties, when they characteristically express themselves in nonpolitical areas such as the arts and academics. Eventually, when a substantial number of individuals reach their forties and fifties, the psychoclass is more likely to make itself felt directly within politics and key institutions. If the psychoclass is to be of crucial historical significance, it moves into the triumphant phase. This is a time of optimism, growth, and substantial reform and reconstruction of society. When the individuals of the triumphant class grow older, they are eventually challenged by a new, emerging psychoclass. The triumphant psychoclass moves into the reactive stage concurrently with the rebellious phase of the new group. Fig. 12 illustrates the correspondence between the psychoclasses and their respective triumphant phases as follows: (1) psychic control: Progressivism, (2) aggressive training; the New Deal, (3) vigorous guidance: the Great Society, (4) delegated release: still in the rebellious phase. Fig. 13 adds the psychophasic dimension.

Fig. 12. Psychoclassic Periodication of Twentieth-Century America

It is possible to derive several generalizations from this structure. First, the triumph phase comes when a majority of a psychoclass has reached middle age, and a new psychoclass reaches the triumph phase approximately every thirty years, or every generation. The triumph of psychic control occurs at the turn of the century, at the time when a majority of the psychoclass has reached middle age. The next period of intensive reform begins in 1933. Finally, the triumphant expression of vigorous guidance occurs with the articulation of the Great Society in the early and mid-1960s.

We may also specify the phase of the cycle where the greatest social instability develops; we find that *without exception* major historical traumas occur during the overlapping phases of reaction and rebellion. A list of the major social traumas since the turn of the century shows that each incident falls within this stage of the cycle: the Spanish-American War, World War I, nativism and the

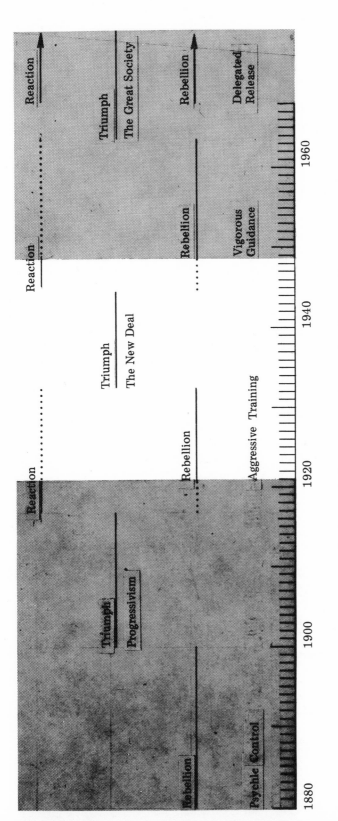

Fig. 13. Psychophasic Periodization of Twentieth-Century America

red scare of the 1920s, the Teapot Dome scandal, the stock-market crash and the onset of the Great Depression, World War II, Hiroshima, the Korean War, McCarthyism, and the Vietnam War. Triumph periods, in contrast, are times of construction and of the realization of human potentialities.

A leader—during any phase of the historical cycle—if he is to be effective must literally represent his psychoclass, which remains his hardest core of support. This psychic constituency may be understood in terms of what psychoanalysts have called "projective identification." Masses of individuals of the same psychoclass share similar projections and propensities for action in specific directions, creating a source of power which a leader acts upon. When a psychoclass moves toward dominating a period of history, its leaders therefore also become strong. Such leaders include Theodore Roosevelt, Woodrow Wilson, Franklin Roosevelt, and, in a qualified sense, Lyndon Johnson—all subjects of the following pages.

A word of caution is in order. Not every follower of the progressive banner, for example, was a member of the control psychoclass. Those individuals who created the progressive system were expressing their basic psychological natures and attracted, therefore, almost the entirety of their psychoclass. Yet individuals of a lower psychoclass may have been attracted to particular aspects of the Progressive phenomenon, such as the war in 1898 or trustbusting, and used these activities for the expression of their own personalities, for their own purposes, often fluctuating in their ideological allegiances.

## I. PROGRESSIVISM

Before beginning a discussion of Progressivism proper, it will be useful to reiterate the basic themes of psychic control and to posit the logical effects of the submode upon the individuals who form the psychoclass. The novel aspects of the childhood experience of psychic control during the period from 1840 to 1880 involved a more intimate association among members of the primary family in which the child was monitored and molded through psychological as opposed to physical means. The experience included an obsession with focusing energy into proper channels and most of all the creation of a deep superego structure, such that the conscience was an integral and dominant aspect of the child's personality. Initial proximity to the mother, characteristically followed by her withdrawal, created severe anxiety—a lifelong fear of being abandoned. There was a high level of repression, and the socially acceptable means of alleviating the resulting hostilities and frustrations were severely limited. The highly cathected relations—the delicate, dependent mother; the virile, efficient, but distant father who is idealized by his children; the helping daughter; the hard-working son—all of these roles in the family constellation produced an "explosive intimacy."[2] We have summarized the archetypal resulting personality as anxiety-prone, with elements of compulsion, in extreme cases suffering hysterical disorders. It developed a relatively thoroughgoing system of defenses, including repression, denial, projection, and displacement. Most individuals of the control psychoclass experienced a lifelong pattern of repression, marked by an awareness of "something" being suppressed just below the surface and an ever-present explosive capacity that was sometimes directed against the self, at other times directed outward—the two extremes being the depressive personality and the orally enraged, phallically aggressive character.

Examining the social contributions of the control psychoclass we see that the organizing submodal themes are expressed in adult form as follows: (1) increased family intimacy and cohesion lead to a desire for intimacy on the social scale, the "urge for consolidation"; (2) superego delegation leads to a moralization of society and a new obsession with right and wrong; (3) the "spermatic economy" leads to a defense against the fear of loss of energy, taking the forms of phallic politics, the "virility impulse," the application of previously unknown levels of individual energy utilization, and new efficiency ethics; (4) the soft side of control leads to a relative improvement in social welfare and the invention of the regulatory state. These themes will be elaborated in the following sections.


## THE URGE FOR CONSOLIDATION

Just as the control family sought a greater intimacy among individuals within the family, so did the control psychoclass seek to unify society through the growth of its organizations and the fluidity of their interactions. The concept of an "urge for social consolidation" appears as a major theme in traditional historians' thought concerning the Progressive years. Wiebe's *Search for Order* is reflective of many historical studies. Antebellum America, he states, was a society conspicuously lacking a sense of discipline. Arguing that the United States of the Reconstruction period was a "society without a core," afflicted by a "general splintering process," Wiebe shows that the nation was incapable of facing the challenges of urbanization, industrialization, and immigration. Wiebe finds this lack of social planning and cooperation dangerous. America was little more than a group of "island communities," without the institutions and attitudes necessary to cope with change. Imperative new values like "regularity, system, continuity . . . clashed increasingly with the old." Wiebe summarizes his thesis as follows:

> By contrast to the personal, informal ways of the community, the new scheme derived from the regulative, hierarchical needs of urban-industrial life. Through rules with the impersonal sanctions, it sought continuity and predictability in a world of endless change. It assigned far greater power to government—in particular to a variety of flexible administrative devices—and it encouraged the centralization of authority. Men were now separated more by skill and occupation than community.[3]

Wiebe argues that "beneath all these surface ripples of rapid change there lay a deep-flowing current, which gave unity to the period as a whole."[4] This unity was built on the new urge for social consolidation. Wiebe uses terms similar to those applicable to the psychic control childhood experience: "The same broad pattern prevailed . . . the initial efforts to impose a crude order, the desire for regularity and predictability, the need for a government of continuous involvement, and the emphasis upon executive administration."[5] Behind rationality lay a "mystic social strength and large doses of force." Wiebe uses the language of increased controls and imperatives, of "binding obligations," of "cohesion." He quotes Theodore Roosevelt on America's place in the world:

> If a nation shows that it knows how to act with reasonable efficiency and decency in social and political matters, if it keeps order and pays its obligations, it need fear no interference from the United States. Chronic wrongdoing, or an impotence which results in a general loosening of the ties of civilized society, may in America, as elsewhere, ultimately require intervention by some civilized nation, and in the Western Hemisphere the adherence of the United States to the Monroe Doctrine may force the United States . . . to exercise an international police power.[6]

Another historical survey, Samuel Hays's *Response to Industrialism, 1885-1914*, sketches the evolving discipline of industrial methods and the attendant rise of specialization:

> To the uncritical observer, the record of industrialism has been written in the production statistics, the accomplishments of investor-heroes, and the rising standard of living of the American people. Even more significant, however, were the less obvious and less concrete changes: the expansion of economic relationships from personal contacts within a village community to impersonal forces in the nation and the entire world; the standardization of life accompanying the standardization of goods and production; increasing specialization in occupation with the resulting dependence of people upon each other to satisfy their wants.[7]

Thus Hays expands the view of an expanding, more intricate web of interrelationships, a weaving together of mutual dependencies that had the family of a few decades earlier as its prototype.

The historian John Garraty touches upon the new urge for discipline and the strengthening of interrelationships in his widely read *The New Commonwealth, 1877-1890*. He believes the title *New Commonwealth* is justified because of a basic change America underwent between 1877 and 1890: "This change took the form of a greatly expanded reliance by individuals upon group activities. Industrialization with its accompanying effects—speedy transportation and communication, specialization, urbanization—compelled men to depend far more than in earlier times on organization in managing their affairs, to deal with problems collectively rather than as individuals."[8]

George Fredrickson, although placing the change earlier and exaggerating embryonic expression in the 1860s and 1870s, observes similar dynamics in *The Inner Civil War: Northern Intellectuals and the Crises of the Union*. In contradistinction to antebellum humanitarian appeals, the United States Sanitary Commission was a representative group of the new "discipline intellectuals." The Commission was concerned with the "matter of teaching order and discipline and in its operation the Commission showed an almost excessive concern for the preservation of discipline in all its forms." Fredrickson continues: "A less tangible influence on the Sanitary philosophy came from its encouragement of a new attitude towards suffering. The Commission's concept of a 'scientific' philanthropy with its tough-minded 'realism' and emphasis on discipline and efficiency could lead to a genuinely hard-hearted approach to the problems of the unfortunate—an approach which could be justified in terms of 'scientific' social theories."[9] Thus, the imposition of mental discipline, stemming from the socialization childhoods beginning in the 1830s and 1840s, was the basis for the more developed urge for social consolidation.

Samuel Haber's treatment of the evolution of professionals in America is an additional example of the movement toward increased organization and consolidation. Although he observes a nadir in professional consciousness from 1830 to 1880, he finds that new forces emerged during the later portion of that period: "Not only did new professions seem to appear more rapidly, but the old and new professions took on a fresh spirit and moved effectively towards legislation enactments that restricted entry into their calling and placed control into the hands of the professionals themselves." Haber continues: "A contrast between the 1830s and the 1880s is revealing. By almost any standard both were decades of turbulent expansion. Yet while in the 1830s this growth was wide open and uncontrolled, in the 1880s it was tempered by new and distinctive restrictions."[10] The hallmark of the progressive impulse was the rise of a new class of professionals, experts in specialized fields of government, science, and management, men first relied on in Washington by the expert commissions of Theodore Roosevelt's administration. They worked with fervor and dedication to better society through their own training, using science in combination with zealous moral purpose.[11]

Cultural historian John Higham describes a development that can be called the logical outcome of psychic control. His article, "From Boundlessness to Consolidation," details the necessary process of the determination of limits as a basis for organization during the latter part of the nineteenth century. Higham calls to mind Daniel Boorstin's analysis of the *vagueness* of pre-Civil War America, with its characteristic lack of firm boundaries or categories—a situation described by David Donald and Stanley Elkins as "anti-institutionalism." Higham writes of the "gathering restrictions," the necessity of masking aggressions, and "the necessity to conform to the discipline of the machine"—the time clock, introduced into the factory in the 1890s, was a symbol of increased vigilance over daily affairs.[12] Henry May identifies the central moralistic quality of the Progressive years: "The first and central article of faith in the national credo was . . . the reality, certainty, and eternity of moral values." But he also recognized the urge for consolidation and unity, transposing the new intimacy of the family onto the social sphere: "For more than most periods of history, more than any since the Civil War, the early twentieth century was a time of sureness and unity."[13]

Historians of the Progressive era accurately reflected the values of the Progressive generation themselves. Symbolic of the urge for control and consolidation is this statement by Professor Charles Van Hise in *Concentration and Control*: "In conclusion, there is presented as the solution of the difficulties of the present industrial situation, concentration, cooperation and control."[14] Senator Albert J. Beveridge, addressing the Senate in 1900, composed a suitable motto for consolidation within a moralistic context: "We will not renounce our part in the mission of the race, trustee, under God, of the civilization of the world. . . . He has made us the master organizers of the world to establish system where chaos reins."[15]

## ENERGY AND THE SPERMATIC ECONOMY

One of the primary aspects of the psychic control submode was the ethic that the body contains a fixed quantity of energy which must not be squandered but rather be directed into socially useful activities. This economic attitude toward energy and sexuality had profound effects on the control psychoclass. The fears of not meeting one's energistic potential and of squandering one's precious force were met in several ways. One of the most effective means of personal defense, especially for young males, was aggressively to assert power, and continually to prove that resources were available. Some historians have called this display of force "the virility impulse." James McGovern writes:

> This may be described as an exaggerated concern with manliness and conventional concomitants—power and activity. Social Darwinism is usually called upon to explain the phenomenon without inquiring why, in personal terms, it was so attractive to its supporters. Symbolically, the period begins with Roosevent's charge up San Juan Hill and ends with his loathing of cowardly officials for refusing his offer to lead a cavalry charge across No Man's Land. . . . It was a time when the Big Stick and the Bull Moose captured the public's favor. Above all, however, the period was marked by activity—strenuous and dedicated effort to alter America and the world.[16]

Similarly, Joe Dubbert describes a masculinity crisis in which men raised under the ethic of righteous living sought to affirm their masculine identity through hard work.[17] Both writers pinpoint an energy which by contemporary standards seems abnormal and a rationalization for frenetic activity which testifies to the need to defend against completely repressed primal pains. According to Higham, the new energy was symbolic of "a new hunger to break out of the frustrations," to "be young, masculine, and adventurous."[18] Terrified of "feminine" passivity, the males who dominated political and social life strove to assert the power of America as individuals.

The display of force and energy took many forms. It certainly was a crucial variable in the impetus to push America into the world arena and make her a world power. Howard K. Beale's study, *Theodore Roosevelt and the Rise of America to World Power*, observes the recurrent associations in this period of femininity with peace and of masculinity with war. A cult of strenuosity and vigor came to pervade American life; inactivity was considered flaccid and weak—opposed to the manliness of a disciplined and forceful existence. Politics, domestic and international, was conceived of in terms of power and the ability to mobilize energy.[19] Another historian speaks in the same terms: "It was in the nineties that the historic expansionist impulse drove Americans far beyond their own boundaries to acquire territory on the shores of Asia. . . . Most Americans faced the new century with exuberant optimism . . . all heralded America's coming of age." Every observer dwelled on words like "power," "strength," and "supremacy," which suddenly became indispensable to discussions of any aspect of the American scene.[20] A contemporary spoke of "the mystique of war," which in a positive sense organizes physical strength, and of "power" as the essence of the state.[21] Howard Mumford Jones went so far as to entitle the period from 1865 to 1915 the "age of energy." The dominant image of the period was the mechanical motor, symbolizing the triumph of science, efficiency, and speed as American ideals; and the *social* machinery included an unprecedented number of associations and societies. Similarly, one of the most important texts of the Progressive period, invoked by Theodore Roosevelt as an ideological base, has been described in these terms:

> Both the rhetoric and philosophy of *The Promise of American Life* make it a proper code for the Age of Energy. The rhetoric, though free of the intemperate language of even Roosevelt, used terms such as "energy," "development,"

"progress," words implying the recognition of power and "promise."[22]

And, according to the same writer, Theodore Roosevelt embodied the period's "restlessness, its ambition, its curiosity, its extraordinary faith in activism rather than in contemplation."[23]

## INTELLECTUAL CURRENTS

Psychic control themes—such as the centrality of conscience, the urge for discipline and intensive socialization of culture in the form of consolidation, and the obsession with energy—may be found in the intellectual currents and formulations of the Progressive era. Lester Ward's *Psychic Factors in Civilization* (1892) is concerned with the proper use of energy, the avoidance of energistic waste, and the proper competition of men through associations of individuals: "The paradox therefore is that *individual freedom can only come through social regulation.*"[24] Ward stresses the impetus for control of the social structure and the proper direction of energy.

Charles Horton Cooley likewise concerns himself with the necessity of directing and socializing energy into the proper spheres: "We are born with a vaguely differentiated mass of mental tendency, vast and potential, but unformed and needing direction." Making the case for the power of the great man in history, Cooley states his arguments in terms of an inordinate amount of the civilization's energy locked within such an individual: "There is explosive material stored up in him, but it cannot go off unless the right spark reaches it." In mystical language cloaking the realities of home life, he traces latent personal energy to a system of "personal impressions": "Most people will be able to recall vague yet intensely personal impressions that they have received from faces—perhaps from a single glance or a countenance that they have never seen before or since—or perhaps from a voice." When a great leader appears, "energy is tapped, an instinct is disengaged, the personal suggestion conveyed in the glance is felt as a symbol . . . that can unlock hidden tendencies. It is much the same as when electricity stored and inert in a jar is loosened by a chance contact." The Anglo-Saxons, he insists, are a strenuous people who "are born to action."[25]

The obsession with energy and its association with power and progress achieved expression in a new concern with the conservation of resources. Frederick Taylor, in *Scientific Management* (1911), explicitly describes the similarity between the necessity of conserving and directing human effort and the necessity of conserving natural forces. Taylor writes: "We can see our forests vanishing, our water-powers going to waste, our soil being carried by floods to the sea; and the end of our coal and our iron is in sight. But our larger wastes of human effort, which go on every day [are caused by] such acts as blundering, ill-directed, or inefficient [administration] . . . . It is only when we fully realize that our duty, as well as our opportunity, lies in systematically cooperating to train and to make this competent man . . . that we shall be on the road to national efficiency."[26] Theodore Roosevelt likewise writes: "The method of reckless and uncontrolled private use and waste has done for us all the good it ever can; and it is time to put an end to it before it does all the evil it easily may. We have passed the time when heedless waste and destruction and arrogant monopoly are any longer permissible. Henceforth, we must seek national efficiency by a new and better way, by the way of the orderly development and use, coupled with preservation of our national resources, by making the most of what we have for the benefit of all of us." On another occasion Roosevelt writes: "As a people we have not yet learned to economize. One of the virtues we Americans need is thrift." Roosevelt connected conservation to efficiency, stating in a Presidential speech: "Finally, let us remember that the conservation of our national resources, though the gravest problem of today, is yet but part of another and greater problem to which the Nation is not yet awake . . . the problem of national efficiency."[27]

The first formalized conceptualization of the science of industrial efficiency emerged during this period. Samuel Haber notes that the efficiency ethic of the Progressives was tied to other values such as moralism and the concern with the proper use of energy: "The Progressive era is almost made to order for the study of Americans in love with efficiency. For the Progressive era gave rise to an efficiency craze—a secular Great Awakening, an outpouring of ideas and emotions in which the gospel of efficiency was preached without embarrassment. . . . the word signified the energy input-output ratio of a machine."[28] Industrialization was associated with morality; as Robert Wiebe states, " 'Industrialize Society Without Commercializing Souls,' could have served as the era's motto."[29]

Herbert Croly, one of the most influential thinkers of the Progressive years, whose writings became the gospel of the

Progressive Party in 1912, created an ideology which may be summarized as follows: (1) individuals are only as effective as their institutions; (2) individuals cannot cooperate without the state and society; (3) an absolute code of ethics is essential; (4) social imperatives take precedence over personal desires; (5) control of the physical and instinctual self is essential.[30] Croly's themes—moralism, energy, control of the passions, the desire for an increase in social solidarity and organization through the hard work of determined and competitive individuals—are the essence of psychic control.

This chapter is concerned with superego delegations, but the pragmatic system of William James must first be placed in perspective. Many assume that in devising a philosophy of pragmatism calling for the abandonment of rigid ethical codes in favor of a sensitivity to the contextual relevance of values, James became a moral relativist. Such an interpretation ignores the intense moral quality of James's thought. In "The Will to Believe" (1897), James states:

> *Moral questions* immediately present themselves as questions whose solution cannot wait for sensible proof. A moral question is a question not of what sensibly exists, but of what is good, or would be good if it did exist. Science can tell us what exists, but to compare the *worth*, both of what exists and of what does not exist, we must consult not science, but what Pascal calls our heart.[31]

Thus James states that moral qualities may never be replaced by science and that they hold an importance apart from empirical reality. Morality is brought to an even more refined level than dogma, a level at which the individual must be sensitive to his own conscience.

Another intellectual manifestation of superego delegation came to be known as the "social gospel." The social gospel communicated to the clergy that it was their moral obligation to take an active part in the betterment of society. The goal of such an ethic was to pinpoint and define evil in urban-industrial society and, with energy and zeal, to weed it out. The church was to concern itself with mankind's collective as well as individual betterment. Walter Rauschenbusch insists, in *Christianity and the Social Crisis* (1907), that the preacher should actively articulate pressing social and political issues. It is the task of society to improve itself through the betterment of its institutions, and it is the task of the clergy to articulate moral problems.

## THE PHALLIC POLITICS OF THEODORE ROOSEVELT

Theodore Roosevelt encapsulates the expression of psychic control. Much of the secret of his appeal lay in the success of the phallic-narcissistic personality as a resolution to the stresses of psychic control. As the child was programmed to repress hostility and divert it into socially useful areas, to be an instrument of progress, monitoring his actions for the social good, so Roosevelt directed his hostile feelings into campaigns for "the right," disciplined his mind and body for the task, and achieved the realization of social consolidation, affirmation of energy, and a stringent code of ethics.

The Spanish-American War served as an arena for the expression of Roosevelt's and his control psychoclass's basic natures. Roosevelt repeatedly stated that the war was personally crucial to him, one of the most important events of his life. Fighting was an imperative: "I have a horror of bluster which does not result in a fight; it is both weak and undignified." Howard K. Beale describes Roosevelt's attitude toward war: "He would have hesitated to proclaim openly that he liked war. Yet there was something dull and effeminate about peace. A civilized tradition drew him back from open advocacy of war. Yet personally he gloried in war, was thrilled by military history, and placed war-like qualities high on his scale of values. Without consciously desiring it, he thought a little war now and then stimulated admirable qualities in man."[32] Roosevelt stated on one occasion that he would have left his wife's deathbed to answer the call; using typically phallic imagery he said that war "is my chance to cut my little notch on the stick that stands as the measuring rod in every family."[33]

Gerald F. Linderman, in *The Mirror of War: American Society in the Spanish-American War*, shows keen insight into the Progressives' martial motivation:

> The most compelling aspect of any problem remained its moral facet; since social evil resulted from the individual's failure to act as he should, locating the right and the wrong within a question was always the first and often the only step in formulating the proper response. In ways lost to our century, both understanding and motivation had clear moral dimensions. . . . The objective was not proficiency in the use of weapons . . . but the hardening of bodies. It was assumed that each man moving to meet the enemy would struggle with himself to mobilize the highest ideals of which he was capable, to conquer the quaking and thinking enemy

within. Training was a method to prevent the intrusion of irrelevant physical factors into that essentially moral encounter with oneself and then with the Spaniard.[34]

That the moral quality of the war was yet another superego delegation of the control submode becomes obvious when examining its supporters' rationalizations. Roosevelt felt war was a means of purging an internal devil: "There is not one among us in whom a devil does not dwell; at some time, or at some point in time that devil masters each of us; he who has never failed has not been tempted; the the man who does in the end conquer, does painfully retrace the steps of his slipping, when he shows that he has been tried in the fire and has not been found wanting."[35] On another occasion Roosevelt said that "the war with Spain was the most absolutely righteous foreign war in which any nation has engaged during the nineteenth century."[36] By 1910, William James was so enamored by the positive qualities war engenders in men that he wrote an article, "The Moral Equivalent of War," in which he sought the means to transfer the positive martial qualities of "order and discipline," the tradition of service and devotion, of physical fitness, exertion, and universal responsibility" to peacetime[37]

Because the moral arguments of entering a war with Spain were flimsy and ambiguous, Roosevelt sought to articulate various ways in which the fight would satisfy the dictates of conscience. He wrote:

> To speak with a frankness which our timid friends would call brutal, I would regard a war with Spain from two standpoints: first, the advisability on the grounds both of humanity and self-interest of interfering on behalf of the Cubans, and of taking one more step toward the complete freeing of America from European domination; second, the benefit done our people by giving them something which isn't material gain, and especially the benefit done our military forces by trying both the Navy and Army in actual practice. I should be very sorry not to see us make the experiment of trying to land, and therefore feed and clothe, an expeditionary force, if only for the sake of learning from our blunders. I should hope that the force would have some fighting to do; it would be a great lesson, and we would profit much by it.[38]

The war also served the forces of consolidation. Reformer Jacob Riis reminisced:

The cowboy, the Indian trailer, the packer, and the hunter who sought and killed the grizzly touched elbows with the New York policeman who, for the love of adventure had followed his once chief to the war, with the college athlete, the football player and the oarsman, the dare-devil mountaineer of Georgia, fresh from hunting moonshiners as a revenue officer, and with the society man, the child of luxury and wealth from the East, bent upon proving that a life of ease had lulled neither his manhood nor his sense of common citizenship.[39]

The war had a breathless quality, from the raucous, high-pitched propaganda in the Hearst press to the declaration of war, the relatively fast-paced fighting, and the successful termination. America danced a manic celebration of national self-congratulation as its efficiency, power, and moral nature were affirmed. The war had all the elements of a puberty rite, proving that America was now an adult, capable of autonomy and leadership, capable of protecting the passive and the weak (the prostrate, helpless, colonial Cuba), capable of warding off the immoral use of force.

Roosevelt's Presidential years heralded in a period of true phallic politics as Roosevelt and his countrymen gloated over their swift victories. His speeches and writings were filled with words like "flaccid," "potent," "soft," "hard," "virile," "manly," and his actions displayed the sense of drive which characterized his era. As a national defense against "the spermatic economy," the fantasy that the body's energies are fixed in quantity, Roosevelt offered a counterfantasy of omnipotence and indestructibility. Fear of losing vital force was warded off through the constant display of force. The fleet was sent around the world, blatantly displaying to all nations the might of America. During one Army-Navy football game, Roosevelt led his cabinet in jogging across the field. He once issued a directive that each officer in the service should be able to ride one hundred miles in three days; to answer the grumbling the edict evoked, he rode the full one hundred miles, in the middle of winter, in one day.[40] And in a characteristic melange of morality and force, Roosevelt declared: "In my judgement the most important service that I rendered to peace was the voyage of the battle fleet around the world."[41]

Roosevelt spoke often of the strengths required of a nation which is to do great work and be a great world power, of a people who must be neither "cravens nor weaklings." He said that "there is no place in the world for nations who have become enervated by soft and easy life, or who have lost their fibers of vigorous hardiness and manliness."[4][2] The fighting virtues were supreme, a necessary accompaniment to an industrialized nation. Warfare was seen as a means of civilization; in a statement of massive denial, TR declared the most righteous of all wars to be "the war with the savage." One writer has said that Roosevelt "dreamed of a world in which imperial powers could live at peace with one another and cooperate to control colonial peoples—by war if necessary." The desire for the subjugation of the primitive is understandable in terms of modal dynamics, for, in conquering the primitive, the Rooseveltian was conquering his own primitive side, waging war on his own unacceptable and antisocial impulses—whether sensual, aggressive, or rebelling against society's values. With the triumph of the articulated and conscious self, the threatening, visceral, unconscious self was covered and the defense system rendered potent.

What seems humorous, absurd, or barbaric by contemporary standards, a mere fifty years later, judged by individuals of a more advanced psychoclass, held glamour and conviction for many of Roosevelt's generation. The conservative or the refined might pull away from the crudity of his adventures, but the vast majority was fascinated. Reports of his continual affirmation of sexual identity were frequent; for example, he wrote from Texas during 1901:

> Soon we saw the lion in a tree top, with two of the dogs so high up among the branches that he was striking at them. He was more afraid of us than of the dogs, and as soon as he saw us he took a great flying leap and was off, the pack close behind. In a few hundred yards the dogs caught him, and a great fight followed. They could have killed him by themselves, but he gashed four of them, and for fear he might kill one I ran in and stabbed him behind the shoulder, thrusting the knife you loaned me right into his heart. I have always wished to kill the cougar as I did this one, with dogs and a knife.[4][3]

Reading the diary which Roosevelt kept on an African trip in 1909 is somewhat like reading a score card. The important fact to the keeper of the diary was the number of animals killed. During one period, Roosevelt alone killed four big game animals a day for several weeks; he once killed seven giraffes in a single day. The hunter was greeted as a hero upon his arrival back in the United States.[4][4]

John Morton Blum's selection of materials in *The Republican Roosevelt* aptly identifies the most basic elements in the thinking of this period. Uncontrolled competition was no longer sanctioned because of the moral and energistic implications: "To a degree selection was most rigid, [Roosevelt] pointed out, where fecundity made the least progress . . . where the struggle . . . was too intense, energy was dissipated in seeking bare existence, and national progress was inhibited . . . a declining population . . . endangered a nation." Roosevelt operated under an ethic of social scope; the individual had a "rational interest in conduct subordinate to the welfare of society, for in the process of social evolution men had reached the stage where they felt more 'shame and misery from neglect of duty, from cowardice or dishonesty' than could be offset from the gratification of individual desires." Social efficiency was felt to derive from "love of order, ability to fight well and breed well, capacity to subordinate the interests of the

Thus social interest was rationalized in terms of energy and morality, the two dominant themes of psychic control. One must maximize the energy of a community to ensure change, which is to be guided by strict moral codes. Blum states that Roosevelt felt that "his life . . . was a quest for the moral." Additionally, Blum points to the themes of "institutionalization," "associationalism," and, in another formulation, "consolidation, administration, stability." He summarizes the Rooseveltian and Progressive platform: "Preparedness, as Roosevelt preached it, rested upon a foundation of physical strength; preserved and developed natural resources, a large—indeed an increasing population, and maximal industrial productivity. To this he added moral resources, especially for women the desire to bear children and for men those inevitable attributes of proper male character, of 'the right stuff,' such as renunciation of ease, the capacity to fight, the willingness to sacrifice life."[4][6]

Joseph Gardner describes the extent to which all of Roosevelt's attempts to reconcile his contradictory drives still left him self-divided:

He was very nearly obsessed with power, more so in the period after he left the White House than during the years in office when power—often as much power as he wished to exercise—was within his grasp. Yet Roosevelt was a highly moralistic man. Deep within, he must have sensed that there was something dark and almost unnatural about the craving for power, something not spoken about but best ignored. No one can even know the inner turmoil he endured as the two conflicting natures struggled for supremacy. When the desire for power overcame his ... real reluctance to return to office, the Colonel would begin to elaborate excuses for what many consider his erratic and contradictory behavior.[47]

Roosevelt's contemporary John Dewey phrased it this way: "Roosevelt was the man of action. In that he incarnated his time ... the age was delirious with activity." All should "take up and notice ... if evils existed it was because men did not act promptly and intensely enough."[48] This perfect "clarity of conscience"[49] came about through the successful incorporation of the demands made by a severely didactic generation of parents, the child's hostilities being redirected in the very act of achieving parental demands. Owen Wister remembered Roosevelt's penchant for viewing his own writings moralistically, and he remembered Roosevelt's objection to bad language while a student at Harvard. Tolstoy included too many intimate details of his characters' lives, Roosevelt felt, and he warned a novelist friend that some of the more unseemly aspects of life are intolerable in art.[50]

Roosevelt produced a surprisingly large volume of writings which speak for many of his own submode, a corpus of literature strikingly manifesting resolutions stemming from the psychic control childhood experience. The virility impulse seeps out of the pages of Roosevelt's writings, but it is nowhere more apparent than in *The Strenuous Life*, a Spartan testament of self-discipline. Roosevent continually weaves the connection between morality and strenuous activity which is the staple of psychic control: "Peace is a great good; and doubly harmful, therefore, is the attitude of those who advocate it in terms that would make it synonymous with selfish and cowardly shrinking from warring against the existence of evil."[51] There are iron laws of morality which bind the righteous to practice what is preached. Key qualities are vigor of body and mind, but even above these is the quality of character, which is defined in terms of action, the willingness to fight against evil. The good boy is one who is "clean-minded and clean-lived," who, "in holding contempt for the coward, holds a fearful blow against evil," who will show "tenacity" and "fixity of purpose." The law of life is work, and "work itself, so far from being a hardship, is a great blessing." *The Strenuous Life* concludes its ideology with another fantasy created by the intimate family, the fantasy of oneness on the social scale, of national unity: "On the whole, we shall all go up or go down together.[52]

Besides the testament of *The Strenuous Life*, Roosevelt betrays his early conditioning in his autobiography, filled with dynamics

whose origins lie in the 1860s. Overflowing with the typical
idealizations of parents—more memories of the father, expressions
of positive feelings toward the mother, though in less
detail—Roosevelt's autobiography presents a childhood which
taught him the importance of morality and training. Proud of his
ability to overcome childhood infirmities through effort, he
presents a life of nonstop activity—from rowing in the summer,
boxing and wrestling all year, to jiujitsu and hunting while holding
political office. Morality must be central to political life: "no man
can lead a public career really worth leading, no man can act with
rugged independence in serious crises, nor strike at great abuses,
nor afford to make powerful and unscrupulous foes, if he is
himself vulnerable in his private character."

It is also of interest that Roosevelt—in his autobiography and
elsewhere—sees nothing wrong with bigness in society, with large
structures which may efficiently and completely add to national
development, but he insists that those structures be *controlled.*
Thus the vigilance of mind over body is to be externalized to
social concerns, with the vigorous development of structures of
organization which are watched and guided by some greater force.
The corporation is almost personified—a force for societal good if
controlled, an evil to be brought to justice if not.


A PSYCHOCLASS RESPONDS

A telling method of determing the historical significance of a
personality is to identify the nature of emotional reactions to the
individual. Logically, Roosevelt's resolutions appear and were
proven to be viable in reference to his childhood experience,
creating defense structures which not every individual was able to
approach. Yet it is apparent from a look at those who came into
contact with the man that he had tapped one of the most
important dynamics which any leader can possess, that he
represented an ego ideal to many of his constituents, an example
of a means of integrating behavior which may not only stave off
pains but also operate within the world with remarkable efficacy.
People generally expressed his impact in terms of energy. An
English doctor related that ordinarily he felt some of his vital
force go out of him each time he treated a patient. After treating
Roosevelt, however, for the first time in his life he was
invigorated; it seemed as if "some kind of vital energy had passed
from him into me instead of me into him!" A naturalist who was
with Roosevelt during one of the big game hunts was surprised

that "the fact that the Colonel was with us gave us energy to do things we couldn't possibly have done otherwise."[5 3]

Roosevelt's presence was not merely noticed or felt, it was experienced. One comment of a visitor to the White House during Roosevelt's presidency is typical: "His personality so crowds the room that the walls are thin and threaten to burst outward . . . you go to the White House—you shake hands with Roosevelt and hear him talk—and then go home to wring the personality out of your clothes." William Allen White felt an inspiring force:

I went home from our first casual meeting . . . I was afire with the splendor of the personality I had met and walked up and down our little bedroom at the Normandy trying to impart to her [his wife] some of the marvel that I saw in that young man. . . . I have never known a man as he, and shall never again. He overcame me. And in the hour or two we spent together, he poured into my heart such visions, such ideals, such hopes, such a new attitude towards life and patriotism and meaning of things, as I had never dreamed men had.[5 4]

The concept of the transference of energy is vital:

One never gets away from Mr. Roosevelt's personality. It sticks by me, so when he comes into a room and stands as he always does for one second before doing something characteristic, he electrifies the company and gives one just the sensations which a pointer does when he first quivers and takes a stand on quail. No matter how worn out and tired out he might be, suddenly to see a pointer whirl and come to stand, electrifies me instantly so nothing will do unless it be to see the President enter a room.[5 5]

Woodbury Kane was a Harvard man, the pinnacle of Eastern polish and conformity to his elitist class. He knew Roosevelt when they were both students, but Kane, an independent sort who felt admiration or closeness to few, had a distinct distast for Roosevelt. Roosevelt was upper-crust, but he somehow went beyond the confines of his own class. This put Kane off: a young Harvard man and member of the Porcellian Club should be well mannered and refined and should arrange his day with the expected proportion of work, fashionable leisure, and sport. Roosevelt was out of line and even had the audacity to run through Harvard Yard instead of proceeding at the expected walk.

Yet even Kane came under Roosevelt's spell several years later when he became a member of the Rough Riders. He had come

face to face with Roosevelt's full force of power. A few years after
the war, when Roosevelt was receiving an honorary degree at
Harvard, Owen Wister confronted Kane: "When we were in
college, you didn't seem to like him much. How do you feel
now?" Kane immediately countered: "If I were crossing the
Brooklyn Bridge and he ordered me to jump over, I'd do it
without asking why." The President, who was walking just in front
of the two men, said, "What are you fellows dangling behind for?
Come alongside." Wister had time to ask Kane before they reached
the president, "Complete surrender?" "Absolutely, old man,"
Kane replied.[56]

At the opposite end of the social spectrum, Roosevelt's servants
felt much the same way. James E. Amos, who wrote *TR: Hero to
His Valet*, confessed there was nothing about the man to which he
did not feel drawn. A White House servant testified: "There he is
. . . I don't know what there is about the man which makes me
feel so. I have seen a good many Presidents come and go in this old
house, and I like them all . . . but I declare I feel as if I could go
twice as far and twice as quick whenever he asks me to, and do it
twice as gladly."[57] One man said that his force was "an
inexhaustible ardor that expressed itself in the love of life. . . .
Men felt it in him as they felt it in their first love, or in the birth
of a first child, or the first challenge of death, and went from his
presence with a sense that their lips had been touched with
burning coal and they had been capable of doing what they had
not dreamed they could." One man said simply, "I have seen
Niagara and I have seen Roosevelt."[58]

## WOODROW WILSON AND THE FINAL YEARS
## OF CONTROL TRIUMPH

The Presidency of Woodrow Wilson corresponds to the final
years of triumph of the psychic control psychoclass and the onset
of its reactive stage during and shortly after World War I. Many
observers have noted the apparent dissimilarity between Wilson
and Roosevelt. Wilson did not always reach out with the
Progressive urge for consolidational growth, the acceptance of
urbanization or of large societal structures, nor did he engage in
the politics of physical and military strength. Wilson noted, "I do
not know how to wield a big stick."[59] On another occasion he
observed that Roosevelt "appeals to their imagination; I do not.
He is a real, vivid person, whom they have seen and shouted
themselves hoarse over and voted for, millions strong; I am a

vague, conjectural personality, made up more of opinions and academic prepossessions than of human traits and red corpuscles."[60] Roosevelt was seen by many as a nationalist in the Progressive tradition—urban, accepting big organizations as inevitable—while Wilson was seen to adhere to the traditional Jeffersonian values idealizing agrarian life and the small businessman.

Yet such differences are largely illusory; the similarities between the two men—who represented the same psychoclass—are far more striking. James Weinstein, in *The Corporate Ideal in the Liberal State: 1900-1918*, rightly observed that Wilson accepted consolidation just as did Roosevelt. "The differences [between the two Presidents] were largely rhetorical . . . Wilson's position in the trust question in 1912 was a synthesis of the positions of Taft and Roosevelt. Acknowledging the demise of the individual, entrepreneurial competition, Wilson affirmed and insisted upon reasonable inter-corporate competition."[61] Two books published in 1912 show the essential similarities between Wilson and Roosevelt. Roosevelt's dedication to the consolidation ethic is evident in his acceptance of the views of Charles Van Hise's *Concentration and Control: A Solution of the Trust Problem in the United States.* Hise stated that the answer to the trust problem was not the disolution of large industrial organizations, but rather their control through equally large government.[62] By the same token, Colonel E. M. House, who would become Wilson's closest advisor and confidant, published *Philip Dru, Administrator*, a novel containing a new hero, the individual efficiency expert. As a presidential advisor, Dru abandons earlier states' rights views in favor of a vigorous, powerful federal executive and more national contol, including nationalization of the telephone and telegraph systems. In the words of Arthur Schlesinger, Jr., the new breed of administrator "set up a nationalism so comprehensive, that it might well have given Theodore Roosevelt pause."[63] Wilson repeatedly articulated his view that consolidation was the only road to progress; as early as the 1890s, while still a professor at Princeton, Wilson stated: "Society is not a crowd, but an organism; and, like every organism, it must grow as a whole or else be deformed." Later he wrote, "elaboration of business upon a great cooperative scale is characteristic of our time." The legislative and administrative record of the Wilson presidency, which saw the enactment of more of the Progressive platform of 1912 than Theodore Roosevelt's administration, attests to Wilson's basically Progressive ideology.[64]

Fundamental difference did exist between Wilson and Roosevelt, but it was not ideological. The difference lay in the means of expressing their similar psychic control personalities. While Roosevelt found many outlets for expressing the different facets of his personality, from the virility ethic and the aggressive oral personality to phallic politics and intense morality, Wilson focused his expression into fewer spheres. But even though Wilson abandoned visceral phallic politics and never made the resolutions of the aggressive oral personality, he did stress the aspects of control involving high standards of achievement, competition, and morality, as well as the power dynamics and the urge for consolidation which define the control executive.

Wilson's enacted superego delegations were so intensive that he even overpowers Roosevelt in this regard. Wilson is quoted in Roosevelt's autobiography as follows:

"You know there is temptation in loneliness and secrecy. Haven't you experienced it? I have. We are never so proper in our conduct as when everybody can look and see exactly what we are doing. If you are off in some distant part of the world . . . you adjourn your ordinary standards. You say to yourself, 'Well, I'll have a fling this time; nobody will know anything about it.' . . . but if you saw one of your immediate neighbors coming . . . you would behave yourself until he got out of sight. The most dangerous thing in the world is to get off where nobody knows you. I advise you to stay around among the neighbors and then you may keep out of jail."[6][5]

In this statement, Wilson articulated the social nature of the conscience formed in the explosive intimacy of the control family. Conscience was seen as the product of adult vigilance, and, although thoroughly instilled in the individual, it loses some of its vitality in the vacuum of seclusion.

More than any other figure of his time, Wilson personified the moral aspects of Progressivism. Henry F. May describes the importance of these: "The first and central article of faith in the national credo was, as it has always been, the reality, certainty, and eternity of moral values."[6][6] If Progressive leaders were "essentially moral crusaders," then Wilson led the way and articulated the loftiest of goals. Wilson said that "it is moral force that is irresistible. It is moral force as much as physical that has defeated the effort to subdue the world. Words have cut as deep as the swords." In reference to a world war Wilson at first desperately tried to avoid, he said, "Like the rivulets gathering into the river and the river into the sea, there came from communities like this streams that fertilize the consciences of men, and it is the conscience of the world that we are trying to place upon the throne which others would usurp."[6][7] Wilson said that "the force of America is the force of moral principle . . . there is nothing else that she loves, and . . . there is nothing else for which she will contend."[6][8] John Morton Blum describes Wilson's belief in the clarity and potency of the forces of right and wrong in a study aptly titled *Woodrow Wilson and the Politics of Morality:* "This was an unintended legacy of Wilson's moralism. His basic, lifelong faith was in the individual as a distinct moral agent, inspired by and accountable to God, in the individual as the special object of a Christian education."[6][9] Once, when a cabinet member suggested a diversion to get away from the particularly tedious task of government at hand, Wilson answered that his boss would not allow it; when asked who his boss was, he answered, "my conscience."[7][0] Wilson's language often carried a moral or even Biblical tone: government "cleanses;" Wilson would "let the sun shine through the clouds again as once it shone;" he spoke of "opening doors" and "letting up the blinds," or of "catching the beast in the jungle."[7][1]

In the true spirit of the psychic control psychoclass, Wilson saw himself as an individual concerned with the constructive uses of power and organization for explicitly moral purposes. He directly refuted the mistaken view that he was primarily a "thinker" or intellectual for whom action was secondary to more sedate rationality:

I have a strong instinct of leadership, an unmistakably oratorical temperament, and the keenest delight in affairs. It has required very constant and stringent schooling to content me with the sober methods of the scholar and the man of letters. I have no patience with the tedious toil of what is known as "research;" I have a passion for interpreting great thoughts to the world; I should be complete if I could inspire a great movement of opinion, if I could read the experiences of the past into the practical life of the men of to-day and so communicate the thought to the minds of the great mass of people so as to impel them to great political achievements. . . . My feeling has been that such literary talents as I have are *secondary* to my equipment for other things: that my power to write was meant to be a handmaiden to my power to speak and to organize action.[7][2]

On another occasion Wilson expressed his view of the importance of morality and of retaining one's principles in the face of opposition:

> I never went into battle; I was never under fire; but I fancy that there are some things just as hard to do as to go under fire. I fancy that it is just as hard to do your duty when men are sneering at you as when they are shooting at you. When they shoot at you, they can only take your natural life; where they sneer at you, they can wound your living heart, and men who are brave enough, steadfast enough, steady in their principles enough, to go about their duty with regard to their fellow-men, no matter whether there are hisses or cheers . . . are men for a nation to be proud of. . . The cheers of the moment are not what a man ought to think about, but the verdict of his conscience and of the consciences of mankind.[7 3]

In his own way, Wilson possessed the inner combustible engine geared for social service which was Roosevelt's hallmark and a quality common to the control psychoclass. Wilson rightly viewed himself as an intense and passionate individual. At a 1914 meeting of the National Press Club, he countered the false impression that he was at times staid or emotionally imperturbable: "I am not aware of having any detachable apparatus inside of me. On the contrary, if I were to interpret myself, I would say that my constant embarrassment is to restrain the emotions that are inside of me. You may not believe it, but I sometimes feel like a fire from a far from extinct volcano, and if the lava does not seem to spill over it is because you are not high enough to see the caldron boil."[7 4] Wilson's political existence was dynamic; he retained the spirit of control and discipline while carrying forth a relatively nurturing (progressive) domestic policy. He spoke of the "inevitable law of change, which is no doubt a law of growth, and not decay" and the necessity of discipline and ordered skills. He called for a new genuineness, which he defined as "pith and strength of fiber," and urged control of the environment: "It is exercise and discipline upon such a scale, too, which strengthen, which for ordinary men came near to creating, that capacity to reason upon affairs and to plan for action . . . steam and electricity have reduced nations to neighborhoods."[7 5]

Wilson indicated in his book, *The New Freedom*, that he recognized the necessity for complexity, for corporations and large structures. Rather than dismantle the large industrial unit, he sought to regulate it. The "energy of concentration" would diffuse throughout his government. This energy would aid in the "intimate, instinctive co-ordination of the organs of life and action." He wrote: "I am not jealous of the size of any business that has *grown* to that size. I am not jealous of any process of growth, no matter how huge the result, provided the result was indeed obtained by the processes of wholesome development, which are the processes of efficiency, of economy, of intelligence, and of invention."[76] As Arthur Link notes, Wilson's Presidency saw the enactment of many of the policies of Roosevelt's "New Nationalism," from Progressive legislation regulating living and working conditions to a tariff commission, aid to education, monetary controls, and a war of grand national purpose and morality.[77]

## THE REACTIVE PHASE:
## WOODROW WILSON AND WORLD WAR I

A telling means of discerning when the social expression of a psychoclass has moved from the triumphant to the reactive stage is to locate the time when its individuals cease to solve the problems that were formulated during the stage of rebellion and partially solved during the period of triumph. The approach of Wilson and his psychic constituency to the First World War serves to illustrate the growing bankruptcy of the Progressive impulse. World War I is thus used within this analysis to illustrate the move of psychic control from the triumphant to the reactive stage. The concern here is not to posit a detailed psychogenic cause of World War I—such requires a separate, detailed work—but to use the war as an aid in the psychogenic periodization of twentieth-century American history.[78]

Wilson's approach to war illustrates vividly the limitations of control superego orientations, as well as the limitations of the urge for consolidation as it became exaggerated into a grandiose fantasy of "oneness." As America drifted toward war, and Wilson saw the onset as inevitable, he increasingly articulated involvement in strictly moral terms. By the time of the war's conclusion, when Wilson strove to realize his dreams of consolidation, he argued for a League of Nations justified on the loftiest of moral grounds.

Wilson sought to achieve a universality for the concept of Americanism: "America is made up of the peoples of the world and she said to mankind at her birth, 'We have come to redeem the world by giving it liberty and justice.' Now we are called upon to redeem that immortal pledge."[7][9] Striving for a sense of unity was nothing new to the President, and he had called for the same process on the national level: "And so my interest in politics . . . is that there is some prospect that we shall end the misunderstandings in America; that we shall bring classes to comprehend one another; that we shall bring about common counsel again; that we shall cease- the fruitless contests of interest with interest and unite all interests upon a basis, not of generosity but of mutual understanding and of mutual comprehension, and put all through the life of America again the sense of brotherhood, a sense of common enterprise in behalf of mankind."[8][0] Now, these sentiments would be transposed to the international arena; and in the pursuit of the ultimate goal of morality—eternal peace on earth—nations would learn to interact, to make the dream of a world community a reality. Wilson insisted that "the only hope for mankind" is international morality in which "America shall show the way."[8][1]

Wilson saw his own increasing rigidity as a determined practicality:

> The stage is set, the destiny closed. It has come about by no plan of our conceiving, but by the hand of God who led us into this way. We cannot turn back. We can only go forward, with lifted eyes and freshened spirit, to follow the vision. It was of this that we dreamed at our birth. America shall in turn show the way. The light streams upon the path ahead, and nowhere else.[8][2]

Increasingly, Wilson associated his aims with what he perceived as America's divinely legislated work: "Why has Jesus Christ so far not succeeded in inducing the world to follow his teachings in these matters: It is because He taught the ideal without devising any practical means of attaining it. That is why I am proposing a practical scheme to carry out His aims." James David Barber juxtaposed some of Wilson's language in furthering the passage of the League:

> "The facts are marching and God is marching with them. You cannot resist them. You must either welcome them or subsequently, with humiliation, surrender to them. It is welcome or surrender. It is acceptance of great world conditions and great world duties or scuttle now and come back afterwards. . . . I wish they could feel the moral obligation that rests upon us not to go back on those boys,

but to see the thing through ... to the end and make good the redemption of the world. For nothing depends upon this decision, nothing less than the liberation and the salvation of the world. ... I am ready to fight from now until all the fight has been taken out of me by death to redeem the faith and promise of the United States. ... I know that the whole world will lose heart unless America consents to show the way."[8] [3]

One biographer says that Wilson "not only keenly felt [that] the great misery of war ravaged mankind: he was possessed by the idea that it was his God-given mission to ameliorate it by so reordering the relations of the nations of the world."[8] [4] In a moment of doubt, Wilson said, "If I were not a Christian, I think I should go mad, but my faith in God holds me to the belief that He is in some way working out His own plan through human perversities and mistakes." Wilson had always "*needed* to do immortal work."[8] [5]

Such is the intensive nature of the morality behind the First World War. The implications of psychic control are even more strikingly illustrated here than in the case of the Spanish-American conflict. The leaders of the First World War—the men who articulated its nature and its purposes—were weaned on the progressive childhood of the mid- to late-nineteenth century, an experience which taught them that they were worthless, loveless creatures if they did not fight for what is right. Imprinted into this generation was not only the sense of, but also the delegated duty to achieve, what is right. But the crusader spirit proved insufficient for Wilson's goals, and he, as well as the control psychoclass, was left with an unsolved problem and a pervasive feeling of moral exhaustion.

Thus a period of the American experience is completed, one in which national triumph reigned for close to two decades, in which the emergency of modern America was heralded literally with a bang. The fiery fuel of affective politics, the rabid crusades and muscular exercises, were fitting to a culture as it moved from a more open and capitalist economy to the maturer stages of its socialization. The major step from rugged individualism to social concern and responsibility was taken as governmental agencies were created to aid in the weaving of a strong, complex national organism. It was a breathless period, with the qualities of adolescence and initiation. America became a world power, abandoning the innocence of isolation, taking on the responsibilities of power and influence, achieving an energy and identity which made the assimilation of an influx of population possible. The relative increase in child nurture of psychic control also found political expression. New democratic measures were furthered by the Progressives, who were responsible for the direct primary, popular election of senators, the income tax and governmental control of trusts and utilities.

Yet the muscular moralism of the Progressives would soon outlive its purpose. Jingoistic nationalism, created by an unprecedented sense of national solidarity, was a potentially dangerous force. Likewise, stringent morality, fueled by an overburdening sense of guilt and an explosive level of energy, proved to be not always an ideal means of solving complex problems. Superego delegations bred simplified prescriptions for progress and movements which served to fragment the drive for unity—the drive which motivated the very individuals who formed inflexible ideologies. The socially realized superego encouraged belief that personal morality could be legislated. Likewise, explosive energy had difficulty catching up with itself and often created a lack of equilibrium between the enthusiastic planting of seeds and their vigilant nurture. The Progressive psychology could easily overextend itself through sheer drive.

## II. THE NEW DEAL

### REACTION AND REBELLION IN THE TWENTIES

This section is intended to illustrate the transformations and dislocations of culture involving the rebellious phase of the aggressive training psychoclass during the 1920's, its triumph during the thirties, and the onset of its reactive stage upon the onset of World War II. Such is a story of the social enactment of ego as opposed to superego tasks, and the realization of the major themes of aggressive training.

Historians present a virtual consensus in portraying the twenties as a period of "reaction." Warren G. Harding's words are often quoted as characteristic of the temper of the times: "America's present mood is not heroics . . . not nostrums, but normalcy; not revolution, but restoration; not agitation, but adjustment; not surgery, but serenity; not the dramatic, but the dispassionate." Jules Abels wrote:

This swift turn about in national psychology is one of the most remarkable phenomenon in our history. It rejected not only Wilson's international program to secure everlasting peace, but also the spirit of his domestic program. The reaction against Wilson swung America away from the reform that had been the keynote of our national policy from Theodore Roosevelt's time at the beginning of the century. . . . In the history of the nation, it is possible to discern a certain rhythm—political action followed by reaction, movement followed by rest. The Coolidge Era was indisputably one of reaction and rest.[86]

Writers point to diverse phenomena such as the disillusionment of the intellectuals, the satires of Mencken and Lewis, the corruption of the Teapot Dome scandals, the lack of distinction of Harding and Coolidge and the inflexibility of Hoover, the growth of Ku Klux Klan, the red scare, nativism, and the "flapper" mentality. Many studies label the period the time of "Normalcy," or the "Era of Excess."[87]

A few analyses do attempt to delineate the persistence of the Progressive impulse during the twenties. Clarke Chambers calls the period a "seedtime of reform," making the case that social-welfare programs moved forward within the context of voluntary associations and agencies. Arthur Link's article "What Happened to the Progressive Movement in the 1920's?" also finds Progressive persistence, but his case to mitigate the reactive nature of the 1920s is made only by insisting upon minimizing the cohesion of the earlier Progressives.[88] Others stress material growth, citing the development of electrical power for the home, the number of Americans owning cars, the development of telephone service, the increase in median real income, as well as the existence of achieving heroes such as Henry Ford and Charles Lindbergh.

Yet identifying the evolutionarily significant aspects of the 1920s does not come merely from searching for the persistence of the older Progressivism, or simply pointing to material prosperity, but comes rather from observing the development of new individuals of the aggressive training psychoclass who would come to fore in the 1930s. Because their attitudes and ideas were not fully articulated until the early thirties, when they were brought to positions of power in Washington, the training psychoclass will be discussed in the context of the New Deal, the second triumphant stage of the twentieth century.

## THE TRAINING PSYCHOCLASS

Before a discussion of the New Deal proper, a reiteration of the definition of aggressive training, as well as an explanation of its psychoclass ramifications, will be helpful. In part one, I defined aggressive training as follows:

(2) *Aggressive Training* (c. 1880-1910): The soft side of
the second submode lies in the reduction in the intensity of
authority bonds and parental projections, in which
intergenerational relations rely less on the imposition of open
guilt patterns and on stringent emotional and instinctual
controls. Distancing measures are reduced somewhat and
previously internalized tensions are focused outward and
manifested in a new concern with the child's place in society.
In the process of child rearing, "the child within the parent"
becomes less threatening, requiring less drastic defense
structures. The resulting aggressive child has more flexibility
and autonomy than his controlled predecessor, is less
didactic, wishes to promote societal organization in a more
pragmatic manner, has less (though still considerable)
compulsion to take personal control and to affirm personal
strength through powers of mind or body. Thus the child's
social attempts are characteristically more successful, less
resembling personal virility-puberty rites. The hard side lies in
the fact that though the child is not psychically *controlled*, it
is aggressively *trained*. Articulated parental standards of
achievement reach new levels of refinement and the
aggressive and competitive pursuit of goals is stressed. The
discipline earlier associated with control of instinct is now
directed to the facility and potency of social interaction. The
child must still fight his way to adulthood. The primary
delegated missions are those of the ego.

The ramifications of such a psychogenic structure are clear and
umambiguous. On the soft side, we see an individual better able to
abandon what was earlier known as "rugged individualism"
because of greater social skills and a less precarious sense of
autonomy. The aggressive training psychoclass may therefore
cooperate to a higher degree than the control individual in areas
effecting more areas of life. Because the training psychoclass has
received more nurture—better education, more caring infant
treatment, more access to parents—it is more willing to create a
nurturing social structure. The emotional texture of training is less
explosive than control due to lessened repressions and the ability
to express anger before it builds into rage. The training conscience
is less domineering and overpowering because its primary missions
are ego tasks; these include abilities of cooperation and
organization and the defusing of explosive intimacy. Because of
his decreased fear of retribution as a consequence of failure, the
training individual can afford to be experimental at times—to alter

his behavior and then analyze the results.

An essential aspect of the softening effect of the training psychoclass is its ability to abandon the impulses stemming from the spermatic economy. Since the training individual is not raised on the notion that the misdirection of vital force leads to disastrous consequences, the ethic of the nobility of saving dissipates, and the view that it is possible to compound resources emerges—an emotional stance with profound implications for the economy and government spending. The aggressive abandonment of the spermatic economy does not lead to extravagant installment purchases and the watering and uncontrolled issuance of stock, but rather to a vigilant, careful effort to enact measures necessary to stimulate development.

On the hard side, the training psychoclass is precisely that: *trained.* Society, though more cooperative on the group level than in the past, is highly competitive, hierarchical in role and position, and achievement-oriented. The trained individual is also aggressive, and, although he is less fueled by pure will and the energy of displacement, he is ultimately concerned with meeting a demanding schedule, remaining active, and perfecting a unified nationalism. The welfare state, a product of the softer aspects of training nurture, is nevertheless limited in scope; the entirely subsidized individual must become lazy and fail to achieve. Social nurture is contingent upon hard individual effort.

## THE ESSENTIAL UNITY OF THE NEW DEAL

Much has been written concerning the supposed "stages" of the New Deal, and different historians attribute varying degrees of divergence between each of them. Common is the view that there is a division between the First New Deal, from March 1933 (including the first three months, known as the "Hundred Days") to the summer of 1935, and the Second New Deal, from 1933 to 1940. The First New Deal is often considered as primarily concerned with relief and recovery, creating such agencies as the Public Works Administration and the Federal Emergency Relief Administration, and the Second New Deal as concerned with such reforms as the Tennessee Valley Authority and the Social Security and Fair Labor Standards Acts.[89] William Leuchtenburg takes note of the almost conservative nature of the Hundred Days and its concern with balancing the budget.[90] Schlesinger notes that the Second New Deal was not as radical as the first, less planned and activist, more capitalistic, forging a coalition between lawyers of the Brandeis school and those steeped in Keynesian economics.[91] Others observe the shift from a directed to a compensated economy, and consider the Second New Deal the more radical phase. Still other writers speak of a New Nationalism phase (from 1933 to 1935) and a New Freedom phase (from 1935 to 1938).[92]

Yet the existence of "stages" or "phases" of the New Deal is more apparent than real, and more reflective of particular phases of completeness of expression of a unified world view than a qualitative change in meaning. When examining the New Deal in the light of the training psychoclass, the unified themes are visible. The new qualities of the New Deal are precisely the same innovations which marked the childhoods of the individuals who created the novel structures. These qualities center around the ego qualities involving a new prominence or rationality over self-justification and conscience, new abilities to organize and experiment, a new flexibility and pragmatism, the dissolution of the spermatic economy, and a growth in empathy on the social scale which takes Progressivism a step further—from regulation to the embryonic welfare state. The hard side of the New Deal involves the militaristic quality of many of its programs and policies, such as General Johnson's National Recovery Administration, the perpetual activism, the relatively rigid bureaucratization, an aggressive paced offensive strategy, and the connection of welfare with the imperative of individual effort.


## THE EXPERIMENTAL NATURE OF THE NEW DEAL

The control psychoclass, which was tied to dictates of a rigid superego, obsessed with affirming personal strength, and steeped in an ethic of progress, was not equipped to break its ties to the past to the degree that the New Dealers broke away from the tradition of strict ideological commitment. The competitive and achievement orientations of aggressive training, for all the pressures placed upon the child, called for more personal expression and creativity on the part of the child in formulating these goals. The training psychoclass was the product of a group of adults who created a child study movement, for example, which proudly announced that the child's energies are not necessarily threatening to society and that an older generation cannot impose its will completely upon the young, who possess tendencies or "germs" of potentialities. Granted more room to move, the child is better able to experiment, and thus mitigate his fears concerning possible failure.

The experimental nature of the New Deal is evident in the very language of the New Dealers. As Richard Hofstadter observes, the Progressives of the previous generation used words which centered about superego qualities: *patriotism, citizen, law, character, conscience, soul, morals, service, duty, shame, disgrace, sin, selfishness*. The New Dealers, in contrast, used such vocabulary as *needs, organization, results, techniques, realism, morale, skill, expert, habits, practicality, leadership*—in other words, the *semantic* expression of aggressive experimentation.

Franklin Roosevelt himself stated, "Take a method and try it. If it fails, try another. But above all, try something."[93] The pattern of trying without fear of failure is the precise pattern established in Roosevelt's boyhood. The following story related by his mother Sara applies equally well to the mature executive Roosevelt, who moved from coordinator of industrial and labor interests, scrupulously balancing the budget and limiting production, to being the spokesman for the limited welfare state and an experimenter with inflation and Keynesian economics. Roosevelt's mother related:

Finally, a little alarmed, I asked him whether he was unhappy. He did not answer at once and then said very seriously, "Yes I am unhappy." When I asked him why, he was again silent for a moment or two. Then with a curious little gesture that combined entreaty with a suggestion of impatience, he clasped his hands in front of him and exclaimed, "Oh, for freedom!" That night, I talked it over with his father who, I confess, often told me I nagged the boy. We agreed that unconsciously we had probably regulated the child's life too closely, even though we knew he had ample time for exercise and play. Evidently he was quite satisfied with what he did with his time, but what worried him was the necessity of conforming to given hours. So the very next morning I told him that he might do whatever he pleased that day. He need obey no former rules nor report at any given intervals, and he was allowed to roam at will. We paid no attention to him, and, I must say, however, a very dirty, tired youngster came dragging in. He was hungry and ready for bed, but we did not ask him where he had been or what he had been doing. We could only deduce that his adventures had been a little lacking in glamour, for the next day, quite of his own accord, he went contentedly back to his routine.[94]

Here are the elements: sufficient perspective to judge the oppressiveness of a situation, without self-castigation, without fear of the consequences of the altered behavior; a willingness to experiment and plan for altered action; an evaluation of the effects and meaning of such alteration; and, finally, a willingness to simply abandon the change if it does not work.

Those who worked closest to Roosevelt observed his pragmatic and experimental approach to problems. Raymond Moley wrote: "Roosevelt's approach to the problems of society and the nation was essentially pragmatic. He considered serious questions with that carefree and tentative and experimental attitude which suggests a comparison with William James."[9 5] Roosevelt himself stated that he had no plans to "put our economic policy in a single systematic straightjacket."[9 6] And with this characteristically experimental attitude, he articulated the desires of his psychoclass. One individual heard Roosevelt say that "public life was a lot of sweat; but it doesn't have to worry you. You won't always be right, but you must not *suffer* from being wrong."[9 7]


EGO CONSOLIDATION

Whereas the superego consolidation of the Progressive years led to a development of social structures created largely for moral purpose, qualitative improvements of the entire structure of society in terms of the new orientations contained delegated *ego* qualities. The New Deal generally, and Roosevelt as an administrator specifically, reflects these qualities. Ego developments involved qualities of coordination, flexibility, and practicality. Historians consistently speak of the integration and organization of the Brain Trusters: "The New Deal of 1933 had rested on a faith in centralized co-ordination—on the notion that modern man must therefore produce an integrated policy."[9 8] Otis Graham, Jr. comments upon the essential differences between the older and newer generations of reformers: "A basic progressive belief was in the possibility of a conscious re-ordering and subsequent control of society and its direction, a re-ordering accomplished by a public awakened . . . backed by right values . . . Always preferring exhortation to analysis, they might well be thought of as a kind of secular clergy." Graham continues that it was up to the next generation to achieve the practicality of government functioning necessary to enact the kinds of progressive measures the early reformers could envision but only partially enact.[9 9]

Roosevelt reminisced in 1938: "By 1935 I became convinced, however, that it would take an overhauling of the entire administrative mechanism in order to make it run more efficiently and economically . . . It had become apparent that the government was becoming cluttered with a number of uncoordinated, independent units which did not fit into any organized plan."[100]

One of the achievements of aggressive education was a reduction of the authority bonding between teacher and student, parent and child. Relationships of the training psychoclass were therefore less authoritarian and less filled with transferences from the control of early authority figures. Franklin Roosevelt reflected a more advanced ability to interact with individuals than Theodore Roosevelt—finding it less necessary, for example, to constantly prove his strength.

Although Franklin Roosevelt dominated in his executive posts, especially during his Presidential years, he developed a novel sense of interaction and coordination within the government. He sought to dissolve the distance between himself and his staff as well as the general public. The famed fireside chats were a means of reaching out to people personally in a way which mitigated his awesome authority, and he communicated to his staff that he was available. As a matter of fact, he was known to purposely circumvent the White House pecking order for purposes of communicating directly with the lower tiers. The Roosevelt speech was the product of a dozen minds, each interacting and coordinated by the chief executive, who managed to derive a cohesive final product from the interaction.

Descriptions of Roosevelt in office indicate he possessed the ego quality of coordination over the superego qualities of articulating the righteous cause and polarizing positions and separating good from evil. James McGregor Burns speaks of Roosevelt's practicality and his ability to be creative in a "gadget" sense. In other words, spiritual or abstract modes of thought were not the Roosevelt contribution, but rather the pragmatic functionalism which marked the decades preceding World War II. H. Frances Perkins thought of Roosevelt as an artist but was careful to draw the distinction between the traditional and contemporary artists which may be described by the term "automism." She writes: "It describes an artist who begins his picture without a clear idea of what he intends to paint or how it should be laid out upon the canvas . . . his plan evolves out of the material of the painting." John Gunther speaks of the primacy of Roosevelt's identity as a receptor: his ability lay in coordination—again the terms of the ego—and of keeping the channels of communication open; as his authority was not inscrutable, he became approachable and was able to keep in touch with various strata of society. Likewise, Schlesinger identifies Roosevelt's success as an executive with his ability to facilitate and keep abreast of the flow of information and ideas.[101]

## THE SOFT SIDE:
## SOCIAL NURTURE AND COLLECTIVISM

Otis Graham, Jr.'s *An Encore for Reform: The Old Progressives and the New Deal* traces the basic differences between what are in this study termed control and training individuals. The old Progressives, or many of them, could not fully support the New Deal because of their ambivalence about the potential malevolence of the use of new expansion and organization, whether in the form of social welfare or extended bureaucracy. Men like Higham Johnson, William Allen White, Gifford and Amos Pinchot, and Chase Osborn could not support the New Deal as the scope of its functions increased. They feared the loss of autonomy, the encroachment of government upon rugged individuality.[102]

In 1929, in *Individualism Old and New*, John Dewey proclaimed that America was on the brink of entering the collectivist age.[103] By this, Dewey meant that social relations were becoming so intimately interrelated that what affected one affected all, that further social cooperation was a necessity in order to proceed on the path of material and cultural growth. The same writer, several years earlier, urged progressive measures in child socialization so that the child could experience more thoroughgoing peer interaction rather than the horizontal isolation of the control experience. Collectivist ideas were the natural next manifestation of the control psychoclass's urge for consolidation into large groups, coming at a time when the interdependence between these large structures was being perceived. Dewey wrote of the new social organization in 1935:

The only form of enduring social organization that is now possible is one in which the new forces of productivity are cooperatively controlled and used in the interests of the effective liberty and cultural development of the individuals that constitute society. Such a social order cannot be established by an unplanned and external convergence of the actions of separate individuals, each of whom is bent on personal private advantage. . . . Organized social planning, put

into effect for the creation of an order in which industry and
finance are socially directed . . . is now the sole method of
social action by which liberalism can realize its professional
aims.[104]

Collectivism in this sense does not necessarily apply to the private
or public ownership of property but rather to the increased
sensitivity to the successful development of all sectors of society,
and a sensitivity to the shared interests between them.

Though Rexford Tugwell believed FDR fell short of his own
concept of collectivism, FDR was particularly aware of the
necessity of a more advanced view of group interrelations than the
older consolidation view. As early as 1912, as a state senator,
Roosevelt stated: "Conditions of civilization that come with
individual freedom are inevitably bound to bring up many
questions that mere individual liberty cannot solve. We have
required new sets of conditions of life that require new theories
for their solution. . . . I have called this new theory the struggle for
the liberty of the community rather than liberty of the
individual."[105] Roosevelt's man Tugwell wrote: "Government
controls ought to be brought to bear where voluntary ones break
down, where, in fact, the interests of the public conflict with
those of a super-coordinated industry." Two economists of New
Deal temperament phrased it more succinctly: "Neither claims of
ownership nor those of control can stand against the paramount
interests of the community." FDR spoke of interdependence in
his inaugural address of 1933: "If I read the temper of our people
correctly, we now realize as we have never realized before our
interdependence on each other."[106] Leuchtenburg writes of this
stage of government activism: "For the first time for many
Americans, the federal government became an institution that was
directly experienced. More than state or local governments, it
came to be *the* government, an agency directly concerned with
their welfare."[107]

The New Deal and the years of the Roosevelt administration
sought to advance the progression towards the democratic and
creative coordination of bigness. Much of Roosevelt's language
reflects a desire for unity in Washington: he spoke of "the
realization that we are bound together by hope of a common
future" and said that "a true function of the head of the
government of the United States is to find among many discordant
elements that unity of purpose that is best for the nation as a
whole."[108]

THE HARD SIDE:
TRAINING, AGGRESSION, CONTINGENT WELFARE

A harder side of the New Deal coexisted with the softer side detailed above. The militarism which heralded in the twentieth century for America in 1898, and the mechanized warfare of the First World War, did not dissipate during the thirties. The National Recovery Administration, created by Congress in 1933, was led by General Hugh S. Johnson, "who had pictured himself as a sort of benign Mussolini presiding over the economy."[109] Calling for minimum wages and maximum working hours, the N.R.A. encouraged the display of a blue eagle symbol on the shirts of all agreeing employers. "In much the spirit of 1917, the nation participated in N.R.A. parades and rallies."[110]

Roosevelt phrased accomplishment in terms of aggressive achievement. He spoke of the "thrill of creative effort" and, in his inaugural address, said that "if we are to go forward, we must move as a trained and loyal army willing to sacrifice for the good of a common discipline, because without such discipline no progress is made."[111]

A telling reminder that training was still entrenched in the socializing mode of child-rearing is the personal experience of the symbol of training, FDR himself. Aggressive training holds to the view that the child must still make his way in the world, achieve growth through sweat and mettle. Socialization is a job, hard work, which must be accomplished by means of a sequential pattern. The nation was inspired by an individual who overcame personal infirmity. Training his body to hold up under a high-pressure schedule, FDR aggressively pushed his chin outward and attempted to triumph over his sickness every day of his existence. On one occasion, he endured a half-hour wait on his feet when President Hoover unexpectedly arrived late at a White House Governor's Conference. Some felt that Hoover, aware of the protocol requiring guests to stand in waiting, wished to test the possibly next president's endurance; Roosevelt, though in obvious pain, remained standing.[112]

The New Deal's limits on the welfare state were distinct. Just as aggressive training love was conditional to achievement, so was social nurture contingent upon individual effort. The Works Project Administration was created to allow individuals to earn their way during hard economic times. One contributes to one's social security payments by means of employment. Subsidy in any form is an unfortunate symptom of failure and the individual must at all times strive to pull himself up by his own bootstraps and make his own way, even if his work is often socially useless.

By the time a new conflict in Europe once again forced America to turn her attention to the other side of the Atlantic, a full phase of psychoclass expression had been enacted. Triumphant aggressive training had moved beyond the creations of the Progressive generation. Superego factors had moved to developments of the ego, consolidation to collectivism, the spermatic economy to new ideas of energy and government financing, the growth of government to match the scale of industry and society, and the movement toward the welfare state had begun. Yet the limitations of training became apparent. The growth of social nurture was directly proportional to the growth of the nurture of the child within the household from the controlled to training submodes. A sense of collective welfare had not moved to a point to include large subcultures of the population, such as the blacks, who gained little ground in their struggle for civil rights. The fantastic growth of bureaucracy and the sophistication of corporate and institutional structures, made possible through aggressive application of the rationality of the ego, planted the seeds of new problems—problems of conformity, homogeneity, and limitations thrust upon personal expression in a mass society. Such problems would be confronted by the rebellion of a new psychoclass, the vigorous guidance individuals, who, in their rebellion through the late forties and fifties and their short period of triumph in the mid-sixties, would also clarify the nature of the training reactive stage.

## REFERENCES

1. See Appendix.
2. The term is derived from Stephen Kern's "Explosive Intimacy: Psychodynamics of the Victorian Family," in *The New Psychohistory*, ed. Lloyd deMause (New York: Psychohistory Press, 1975), pp. 29-55.
3. Robert H. Wiebe, *The Search for Order* (New York: Hill and Wang, 1967).
4. Ibid., p. 7.
5. Ibid., pp. 228-29.
6. Ibid., p. 245.
7. Samuel P. Hays, *The Response to Industrialism, 1885-1914* (Chicago: University of Chicago Press, 1957), p. 4.
8. John Garraty, *The New Commonwealth, 1877-1890* (New York: Harper and Row, 1968), p. xiii.

9. George M. Fredrickson, *The Inner Civil War: Northern Intellectuals and the Crises of the Union* (New York: Harper and Row), p. 112.
10. Samuel Haber, "The Professions and Higher Education in America: A Historical View," in *Higher Education and the Labor Market*, ed. Margaret S. Gordon, p. 246.
11. Ibid.
12. John Higham, *The Writing of American History* (Bloomington: University of Indiana Press, 1970), p. 78.
13. Henry F. May, *The End of American Innocence* (New York: Alfred A. Knopf, 1959), p. 18.
14. Quoted by Theodore Roosevelt in "A Confession of Faith," in *The Progressive Years: The Spirit and Achievement of American Reform*, ed. Otis Pease (New York: Charles Braziller, 1962), p. 18.
15. Mark Sullivan, *Our Times: 1900-1925* (New York: Charles Scribner's Sons, 1971), p. 48.
16. James R. McGovern, "David Graham Philipps and the Virility Impulse of Progressivism," *New England Quarterly*, 39 (September 1966): 355.
17. Joe L. Dubbert, "Progressivism and the Masculinity Crisis," *Psychoanalytic Review*, November 1974.
18. Higham, *Writing of American History*, p. 78.
19. Howard K. Beale, *Theodore Roosevelt and the Rise of America to World Power* (Baltimore: John Hopkins University Press, 1956).
20. Harold U. Faukner, *Politics, Reforms and Expansion, 1890-1900* (New York: Harper and Row, 1959), pp. 278-79.
21. H. Treitschke, "The Mystique of War," in *Politics*, ed. B. Dugdale (New York: Macmillan, 1916).
22. Howard Mumford Jones, *The Age of Energy: Varieties of American Experience, 1865-1915* (New York: Viking, 1970), p. 422.
23. Ibid., p. 429.
24. Lester Ward, *Psychic Factors in Civilization* (Boston: Ginn, 1892).
25. Charles Horton Cooley, *Human Nature and the Social Order* (New York: Schocken, 1902).
26. Taylor quoted in Otis Graham, Jr., *The Great Campaigns: Reform qnd War in America, 1900-1928* Englewood Cliffs, N.J.: Prentice-Hall, 1971), p. 241.
27. *The New Nationalism: Theodore Roosevelt* (Englewood Cliffs: Prentice-Hall, 1961), pp. 15, 68; Theodore Roosevelt, "The Conservation of Natural Resources," *Proceedings of a Conference of Governors in the White House* (Washington: Government Printing Office, 1909).

28. Samuel Haber, *Efficiency and Uplift: Scientific Management in the Progressive Era, 1890-1920* (Chicago: University of Chicago Press, 1964), pp. ix-x.
29. Robert Wiebe, *Businessmen and Reform: A Study of the Progressive Movement* (Cambridge: Harvard University Press, 1962), p. 9.
30. David W. Noble, *The Paradox of Progressive Thought* (Minneapolis: University of Minnesota Press, 1958), p. 65.
31. William James, "The Will to Believe," in *American Thought: Civil War to WWI*, ed. Perry Miller (New York, Holt, Rinehart & Winston, 1954), p. 158.
32. Beale, *Theodore Roosevelt*, pp. 48, 50.
33. William Henry Harbaugh, *The Life and Times of Theodore Roosevelt* (New York: Collier, 1961), p. 105.
34. Gerald F. Linderman, *The Mirror of War: American Society and the Spanish-American War* (Ann Arbor: University of Michigan Press, 1974), p. 96.
35. John Morton Blum, *The Republican Roosevelt* (Cambridge: Harvard University Press, 1954), p. 161.
36. Henry F. Pringle, *Theodore Roosevelt* (New York: Harcourt, Brace & World, 1956).
37. William James in Pease, *Progressive Years*, pp. 486-90.
38. Elting Morison, ed., *The Letters of Theodore Roosevelt*, vol. 1 (Cambridge: Harvard University Press, 1954), p. 717.
39. Jacob A. Riis, *Theodore Roosevelt the Citizen* (New York: Grosset and Dunlap, 1903), p. 182.
40. Corinne Roosevelt Robinson, *My Brother Theodore Roosevelt* (New York: Charles Scribner's Sons, 1921), p. 278.
41. Morison, *Letters*, 5:721.
42. Beale, *Theodore Roosevelt*, p. 50.
43. Joseph Bishop, ed., *Theodore Roosevelt's Letters to His Children* (New York: Charles Scribner's Sons, 1919), p. 94.
44. Pocket diary of Theodore Roosevelt, April-November, 1909, Harvard University.
45. Blum, *Republican Roosevelt*, pp. 26-40.
46. Ibid., p. 126.
47. Joseph Gardner, *Departing Glory: Theodore Roosevelt as Ex-President* (Charles Scribner's Sons, 1973), p. 221.
48. John Dewey, "Theodore Roosevelt," *Dial*, February 8, 1919.
49. Ibid.
50. Owen Wister, *Roosevelt: The Story of a Friendship* (New York: Macmillan Co., 1930), p. 16.
51. Theodore Roosevelt, *The Strenuous Life* (New York: Century Co., 1902), p. 26.

52. Ibid., p. 317.
53. Lawrence A. Abbott, *Impressions of TR* (New York: Doubleday, 1924), p. 259; Theodore Roosevelt, *The Works of Theodore Roosevelt*, ed. Hermann Hagedorn, vol. 5 (New York: Charles Scribner's Sons, 1926), pp. xvii-xviii.
54. Edward Wagenknecht, *The Seven Worlds of Theodore Roosevelt* (New York: Longmans, Green, and Co., 1958), pp. 107-8.
55. Lawrence A. Abbott, ed., *The Letters of Archie Butt* (New York: Doubleday, 1924), p. 233.
56. Wister, *Roosevelt*, p. 8.
57. James E. Amos, *TR: Hero to His Valet* (New York: John Day, 1927).
58. Frederick S. Wood, *Roosevelt As We Knew Him* (Philadelphia: John C. Winston, 1927).
59. Donald Day, ed., *Woodrow Wilson's Own Story* (Boston: Little, Brown & Co., 1952), p. 148.
60. Gardner, *Departing Glory*.
61. James Weinstein, *The Corporate Ideal in the Liberal State, 1900-1918* (Boston: Beacon Press, 1968), p. 162.
62. Arthur M. Schlesinger, Jr., *The Age of Roosevelt: The Crisis of the Old Order, 1919-1933* (Boston: Houghton Mifflin, 1957), p. 22.
63. Ibid., p. 33.
64. E. David Conan, ed., *The Political Thought of Woodrow Wilson* (Bobbs-Merrill Co., 1965), p. 23; Woodrow Wilson, *The New Freedom* (Englewood Cliffs, N.J.: Prentice-Hall, 1961), p. 101.
65. *The Autobiography of Theodore Roosevelt* (New York: Macmillan, 1913), p. 628.
66. May, *American Innocence*, p. 18.
67. Day, *Wilson's Own Story;* Rear Admiral Cary T. Grayson, *Woodrow Wilson: An Intimate Memoir* (New York: Holt, Rinehart, & Winston, 1959).
68. John Morton Blum, *Woodrow Wilson and the Politics of Morality* (Boston: Little, Brown & Co., 1956), p. 84.
69. Ibid., p. 197.
70. E. M. Bowles Alsop, ed., *The Greatness of Woodrow Wilson* (New York: Rinehart & Co., 1956), p. 83.
71. Wilson, *The New Freedom*.
72. Alexander and Juliette George, *Woodrow Wilson and Colonel House* (New York: John Day, 1956).
73. Arthur S. Link, ed., *Woodrow Wilson: A Profile* (New York: Hill and Wang, 1968), p. 81.

74. Conan, *Political Thought*, p. 13.
75. Wilson, *The New Freedom;* Woodrow Wilson, *On Being Human* (New York: Harper, 1916), pp. 12, 51.
76. Wilson, *The New Freedom.*
77. Arthur S. Link, *A History of the United States Since the 1890's,* vol. 1 (New York: Alfred A. Knopf, 1955); see also Woodrow Wilson, *When a Man Comes to Himself* (New York: Harper & Bros., 1901).
78. For an idea of the potential of the psychogenic approach to war-as-birth, see Lloyd deMause, "The Independence of Psychohistory," in *The New Psychohistory.*
79. Woodrow Wilson, *The Hope of the World* (New York: Harper and Bros., 1920), p. 103.
80. Woodrow Wilson, "The New Freedom," in *A Crossroads of Freedom* ed. John W. Davidson (New Haven: Yale University Press, 1956), p. 381.
81. George and George, *Wilson.*
82. James David Barber, *The Presidential Character: Predicting Performance in the White House* (Englewood Cliffs: Prentice-Hall, 1972), p. 45.
83. Ibid.
84. George and George, *Wilson.*
85. Grayson, *Wilson;* George and George, *Wilson.*
86. Jules Abels, *In the Time of Silent Cal* (New York: G. P. Putnam's Sons, 1969), p. 66.
87. Andrew Sinclair, *Era of Excess* (New York: Harper, 1964); John D. Hicks, *Republican Ascendancy* (New York: Harper, 1960); William Allen White, *A Puritan in Babylon* (New York: Macmillan, 1938); Roderick Nash, *The Nervous Generation* (Chicago: Rand, McNally).
88. Clarke A. Chambers, *Seedtime of Reform* (Ann Arbor: University of Michigan Press, 1967); Arthur Link, "What Happened to the Progressive Movement in the 1920's?" *American Historical Review* 64 (July 1959).
89. Otis Graham, Jr., *The New Deal: The Critical Issues* (Boston: Little, Brown & Co., 1971); Daniel Snowman, *America Since 1920* (New York: Harper and Row, 1968).
90. William E. Leuchtenburg, *Franklin D. Roosevelt and the New Deal* (New York: Harper and Row, 1963).
91. Arthur M. Schlesinger, Jr., *The Age of Roosevelt: The Politics of Upheaval* (Cambridge: Houghton Mifflin, 1960).
92. Snowman, *America.*
93. Barber, *Presidential Character.*
94. Ibid., p. 213.
95. Raymond Moley, *The First New Deal* (New York: Harcourt,

Brace & World, 1966), p. 5.
96. Carl N. Degler, ed., *The New Deal* (Chicago: Quadrangle, 1970), p. 18.
97. Rexford G. Tugwell, *In Search of Roosevelt* (Cambridge: Harvard University Press, 1972), p. 305.
98. Schlesinger, *Upheaval*, p. 212.
99. Otis Graham, Jr., *An Encore for Reform: The Old Progressives and the New Deal* (New York: Oxford University Press, 1967).
100. *The Public Papers of Franklin D. Roosevelt* (New York: Random House, 1938), pp. 183-84.
101. James McGregor Burns, *Roosevelt: The Lion and the Fox* (New York: Harcourt, Brace & Co., 1956), p. 244; Frances Perkins, *The Roosevelt I Knew* (New York: Viking Press, 1946), p. 163; John Gunther, *Roosevelt in Retrospect* (New York: Harper and Row, 1950), p. 3; Arthur M. Schlesinger, Jr., *The Age of Roosevelt: The Coming of the New Deal* (Boston: Houghton Mifflin, 1959), p. 522; Arthur A. Erich, Jr., *The Impact of New Deal Thought on America* (Chicago: Quadrangle Books, 1969).
102. Graham, *Encore.*
103. Schlesinger, *Crisis*, pp. 131-32.
104. Howard Zinn, ed., *New Deal Thought* (New York: Bobbs-Merrill, 1966), p. xxvii.
105. Daniel Fusfeld, *The Economic Thought of Franklin D. Roosevelt* (New York: Columbia University Press, 1954).
106. Ibid.; Alfred B. Rollins, Jr., ed., *Depression, Recovery and War* (New York: McGraw Hill, 1966), p. 65.
107. Leuchtenburg, *Roosevelt*, p. 331.
108. Thomas H. Greer, *What Roosevelt Thought: The Social and Political Ideas of Franklin D. Roosevelt* (Michigan State University Press, 1958), p. 30.
109. Frank Freidel, *America in the Twentieth Century* (New York: Alfred A. Knopf, 1965).
110. Ibid.
111. Rollins, *Depression*, p. 65.
112. See also Elliot A. Rosen, "Roosevelt and the Brain Trust: A Historiographical Overview," *Political Science Quarterly* December 1972; Greer, *What Roosevelt Thought;* Walter Lippmann, *Drift and Mastery* (New York: Kennerly, 1914); James Truslow Adams, *Our Business Civilization: Some Aspects of American Culture* (New York: Albert and Charles Boni, 1929); Rexford G. Tugwell, *FDR: Architect of an Era* (New York: Macmillan, 1967); Edgar Eugene Robinson, *The*

*Roosevelt Leadership, 1933-1945* (Philadelphia: Lippincott, 1955); Frank Friedel, *The New Deal and the American People* (Englewood Cliffs, N.J.: Prentice-Hall, 1964); Morton Frisch, *Franklin D. Roosevelt: The Contribution of the New Deal to American Political Thought and Practice* (Boston: Twayne, 1975).

CHAPTER SEVEN


THE GREAT SOCIETY AND THE YOUTH REVOLT


This final chapter seeks to illustrate the proposition that the two most recent periods in the American twentieth century are expressions of guidance and release psychoclasses. The nature of this task necessitates a relatively brief chapter for several reasons. First, because we are dealing with the recent past and vital documents remain either unavailable or uncollected, few definitive works which seek to define these periods yet exist. Second, and more important, the release psychoclass is still in the midst of its rebellious phase, and it is therefore impossible to trace the completion of its cycle of historical expression.

A third limitation further narrows the scope of this chapter. The psychohistorical study of foreign affairs is a more complex area than the psychohistory of domestic concerns, a complexity which is made all the more difficult because of the relatively unexplored nature of the field. It is already clear, though, that international relations involve dynamics the origins of which reach to the earliest existences of the individuals involved, dynamics originating as early as birth and prenatal phenomenon.[1] Compounding this complexity is the fact that each nation comes to the international arena with its own particular psychoclass composition and history. Therefore, any attempt to periodize America which is inclusive of foreign policy and international relations would be premature.

We can, however, complete the broad periodization of postwar domestic America, and, in the process, observe some complex psychogenic phenomena. First, we may observe the interaction of up to three psychoclasses during one period of time (the late Johnson administration), and second, we may witness conflicting submodal dynamics within the psyche of one individual. Lyndon Johnson presents the case of internal psychic composition of training and guidance qualities, two elements which, it will be seen, did not combine into a unique compound, but rather remained distinct and independently operative within Johnson's mind.

## I.  TOWARDS THE GREAT SOCIETY

### THE TRUMAN YEARS: REACTIVE TRAINING

Upon cursory examination, much of the Truman administration distinguishes itself from the progressive reforms of the New Deal. Truman proposed programs which went a step beyond the New Deal and which seemed to approach at least the verbal or rhetorical expression of dynamics associated with the third submode, vigorous guidance. These programs included abandoning the geneticism and racism of training in favor of proposing civil rights legislation and humane immigration laws, and expanding social nurture by means of national health insurance and federal aids to education as well as in an increased minimum wage. Truman received high scores in Arthur Schlesinger, Jr.'s Presidential rating polls.[2] Some writers attribute positive qualities to the tone and quality of his administration. Cabell Phillips labels the Truman Presidency the "triumphant succession."[3] One textbook asserts that Truman's Fair Deal deserves to be rated on its own terms, that it is distinct in many respects from the New Deal. Several writers associate positive verbal images and phrases with the Truman years such as "Decade of Triumph" or "The Best Years." The post-war years include "shared joy" in the triumph of American values over European fascism and a "rare sense of national unity and superiority."[4]

Yet conflicting and more convincing information associates the Truman administration with the New Deal and places it, therefore, within the reactive phase of the second, or training, mode. Although no psychohistorical work has yet been completed concerning Truman as an individual, he was born in 1884 and is therefore unlikely to have experienced an extremely advanced childhood which would adumbrate vigorous guidance. Truman's innovative support of civil rights and increased welfare nurture (health insurance and a higher minimum wage) may be seen within the context of the reaction phase. By 1950, the oldest guidance individuals were forty, and therefore just entering the political power structure. Truman might have gone as far as to give verbal support to their views, yet the President did not represent a psychic constituency which was able and willing to *institute* such ideals.

The most convincing documentation places Truman and his administration in a reaction phase. Writers stress the lack of faith Truman, as well as the American people, felt in his ability to carry the banner of the fallen Roosevelt. I. F. Stone remarked, "Truman was a man without faith in himself, surrounded by men without real faith in American society."[5] Stone emphasized that Truman was simply a Roosevelt man, but without the latter's power: "The manner was that of a dutiful schoolboy, repeating a lesson letter-perfect but only half understood. Where FDR would have said 'we can and must' with magnetic fire, Mr. Truman said it with a rehearsed lilt . . . . That subtle emanation of spirit, the quality of leadership, just wasn't there."[6] Goulden wrote: "Many of the Roosevelt people treated the new President as somewhat of a bumpkin unworthy of the Rooseveltian mantle; their intrinsic loyalty was not to Truman, but to FDR's programs and ideals. The Trumanites, for their part, bridled at the notion that any decision must be prefaced by the question, 'What would President Roosevelt have done?"[7] Cabell Phillips relates that Truman was initially looked upon as a sort of "caretaker President," even by those on his staff.[8] Another remarked that while an FDR fireside chat seldom evoked less than a tounsand letters, in January, 1946, when Truman denounced Congress for failing to approve key parts of his economic program on national radio, fewer than a hundred letters from citizens around the country resulted. Historian George E. Mowry observed the omnipresence of the Roosevelt image: "Truman fairly peppered his speeches with references to his immediate predecessor—'the greatest president this country has ever had.' " In 1948 in Omaha, Truman spoke to a crowd of 1,000 in a stadium with a seating capacity of 12,000.[9]

Truman was not an unsuccessful President, as the first months of his administration might have portended. The election of 1948 illustrates that Truman was successful in his role as a reaction phase President, preserving rather than qualitatively altering the innovations of the New Deal. The unexpected though marginal defeat of Dewey gave Truman leverage, but this strength never reached the potency necessary for instituting structural reforms. During the early stages of the campaign a *New York Star* editorial showed Truman as a battered but as yet undefeated individual holding a flickering "Liberal torch of FDR."[10] I. F. Stone felt that Truman's "get-tough" policy was a mask for his own insecurity, camouflage for his own surprise at having retained power.[11]

A close Truman associate described vividly the effects of Truman's victory:

> Something happened between Truman's first and second terms that is hard to pin down. There was a change of atmosphere around the White House, a subtle change in the relationship . . . . we were all playing it pretty much by ear. There wasn't much pressure from the outside, from the lobbies and the special interests . . . . They looked on him as just a sort of caretaker President, and they didn't expect him to run for a full term. He seemed for a time to reflect that sort of attitude, too.
>
> And then came the 1948 election, and—my God!—how cocky he was after that . . . . Now he was all bustle and decisiveness and full of big plans, and to hell with the details. This was going to be *his* administration, and he was going to put the Fair Deal right up there in history in letters as big as the New Deal.
>
> But now the outside pressures began to close in on him and on us . . . . it was a new mood and a new climate, and in a way Mr. Truman was a captive of it.[12]

In other words, the sense of triumph was transient, more a momentary flash of confidence than the onset of a new climate. Journalist Joseph Goulden felt that Truman's victory did not vindicate him from the criticisms of Walter Lippmann, who urged him not to run. Highlighting the lack of enthusiasm for Truman was the light voter turn-out. Goulden emphasized that electoral victory was only a "fleeting respite" from mounting factionalism and that Truman was beset by a series of shocks in 1949 such as the concession of China to the Communists and the announcement of the Soviet atom bomb, shocks which ignited a "turbulent bitterness" in America.[13]

In contrast to Truman's vigorous and aggressive personal manner, the record of his domestic administration is described by most writers in terms of either standing still or preserving the New Deal. One observer takes an extreme position: "All his skills and energies ... were directed to standing still ... Where he took vigorous action in one direction, it was axiomatic that he would contrive soon afterward to move in the conflicting direction." Harvard Sitkoff remarks that Truman's seemingly innovative stances on civil rights never moved beyond the level of rhetoric.[14] The editors of a collection of documentary materials on the Truman administration conclude that the Fair Deal, Truman's domestic program, must be judged a failure. After close to eight years in office, Truman could point to only a few tangible domestic accomplishments such as executive orders ending discrimination in the armed services and federal government, a public housing act, a rise in the minimum wage, and a social security measure. The editors add: "But his boldest proposals were ignored, or defeated by Congress."[15] Civil rights legislation, health insurance, agricultural reorganization, immigration laws and aid to education fell through. "His achievements, then," summarized one writer, "seem mainly negative. In a conservative era he helped prevent the repeal of the New Deal and preserved a vision of mild welfare capitalism."[16]

Although Cabell Phillips endorses Truman's measures in foreign policy such as European recovery, NATO, the Berlin airlift, his policy of containment in Korea and the Truman Doctrine, he concedes that Truman did not inspire anyone and that "his tenure, moreover, was the least tranquil, the most bedeviled by partisan strife of any President since Andrew Johnson."[17] Another historian concludes that the Truman years were a haphazard completion of leftover jobs from the New Deal, and that the Fair Deal suffers in comparison with the New Deal and the Great Society.[18]

The eightieth Congress is described as waiting with whetted knives for a lame duck President ready for carving. Eric Goldman feels that when Truman acted, he acted along a "wavering line." Truman's loyalties were torn between the progressive measures of the New Deal and a desire to work with a more conservative Congress. The Truman climate is described as uncongenial to the brightest and most idealistic young intellectuals, a group who swarmed to the Roosevelt administration.[19]

A consensus concerning the national mood of the late forties emerges from the literature. Phillips uses words such as "perplexity" and "fretfulness" and phrases such as "dissatisfaction with things as they were and no clear image of what they ought to be" to describe the overriding mood.[20] Arthur S. Link writes: "Not in many years had the American political scene seemed so confused as during the period between the end of the Second

World War and the elections of 1952."[21] Individuals were filled with a sense of loss, both of lost years and wasted energies, as a result of the war. *Fortune* supported the notion of the Truman period as a reactive era when it concluded in 1949 that the primary tone in the schools was an aversion to taking risks and a "passion for security."[22] Another writer uses the term "mood maybe."[23]

The following comment perfectly summarizes Truman's identity as the successful *reactive* President:

> He was no Roosevelt who, like Moses, led his people through the desert of the depression and the trials of war toward an awareness of their social and international responsibilities. Truman's contribution was rather to be a Joshua, the faithful lieutenant who, after the prophet's meeting with his God and the proclamation of the Tables of the Law, undertook the applications of them.[24]

The complexities of conflicting interpretations of Truman—as weak or strong, as a success or a failure—may thus be resolved by means of the psychogenic cycle. Truman was not a triumphant President, but he did successfully fulfill his reactive role within his stage of the psychogenic cycle. A staunch member of the aggressive training psychoclass, he preserved the contributions of the New Deal, secure in his identity, determined in his actions.

THE 1950s

At this juncture in tracing the psychogenic basis of the periodization of twentieth-century America, we should make note of a particular arithmetical consistency. Just as individuals rarely reach the highest positions of power in American political culture before their late forties, so the triumphant expression of a psychoclass cannot take place until at least its oldest members reach this period in their lives. The oldest control individuals were about fifty in 1900, the oldest training individuals were about fifty in 1930, and in the 1950s, the oldest guidance individuals were only in their forties. As theory predicts, the guidance psychoclass did not make its triumphant mark upon these years but rather in the early 1960s. Because the concern here is with periodization, isolating the triumphant phase of each psychoclass, analysis of the rebellious phase of guidance individuals in the 1950s—expressing themselves in the arts, the world of ideas, and the most liberal wing of the Stevenson followers—will be left in favor of a discussion of those who did dominate Washington and succeeded in carrying forth the reactive period to its conclusion, an order which centered around one individual: Dwight D. Eisenhower.

Most analyses of the fifties overtly or tacitly include the General as a pivotal figure, if not the symbol of the age. It is logical that this training individual who would take up the role of guarding the political order came from the ranks of the modern armed services. Just as much of the New Deal was flavored with military images and concepts—from the NRA to American mobilization at the onset of World War II—an individual without the control lust for battle, but with the training sense of coordination and organization, flavored the 1950s with the military products of the training submode.

Writers concerned with Eisenhower's significance note the fact that his elevation to power was a natural phenomenon of the times, or simply necessary.[25] Arthur S. Link called him the "standard American." To some, Eisenhower's personality was suited to a "holding period." Phrased negatively, his "leadership was put in the service of drift, a man travelling all the time yet going nowhere." Others state that the Eisenhower Presidency neither lost nor gained anything, a verdict likewise applicable to a period which is commonly considered an interstice, neither a move backwards nor forwards. Eisenhower symbolized the "middle-of-the-road" and served to establish "equilibrium."[26] John Gunther, in *Eisenhower: The Man and the Symbol*, emphasized Eisenhower's coordinating abilities, and his talent for conciliation, qualities remarked upon before in reference to the ego consolidation of aggressive training.[27]

Eisenhower should not, however, be placed psychogenically before Roosevelt, and here again, the dynamics of evolution are crucial. Although Eisenhower adhered to the New Deal doctrines, he was considered a conservative while Roosevelt gains historical identity as a liberal. The reality is that the training task had already been innovated and instituted; therefore, the expression of training by the 1950's became a conserving function. Reaction Presidents hold the function of preservation and caretaking, and make the attempt to strike a posture of repose and respectability. The further in time a reactive President comes to office from the triumphant expression of his psychoclass, the more conservative is his function.

There is a consensus in the historical literature as to the relatively slight effect of the Eisenhower years upon the evolution of America, and one's judgment of this reality is colored by one's individual propensity to be thankful when conditions get no worse, or do not degenerate. Images describing Eisenhower and his times inevitably relate to the fact that he refused to move forward. Descriptions of the Eisenhower administration and period, then, are fulled with the imagery of stasis. The *New York Post*'s William W. Shannon remarked: "The Eisenhower years have been years of flabbiness and self-satisfaction and gross materialism . . . . [The] loudest sound in the land has been the oink-and-grunt of private hoggishness." Another writer applied similar imagery of inactivity and softness: "We meander along in a stupor of fat . . . Probably the climate of the 'Fifties' was the dullest and dreariest in all our history." In less derogatory terms, yet remarking upon the general reactive nature of the period, Reinhold Neibuhr observed that Eisenhower symbolized the nation's "complacency."[28] Also describing the lack of innovation in nonderogatory terms, Arthur Schlesinger, Jr. felt that "Eisenhower symbolized and expressed a national desire for repose. Any activist President would have encountered great difficulties in the 1950s . . . The fifties were certainly a time when the cycle was in a phase of quiescence."[29]

William V. Shannon, probably better than any other single writer, summarizes the nature of the 1950s as an interstice in the periodization of twentieth-century America (and therefore places it squarely in the reactive phase of aggressive training). Shannon writes:

> He had not shaped the future nor tried to repeal the past. He has not politically organized nor intellectually defined a new consensus . . . . No national problems, whether it be education, housing, urban revitalization, agriculture, or inflation, will have been advanced importantly toward solution nor its dimensions significantly altered. The Eisenhower era is the time of the great postponement.[30]

On another occasion Shannon observed that "Eisenhower and his administration have lived off the accumulated wisdom, the accumulated prestige, and the accumulated military strength of his predecessors.[31] Walter Lippmann's comment concerning a general societal climate is equally applicable to the administration in Washington: "for the time being our people do not have great purposes which they feel united in wanting to achieve. The public mood of the country is defensive, to hold on to and to conserve. We talk about ourselves these days as if we were a completed society, one which has achieved its purposes, and has no further business to transact."[32] Any efforts at innovation—few as they were—were muddled and confused, as if innovation was no longer within Presidential jurisdiction. Accepting that the New Deal and the Fair Deal were here to stay, any policy besides their preservation within an aggressive training concept of a modest budget was unacceptable and made the administration and the country uneasy.

The lack of innovation in Eisenhower's administration is evident in many areas, but the situation is especially apparent in the administration's failure to find a telling label analogous to the New Deal or the Fair Deal. Terms such as "dynamic conservatism," "progressive, dynamic conservatism," "progressive moderation," "moderate progressivism," and "positive progressivism" were attempted but faded away because of their lack of emotional meaning. Aggressive training had found its expression in the triumphant reordering of society in the 1930s, and it was granted its preservation in the late 1940s and the 1950s. By the mid-1950s, its ethos had reached the middle-of-the-road.

## THE VIGOROUS GUIDANCE PSYCHOCLASS

The broader implications of the third submodal childhood experience of vigorous guidance prove as manageable and lucid as the social implications of the control and training submodes. The major innovations of vigorous guidance, previously described in detail, may be summarized as follows: (1) The new psychology, fueled by the breakthroughs of psychoanalysis and developing concepts in sociology, accepts primary drives as natural and presents the notion of developmental distortion supplementing the more widely accepted unsuccessful repression model of neurosis. (2) Autonomy and individuality are stressed in child-rearing and in psychological developmental systems. (3) Child sexuality is less feared, and considered in greatest probability not harmful, though still not a positive good. (4) Institutional and familial developments point to a more nurturing childhood, in which the child's wishes gain in importance. (5) Montessori's innovations, as well as the innovations of progressive education, stress manipulation of the environment in order to encourage the child's self-development. (6) On the vigorous or hard side of guidance, more refined standards of achievement and the association of self-worth with the mastery of tasks appear. (7) Progress and achievements continue to be related to discipline and work, and even play is conceptualized in terms of development. (8) The child is seen to hold potentialities rather than more rigid genetic traits which may be developed and guided through the proper environmental catalysis.

The corresponding psychoclass reactions on the group scale may be summarized as follows: (1) Environmental sensitivity to the child produces, on the social scale, an increased sensitivity to the environmental means of increasing social nurture. (2) The ethos of individual effort and achievement leads to a more consistent establishment of status according to abilities. (3) Dissolution of the fear of sexuality leads to a more flexible view of energy and the related area of economic and fiscal policy. Because the spermatic economy is left far behind, and the body is no longer seen as a closed system of energy, new energy sources may be tapped both internally (within the body) and externally (natural resources, synthetic resources, and the manipulation of fiscal policies). The result is further protection against severe and sudden economic-energistic collapse. (4) More nurture and empathy within the family leads to increased nurture and empathy on the social scale. The step beyond the ethic that those who work deserve sustenance (e.g., the New Deal's Work Projects Administration) is the belief that if individuals are given the opportunities they will be naturally productive. Social measures, therefore, are apt to project earlier and deeper into individual life in areas such as education and homelife. (5) Because of the belief in the efficacy of environmental alteration in improving the behavior of individuals, institutional-bureaucratic measures are emphasized. (6) The new status based upon performance leads to more subtle means of furthering personal influence within corporate culture. (7) The abandonment of the genetic view of development in favor of the belief in innate potentialities allows for further democratization of culture, and a new ability of a psychoclass to further civil rights and a more general equality of opportunity.

The following pages will show how two Presidents who developed within environments which contained guidance elements expressed these very same dynamics on the political scale.

## KENNEDY AND JOHNSON: ABBREVIATED TRIUMPHANT GUIDANCE AND EXTERNALIZED TRAINING

The analysis of the Kennedy/Johnson years allows for a special view of the expression of vigorous guidance. Yet the guidance cycle did not achieve the clarity of expression of the cycles of control and training. Two factors were responsible for this. First, John F. Kennedy was assassinated after a mere thousand days in office. This event makes a full reckoning of the meaning of Kennedy's administration from the perspective of hard achievements almost impossible. When the same time frame is imposed upon the administrations of Abraham Lincoln and Franklin Roosevelt, much of their greatness is lost. Psychogenic examination of Kennedy, then, must be based on the quality of his leadership and the promises and spirit he successfully communicated and spoke for. Secondly, the problem of submodal combination is evident in both Presidents. Both Kennedy and Johnson received differential care from their mother and father, guidance centering around the mother and training centering around the father. Both of these men split their functioning, producing a schism between training foreign policy behavior and guidance behavior in domestic concerns. Because, as previously mentioned, foreign policy is an even more complex subject than the combination of submodes within individuals, and the purpose of this section is the periodization of domestic America, the more advanced sides of these men will be emphasized. The training sides of Johnson and Kennedy will be brought into discussion only when they clearly impeded the development of the Presidents' domestic goals. The term abbreviated triumphant. guidance is applied precisely because the guidance psychoclass experienced a relatively short duration of triumph. The tragedy behind the experience of the two Presidents, and ultimately a generation of Americans, is that the less advanced foreign policy behavior came to infect or swamp the more advanced domestic actions. In the case of Kennedy, a web of international Cold Warism brought the nation to the nuclear brink after the Bay of Pigs, and his entanglements in Cuba may someday even prove to be related to his assassination. In the case of Johnson, an expensive and unwanted war thwarted the most thorough and elevated programs of structural reforms in American history.

Entirely aside from the issue and ideology articulated by John F. Kennedy and its relation to vigorous guidance is the spirit and enthusiasm which he generated, a spirit which is symptomatic of the emergence of a psychoclass into the triumphant phase. Not since Franklin Roosevelt had a political personality generated such enthusiasm. One textbook indicates, "From its advent, the Presidency exuded brilliance and excitement. Innovative new approaches . . . stirred the public's imagination."[33] The authors conclude, "However history judges his success as a President, John

F. Kennedy set a tone and a style that signified the coming to political maturity of a new generation."[34] Adlai Stevenson likewise characterized Kennedy as "the contemporary man" who possessed "profound modernity."[35] Observers foraged for applicable words to describe his effect and came up with the nebulous concept of "charisma" to describe the intensity of his exhilirating effect on individuals and groups.[36]

The *New Republic* concluded in March of 1961 that "Washington is crackling, rocking, jumping." Arthur Schlesinger, Jr. observed, "The New Frotier gospel of criticism and hope stirred the finest instincts of the young; it restored a sense of renovation and adventure to the republic." John Morton Blum summarizes the tone of the Kennedy administration independently of the contextual policies involved: "In his brief thousand days in the Presidency, he had done much to wipe away the world's impression of his country as an old nation of old men, weary, played out, fearful of ideas, everywhere committed to the status quo, and had revived the idea of America as a young, questioning, progressive land, facing the future with confidence and hope." James David Barber summarizes: "[Kennedy] did manage to express for the nation . . . that we had become too easy, too soft, had drifted long enough."[37] Schlesinger remarks: "Euphoria reigned; we thought for a moment that the world was plastic and the future unlimited."[38]

Kennedy possessed all the qualities of style of the triumphant President. Theodore Sorensen, who many called Kennedy's alter-ego, remarked upon Kennedy's love of the job, but not simply out of the mere fulfillment of a drive for power: "He enjoyed the Presidency, thinking not of its power but of its opportunities." Kennedy is already cemented into the textbooks with the image as a "youthful, vigorous, and confident leader."[39] James David Barber stresses that Kennedy successfully expressed that the nation had drifted for long enough and had become soft, and was ready and in severe need of a new beginning.[40]

Despite his actual behavior and accomplishment, Kennedy successfully projected an image of a strong President ready to begin a new epoch in American history. While campaigning, he told his listeners: "We stand today on the edge of a New Frontier: the frontier of the 1960's, a frontier of unknown opportunities and paths, a frontier of unfulfilled hopes and threats . . . . The New Frontier of which I speak . . . [is] a set of challenges . . . . I believe that the time demands invention, innovation, imagination, decision. I am asking each of you to be new pioneers in that New Frontier."[41] Kennedy stated in his inaugural address, "We observe today not a victory of party but a celebration of freedom, symbolizing an end as well as a beginning."[42] One of Kennedy's sentences included: "striving, risking, choosing, making decisions, engaging in a pursuit of happiness that is strenuous, heroic, exciting and exalted"—language of triumph and construction. Kennedy proclaimed, "There is a new world to be won."[43]

Even though Kennedy's tenure was abbreviated, and even though he received enough paternal training early experience which found expression in foreign policy actions, many of the major facets of vigorous guidance are present in Kennedy's administration. First, when Kennedy implored his fellow countrymen to go forth with "vigah," he appealed to the vigorous guidance notions of achievement. Unlike the moralistic drive of control, or the overtly competitive strivings of training, guidance achievement was based on a new sense of individuality, autonomy and expansiveness. While the quest for space exploration was overtly competitive vis-à-vis the Russians (most international behavior operates on the level of lower psychogenic modes), within the United States, the task was filled with a feeling of freedom. Henry Fairlie writes: "For three years after 20 January 1961, the American people were persuaded that, metaphorically as well as literally, they could shoot for the moon."[44] Although Kennedy invoked the image of Woodrow Wilson when he spoke of achievement, the races of the 1960s were quite secular. When Kennedy was questioned about his desire to reach the moon, he did not answer in terms of the moral necessity but rather in terms of the creativity involved, and the significance of man's almost unlimited capacities for achievement.[45]

If the space quest was turned into a race for preferred military positions, or if nuclear holocaust became a lurking threat, the problem would not be so much a moral problem as a failure in *reason.*[46] Schlesinger summarized the ego qualities of Kennedy using adjectives such as "projective, practical, ironic, skeptical, unfettered, and insatiable." Schlesinger's poll of historians' ratings of the Presidents placed Kennedy as first in the quality of flexibility.[47]

The President gathered a staff as impressive in their personal achievements as the heights to which Kennedy aspired. It was an administration dominated by men of ideas from the university and foundation, rather than the business community as was the case during the 1950s, and the staff had a low median age and a high median energy level. Men including Robert Kennedy, Theodore Sorensen, Arthur Schlesinger, Jr., and Pierre Salinger formed a body of talent which would come to be labeled the "best and the brightest," a group which could easily challenge FDR's brain trust.

Evelyn Lincoln, Kennedy's personal secretary, remarked that the greatest single blow to Kennedy during the years she was with him occurred upon the death of his infant son. The secretary writes with insight that "It wasn't so much grief for his own son, but for a potential which would never be realized."[4][8]

Because fuller expression of guidance dynamics did not come until the early years of the Johnson administration, much of its detail must await a discussion of Kennedy's successor. Yet, even in Kennedy's thousand days, he evidenced a desire to move in two central and vital guidance areas. First, the abandonment of the spermatic economy in full held new potentials for government fiscal and economic policy. I. F. Stone remarked that "The real lesson of the Roosevelt period was that the Keynesian approach was not enough."[4][9] FDR's use of the concept of deficit spending was always rationalized as a necessary evil, an embarrassment which must be resorted to much as the emergency measures of the planned wartime economy. But Kennedy never voiced a commitment to a balanced budget. In his message to Congress in February of 1961, he proudly declared: "This administration is pledged to a Federal revenue system that balances the budget over the years of the economic cycle, yielding surpluses of debt in times of high employment that more than offset deficits which accompany, and indeed help overcome, low levels of economic activity over the years."[5][0] Thus, a new view of the economy had been reached, replacing the Roosevelt-Truman-Eisenhower embarrassments over deficits by the manipulation of the budget as a means of economic stimulus and growth. He added: "The programs I an now proposing will not by themselves unbalance the budget . . . but are designed to fulfill our responsibility to alleviate distress and speed recovery."[5][1]

Related to Kennedy's fiscal measures is a new aura surrounding the man himself involving Kennedy's sexuality and energies. Although the question of extramarital sexual relations was not applicable only to Kennedy, the President's magnetism was related to an overt affirmation of his sexual identity. He enjoyed the screaming teenage girls, and evidenced none of the guilt over his lapses in personal morality which plagued Franklin Roosevelt's relationship with Lucy Mercer. While sexual matters were unmentionable in speech and highly guarded in conduct to the control President Theodore Roosevelt, and sensuality was an embarrassment to the training President Franklin Roosevelt, President Kennedy could proudly appear on stage with Marilyn Monroe as she wrapped her arms around him and alluringly wished him a happy birthday. This pattern of development is consistent with the evolution of views of child sexuality, from the spermatic economy, through ambivalence over sensuality, and finally to the view that sensuality is not harmful.

Kennedy's view of personal energy is likewise a reflection of guidance. Although he proposed an ethic of personal vigor, it had none of the qualities of the phallic politics of Theodore Roosevelt. Not finding it necessary to propose an image of indestructibility like TR who guarded the secret of the blindness in one of his eyes, Kennedy was open about his back problem and his adrenal deficiency, and he felt no aversion to publicly sitting in his rocking chair while TR insisted on leading his cabinet in a jog across a football field, or returning to Washington with the largest number of animals after a hunting excursion.

Another central dynamic of vigorous guidance is the abandonment of the genetic view of inherited traits in favor of the belief in innate potentialities, an ethic, of course, with profound implications for general social nurture. It is a telling fact that this nation's first Catholic President who authored *A Nation of Immigrants* represented a psychoclass who could move beyond the geneticism and racism of aggressive training. Although initially tacit concerning the emerging civil rights struggle, Kennedy gradually moved towards a firm commitment, a commitment which all indications show would have found institutional expression had Kennedy survived to serve a second term. In the words of one observer, for the first time a President "not only gave full executive backing to the enforcement of court decisions but personally identified himself with the goals of the Negro revolution and gave them the full moral support of the Presidency."[5 2]

It will never be possible to state unequivocally that Kennedy would have been able to sustain triumphant guidance for a longer duration than Lyndon Johnson. Indications are that by the latter days of his administration he had committed himself to civil rights, a phased withdrawal from Vietnam, had learned the lessons of the politics of confrontation from Cuba, and was planning to push through Congress a thorough, nurturing war on poverty in the early days of his second administration.[5 3]

The tragedy of Kennedy's death also presents vital psychohistorical questions. Beyond the shock of assassination of a youthful President who "could speak of death like all other subjects, candidly, objectively and at times humorously," who, having come close to death four times, remained unafraid of the prospect, are questions of his psychic constituency. Did much of this psychic constituency share qualities of guidance *and* training and, therefore, identity with the totality of his being, or did he attract individuals separately from each psychoclass, one resonating with his domestic identity, and the progress of the Peace Corps, and the other, to the Cold Warism aggressiveness of his Cold War posture? Whatever the answer—which must await further research—by 1963 we have one indication that Kennedy, at least unconsciously, recognized his own internal conflicts. He quoted the following speech of King John containing a central theme of division and destruction:

> The sun is o'er cast with blood; fair day adieu!
> Which is the sede that I must go withal?
> I am with both: each army hath a hand;
> And in their rage, I having hold of both,
> They whirl asunder and dismember me.[54]

During the years of 1964, 1965 and 1966, Lyndon Johnson carried forth the Kennedy banner and effected the expression of triumphant vigorous guidace, a phase attenuated by the cancerous infection of Vietnam policy during the second half of the decade. James David Barber felt that the division within Johnson, which we have identified as bi-submodal influence, was clear from the opening days of his administration:

> Two themes persisted . . . a tough, hard, militaristic theme and a dedicated humanitarianism—Johnson mean and Johnson nice. Together they add up to a view of the world in which the strong-weak dimension is paramount. Never fully consistent in any philosophical sense, Johnson found a way to let them live together by separating the arenas in which they were operative. To the outer world of foreign-policy, Johnson presented his hard soldierly visage. To the deprived at home, he showed his kindlier face. There were many exceptions, but these were the main themes.[55]

At this point, for purposes of establishing the case of a brief period of triumphant guidance, we will center upon the progressive side of Johnson's psyche. Johnson's Great Society was based on all the logical outcomes of vigorous guidance—the belief in effort, dissolution of the spermatic economy, social nurture, belief in the efficacy of altering environments for progress, and the abandonment of geneticism. The verbal articulation of the Great Society is filled with the progressive social nurturance which matches the relative individual nurturance of vigorous guidance: Johnson proclaimed:

> The Great Society is a place where every child can find knowledge to enrich his mind and to enlarge his talents. It is a place where leisure is a . . . chance to build and reflect . . . It is a place when the city of man serves not only the needs of the body and the demands of commerce but the desire for beauty and the hunger for community . . . Our society will not be great until every young mind is free to scan the farthest reaches of thought and imagination.[56]

The child is given a chance to "find knowledge" and to "enrich his mind," an activity which begins with the inner motivation of the child, but is catalyzed by an amenably structured environment. The young mind should be free to scan the "farthest reaches of thought and imagination."

Johnson stressed the ability of the country to support progress and to allow for the creation of the Great Society: "This great, rich, restless country can offer opportunity and education and hope to all—all black and white, all North and South, sharecropper and city-dweller. These are the enemies—poverty, ignorance, disease. They are enemies, not our fellow man, not our neighbor, and those enemies, too . . . we shall overcome."[57]

The President's speeches are filled with his desire to build a new, nurturing order: "I do not want to be the President who built empires . . . . I want to be the President who educated young children to the wonders of this world . . . . I want to be the President who helped the poor to find their own way and who protected the right of every citizen to vote in every election."[58] He added: "It's the time—and it's going to be soon—when nobody in this country is poor . . . . It's the time—and there is no point in waiting—when every boy or girl . . . has the right to all the education that he can absorb."[59] Johnson stressed that the Great Society "is not a safe harbor, a resting place, a final objective, a finished work. It is a challenge constantly renewed."[60] Johnson elaborated upon the dynamic nature of the Great Society: "I do not believe that the Great Society is the ordered, changeless, and sterile battalion of the ants. It is the excitement of becoming—always becoming, trying, probing, falling, resting, trying again."[61] The elements of guidance are present in these statements: the confidence in institutions and the ethic of the good in providing a proper environment within which the child will naturally meet potential, empathy for the needy, the right of individuals to a minimal level of comfort divorced from the degree of effort they currently put into society and the omnipresent achievement ethic.

The President was aware that he was experiencing a triumphant phase of history. Encouraged by the smashing electoral victory of 1964 (sixty-four percent of the popular vote, a greater landslide than FDR's victory in 1936) Johnson, who had presented himself as a peace candidate, devoted less than one-fifth of his first State of the Union Message to matters of foreign policy and its usual belligerent themes. Instead, the Great Society was articulated giving full expression to an ethic of nurturance. Johnson proudly announced in 1965, "No longer are we called upon to get America moving. We *are* moving."[62]

Johnson summarized his program as the need for rational answers to problems, the realization of the worth of the individual, the necessity of full utilization of resources, and the positive value of economic and social planning.[63] Such ideals were not a collection of empty rhetoric. Goals which aimed to "conduct a war on poverty, to assure every American family an adequate home, to relieve old and poor people of the financial burdens of illnesses, to widen the educational opportunities of poor children, to speed the integration of the black communities"[64] required extensive programs. And these programs came, and even gained institutionalization during the brief years of triumph. February of 1964 brought a progressive taxation bill, June of 1964 brought the most thorough civil rights legislation passed in the twentieth century. Johnson established an Office of Economic Opportunity, conservation acts, and more, which in the words of one text, "was a tribute to the forceful leadership of President Johnson."[65] Legislation also included the Elementary and Secondary Education Act, the Higher Education Act, which extended federal funding of schools, the Housing Act of 1965 which created HUD, and the model cities project which established the federal government as the coordinator of the drive to eliminate urban poverty.[66]

The War on Poverty amounted to a bureaucratic revolution in which agencies such as the Job Corp, Work-Study, VISTA, and Community Action Program, emphasized democratic procedures within a far less contingent, conditional and limited welfare state than was the case during previous decades. Medicare and educational opportunities made new inroads in the problems of poverty and economic insecurity. The general economy reflected this triumph: in 1964 the GNP increased by 7.1%, in 1965 it increased by 8.1%, and in 1966 it increased by 9.5%.[67] If the

1966 elections evidenced a reaction in Congress and a move back to the center, the move, in itself, was not severe enough to undo the revolution in social nurture of the early sixties.

Yet by 1965 the seeds of tragedy in Vietnam were already apparent. Johnson's rhetoric of peace already began to have a paradoxical meaning. He stated: "War is always the same. It is young men dying in the fullness of their promise. It is trying to kill a man that you do not even know well enough to hate. Therefore, to know war is to know that there is still weakness in the world."[68] But Johson's guidance self would rarely again confront his hard, training self. The Tonkin Gulf Resolution of August 7, 1964, already had given Johnson an open hand in escalation, and 1964 marked a geometric increase in troop strength. By 1967, 16,000 Americans had been killed and 100,000 wounded. The Air Force made 24,570 sorties into North Vietnam in 1965; in 1966 it made 94,308.[69]

The latter half of the Johnson administration is correctly labeled by one writer "The Years of Frustration" as his training nature refused to risk humiliation by retreating from Vietnamese soil.[70] Doris Kearns traces a psychodynamic reality in which Johnson's actions became increasingly dominated by his aggressive side. His dream life became obsessed with recurring images of humiliation, scenerios of thousands of people attacking, some shouting and calling him a weakling and a coward; or a dream in which he saw himself vainly swimming about in circles, unable to reach the shore.[71]

Johnson's consensus began to crack as the Congress moved to the center; the nation began to fragment when the massive expenditures in Vietnam thwarted the allocation of funds necessary to carry through the programs of the Great Society. In 1966, Bill Moyers, one of Johnson's most trusted aides, left his post because of the Vietnamese escalation.[72] There is a consensus among historians and journalists that the expense and moral questions of the Vietnam War literally destroyed the sense of unity necessary to continue the development of the Great Society. Arthur Schlesinger, jr. told historian John Garraty: "The irony of Johnson is that, having started out so promisingly, he allowed his domestic program to be derailed by his obsession with the war in Vietnam, an obsession which increasingly monopolized not only his own attention but the resources and concern of the country." The war was "unquestionably at the root of the nation's political disorders." Another writes: "More than anything else, the Vietnam War was the main enemy of the Great Society . . . the bitterness, hostility, and disillusionment generated by Johson's prosecution and escalation of an unpopular war destroyed the consensus on social goals that he had earlier managed to create."[73]

Johnson himself looked back in 1971:

> The Great Society had a real chance to grow into a beautiful woman. And I figured her growth and development would be as natural and inevitable as any small child's. In the first year, as we got the laws on the books, she'd begin to crawl. Then in the second year, as we got more laws on the books, she'd begin to walk, and the year after that, she'd be off and running, all the time growing bigger and healthier and fatter. And when she grew up, I figured she'd be so big and beautiful that the American people couldn't help but fall in love with her.[74]

In this statement, Johnson directly associated his domestic policy with a female identity, and stated his initial confidence that its triumphant expression would grow organically. But only one-half of him was speaking in 1971, the constructive half which built these new structural reforms and therefore spoke for the progressive guidance psychoclass. Yet Johnson remained blind to a harder side, a side which subverted his own plans, a true enemy within.


## II. <u>THE YOUTH REVOLT</u>

### THE DELEGATED RELEASE PSYCHOCLASS

Although this analysis intends to extend the periodization of twentieth-century America only to the end of Johnson's term of office (1968), the effects of the early stages of rebellion of the delegated release psychoclass (fourth submode) must be confronted. By 1965 the oldest members of this group were twenty-five, which precisely parallels the upsurge of the student activist movement. The clash of psychoclasses in the sixties will be seen to be particularly intense in light of the range of psychoclasses interacting: the hard training side of Johnson and its constituency known as foreign-policy hawks (who aligned on the war issue as the political center and right); the guidance individuals such as Bill Moyers who were torn between affiliations to Johnson and younger, more progressive individuals; and finally, the youngest and most progressive voices of dissent, members of the delegated release psychoclass.

It is useful at this juncture once again to summarize a submode and posit its logical effects upon its resulting psychoclass. Delegated release, as the other submodes, involves two sides. On the child-oriented side, this submode reaches unprecedented levels of freedom and autonomy, and the parents reach the insight that the child contains potentialities which may be distorted through improper care. Sexuality moves to a new level of advancement at which point it is seen not only as a nondestructive force, but also a positive good. The father is involved more with infant care, though his presence is still sporadic during infancy.

On the soft side, authority bonding declines severely, and the home is seen as the model of a democracy. Empathy reaches new levels, and the generation of release parents attempt more successfully to understand the nature of infant and child psychology.

On the parent-oriented side, delegated tasks are missions of the id, in which particularly the mother's inhibitions are expressed through the child who acts out frustrated, repressed, and infantile wishes. The mother's frustrations at having major responsibility for early child care are subtly communicated and messages are sent to the child to transcend such a binding environment. Children are therefore a means of achieving vicarious freedom. The child's sexual existence is thus complicated because it becomes a means for the mother to achieve self-expression and psycho-physical equilibrium. Parent and child react with ambivalent feelings, the parent jealous of the child's apparent freedom, and the child ambivalent about the parents' seeming disparity between wish and action.

The soft reaction to such an environment leads to a desire for further democratization of society. Because release stresses the universal impetus *within* the child to develop, it is likely that fewer subgroups within society will be excluded from expression of potential. Authorities are apt to be less accepted on face value but rather are evaluated according to the contents of their pronouncements rather than virtues of their positions. Empathy for the needy will have reached a new level, and it is likely that beyond help for those who work, or welfare allotted on the condition that one takes advantage of such aid by means of vigorous self-application, the release individual will move closer to the ideal of *unconditional human subsidization*, the ethos that the mere fact of being human guarantees one certain minimal standards of care within the greater society. Because of more advanced ego structures, release individuals will be less likely to demand rigid societal structuring. They will better be able to achieve goals through flexibly structured environments and structures amenable to change.

The hard or delegated side of release promises a particular impatience emanating from this psychoclass, a desire for high-velocity change as well as gratification of certain impulses, impulses which are by their nature right and good but which still retain their delegated qualities. Id qualities are therefore stressed in addition to ego abilities so that a *feeling* reorientation within society is called for. Release individuals are still reared under the socializing mode, though, and are still concerned to varying degress with achievement of their parents' goals.


THE ANATOMY OF PROTEST

Literally all of the above qualities form the core of the protest movement which emerged in the mid-1960's, a time when the release individuals reached college and university age in substantial numbers. The first crucial stage in the precise identification of release activity, though, requires a clarification of who exactly the release individual is. The fact emerges that *not all student activists belong to the release psychoclass.* Liebert discusses the distinction between the "idealistic radical" and the "nihilistic radicals." Black speaks of the distinction between activists and dissenters. Albert produces the distinction between "instrumental" activists and "principled" activists. The instrumental are motivated primarily by authority problems and the need to rebel (and be punished). The principled have a more creative vision of humanitarian and societal growth, are better able to function within society, are less destroyed by failure, and are in the long run, more tenacious. Liebert describes such activists: "The commitment of the more 'idealistic' radicals and militants involved newer character traits of hope, will, purpose, empathy, and a flexible relationship with authority," as opposed to aggressivity, and impulse gratification and simple anti-authoritarianism.[75]

Keniston's distinction between the activists and nonactivists is most useful for the purposes of identifying the release psychoclass.[76] The sociologist's distinction allows us to leave out a sizable quantity of youth activity. First, what came to be known as the hippie movement, the Weathermen, the violent radicals, and the commune and counterculture activity fall into the category of the alienated or nonactivist youths. A separate study would be required to identify these individuals' psychogenic origins, but it may be summarized here that nonactivists consist of groups of lower submodal origins than release who were unable to handle the freedoms and sensual explorations of the release psychoclass.

Empirical studies confirm that the activist group are consistently members of the release psychoclass. Their identity as a delegated group is especially apparent in their lack of radical rebellion from their parents, and their repression and acting out of many parental values. Keniston found that the activists he studied remained closer to their parents emotionally than the nonactivists. His descriptions of the activists correspond to the delegated release experience. Keniston writes: "As a group, activists seem to possess an unusual capacity for nurturant identification—that is, for empathy and sympathy with the underdog, the oppressed and the needy ... the dominant ethos of their families is unusually egalitarian, permissive, democratic and highly individuated." While the alienated radical is likely to be a "romantic" who rejects society because of its lack of spiritual fulfillment, the activists "are politically involved, humanitarian and universalistic in values."[77] Keniston describes the constellation of the activists' childhood experience which corresponds to release: "Both father and son are described as expressive, humanitarian, and idealistic. The son identifies with his father, although the son is usually more radical. Such sons are very likely to be radicals in action as well as in beliefs.[78]

Other observations conform to the above. The observer noted that the activists tend to be more secular than others, more politically liberal, and to come from relatively well educated parents. Another states, "Activists in our sample were found to be more independent, service-oriented, artistic, and expressive than other students. Their home life was stimulating." Peterson's 1968 study includes: "Activists perceive in themselves an altruistic sense of responsibility in relation to almost all people, and their interpersonal relationships stress empathy, openness, and honesty."[79]

Some aspects of release activity—experimentation with drugs, sexual experience, and the back-to-nature impetus as well as a recognition of the importance of feeling within corporate culture—have lost their proper perspective within the entirety of the release submode. There were excesses, for release is delegated rather than coming from within and is a submode of socialization, albeit advanced socialization. The child matures with a sense of parental ambivalences over watching him achieve what the parent could only yearn for but not enact; the child matures with a driving force of motivation placed upon natural id drives. But an analysis of the id qualities of the release psychoclass must—as in the case of political activism—carefully isolate release from earlier psychoclass behavior.

James Simon Kunen's *The Strawberry Statement: Notes of a College Revolutionary* is most reflective of the delegated release qualities of activism. In this short account, Kunen states how he attempted to contact the American Ambassador to Vietnam for a month before finally making phone contact. Unintimidated by authority, yet neither in disdain of it, Kunen proceeded to lucidly get his point across to Ambassador Bunker who in turn, frankly admitted to not having gone out to personally meet Vietnam citizens. The Ambassador offered to state his rationale for being in Vietnam in writing and have the communication forwarded to Kunen. Kunen also writes that he climbed a mountain on an outing but felt little elation at having reached the top. He felt none of the Kennedy desire to prove and accomplish a challenge almost for the pure sake of accomplishment.

Although several years will pass before a definitive study precisely elucidates the elements of protest in the sixties, the evidence is strong that the most constructive, cohesive, progressive, and ultimately potent thrust of the youth movement came from the delegated release psychoclass.


PROSPECTS

When the following chart (Figure 14) is read on conjunction with the charts shown in Figures 12 and 13, the major conclusions of this volume are summarized: (see next page)

Little needs to be said concerning the course of events between the latter portion of the Johnson administration and 1976, the publication year of this volume. The psychogenic theory states that the termination of a period of triumph is met by a reactive period overlapping the rebellious phase of a new psychoclass, as well as the possibility of severely dislocating events. Both situations occurred with the election of a reactive president and the traumas of escalated war in Vietnam, the bombing of Cambodia, and the removal of a President from office because of unethical conduct. Nixon's reaction to the rebellious release psychoclass consisted of a rigidified fear of youth radicals—activists and alienated—and the association of them with broad sicknesses of America, failings which were strongly related in his mind to permissive child-rearing.

One measure of the importance of a theory, and a criterion of its scientific nature, is the theory's ability to predict. Based on the

Fig. 14. Psychoclassic Expressions and Limitations

| Psychoclass | Expression | Limitation |
|---|---|---|
| Psychic control | Urge for consolidation<br>Energy and the spermatic economy<br>Intellectual currents of conscience, efficiency and energy<br>Phallic politics of Theodore Roosevelt<br>Wilson's superego delegations<br>Reactive phase: World War I<br>Reaction and rebellion in the twenties | Authority-oriented<br>Strident nationalism<br>Fantasies of omnipotence<br>Didactic moralism<br>Inflexible institutions<br>Violent group fantasies<br>Homogeneous ideals of culture<br>Stereotype sex roles<br>Desire to legislate personal conduct<br>Fear of energy loss |
| Aggressive training | Training psychoclass<br>Essential unity of the New Deal<br>Experimental nature of the New Deal<br>Ego Consolidation<br>Social nurture and collectivism<br>Training, aggression and contingent welfare<br>Truman's reactive training<br>1950s: Eisenhower and reactive training | Establishment of impersonal bureaucracy<br>One must work to achieve sustenance<br>Half-hearted abandonment of spermatic economy<br>Aggressive military imagery and symbols<br>Persistent nationalism<br>Persistent competition<br>Fear of idleness |
| Vigorous guidance | Vigorous guidance psychoclass<br>Kennedy and Johnson: abbreviated guidance, externalized training | Impersonal bureaucracy<br>Persistence of competition<br>Ethic of achievement associated with self worth |

| Psychoclass | Expression | Limitation |
|---|---|---|
| Vigorous guidance (cont'd) | Civil rights, deficit spending<br>Semi-contingent welfare guarantees<br>Environmental stimulus, bureaucratic advance<br>More sensitive democracy<br>Extended equality of opportunity | One must function within extended bureaucratic structures<br>Limited vision of possibilities of collective action and preserved autonomy<br>Limited id expression |
| Delegated release | Delegated release psychoclass<br>Individuality<br>Autonomy<br>Feeling<br>Initiative and creativity<br>Sensual drive<br>Necessity of self assertion and communicative ability | Persistence of association of achievement and self worth<br>Id expression acted out for parents<br>Ambivalencies towards parents persist<br>Others will become clearer in the future |

empirical findings of this study, and conceptualizations based on the psychogenic theory of history, several comments regarding the next two decades are possible. First, a period of structural reform of sufficient degree and success to become a distinct period in the evolution of the American twentieth century is not likely to occur until the 1980s. By 1986, the oldest release individuals will be forty-five, and unless we sufficiently reorient our standards of age and political office, these release individuals will not hold important legislative and executive posts until that time. They may hold more minor positions before the mid-1980s and therefore influence the degree of reaction present in the late 1970s and early 1980s, but the beginning of a new triumphant period will most likely await close to a decade after this writing.

A theory's importance may also be measured by its ability to grow. Much as any force, it pushes research in new directions, defining novel problems. If its insights and hypotheses prove to be incorrect, they are dropped and the theory modified in favor of more consistent formulations. If its insights are born out by empirical reality, old questions are answered and a new set generated. The theory moves to a new stage, and becomes a movement, until, if work proves to be truly cumulative, it forms the basis of a new discipline.

I believe the psychogenic theory of history has by now passed a crucial initial test and has moved to a new stage of development; its basic propositions are supported by painstaking primary research, both here and in deMause's *Journal of Psychohistory*, and a novel set of problems has organically emerged. The first stages involved substantiation that childhood lawfully evolves and that this evolution is the ultimate cause of the evolution of society. Detailed study of the early years allows for a sense of the processes of personality formation within particular modes and submodes. Because the very formative processes may be observed in minute detail, the repetition of traits upon maturation means these dynamics are being expressed in adult personality not caused anew by "outside" forces. This study has detailed the means by which a progressive thread of evolution within the childhood experience in modern America came about and how it was expressed in the form of the progressive periodization.

An entirely new fabric and psychogenic structure within society emerges. The former sociological view has proved inadequate. The perspective that broad forces—economic, technological—of vague "outside" origins act upon individuals precludes in-depth genetic analysis and relegates much of sociological work to description. Such macro forces may now be seen as surface symptoms, results not causes, an epidermis stretching about an architecture or inner core of shared psychic reality. Society is a shared group-fantasy—expressed wishes—in which nothing may be divorced from its emotional significance. There are no objective "non-psychological" laws of economics, culture, politics, or social change, but only psychohistorical dynamics governing individuals and groups. The phenomenon of interaction of psychoclasses is the marrow of social existence. Major affective themes motivate groups of individuals, themes which are defined in submodal childhood experience, and which underlie the synthesis of culture.

The psychogenic theory cracks the shell of this hidden reality and allows for the framing of an entirely new set of questions. For example, what precisely determines when a psychoclass will come to predominance while others are temporarily or permanently swamped? What determines the precise duration of any phase of the psychogenic cycle? Is the interaction of individuals in large groups the same process as the interaction of smaller groups? Are there hidden principles involved in group behavior independent of the dynamics of psychoclass, such as, in de Mause's phrase "the larger the group, the earlier the origin of the expressed fantasy?" Are there subphases of the phases of psychoclass expression just as there are submodes of modal stages of childhood? With adequate analysis, might not *every* institution be traced to its childhood origins? What is the group dynamics of the interaction of nations? Does personality formation extend farther back than is commonly known, to the birth process and prenatal environment? What are the implications of this research upon the psychogenic evolution of psychoclasses? Is it possible to relate modal childhood experience to personality formation in greater detail? Is it possible to facilitate the process of evolution by means of direct social encouragement of advanced parenting? Why do some family lines, groups, and countries become fossilized while others demonstrate continual progress? Is there a psychogenic theory of war, or does each war play a unique function in the evolutionary process? Why do primitive (paranoid) leaders often gain predominance in more advanced cultures? What are the processes of the interaction of psychoclasses? May one psychoclass, for example, receive delegated tasks from another? Such are only a few of the questions spawned in extending initial psychogenic propositions.

One comes away from the psychogenic theory and the study of American childhood in an unaccustomed mood of optimism. Although such a study discovers a previously hidden and violent past, it re-humanizes history and presents the potential of unlimited continued progress, a highly unpopular view today. Man is revealed as the architect of his own fate rather than being the product of his institutions. This study has shown the substages of the socialization mode, for example, to manifest continual—though far too slow—enlightenment. Perhaps in a generation, if evolution is not obstructed by our own culture's remnants of a brutal past, it will be possible to conceive of a volume entitled "Beyond Socialization." It might be based on the notion that history does not cause emotions, but emotions cause history. It might trace the history of violence, for example, from cannibalism, murder, and the socially-condoned murders of war, to the successful elimination of socially-organized destructive impulses, to, finally, the dissolution of the basic impulse. Only then will the psychoses of history become comprehensible, and the world's fears of a general holocaust be relieved.

REFERENCES

1. See the Appendix and deMause's "The Independence of Psychohistory" in *The New Psychohistory*.
2. "An Evaluation of Presidents: An Extension of the Schlesinger Polls," *Journal of American History*, LVII (June, 1970).
3. Cabell Phillips, *The Truman Presidency: The History of a Triumphant Succession* (New York: Macmillan, 1966).
4. Norman L. Rosenberg et. al., *In Our Times: America Since World War II* (Englewood Cliffs: Prentice-Hall, 1976), p. 34; Joseph C. Goulden, *The Best Years: 1945-1950* (New York: Atheneum, 1976); Cabell Phillips, *The 1940s: Decade of Triumph and Trouble* (New York: Macmillan, 1975).
5. I. F. Stone, *The Truman Era* (New York: Random House, 1953), p. xxi.
6. *Ibid.*, p. 58.
7. Goulden, *Best Years*, p. 99.
8. Phillips, *Truman Presidency*.
9. Goulden, *Best Years*, p. 215; George E. Mowry, "The Uses of HIstory by Recent Presidents," *Journal of American History*, LVII (June, 1966), p. 11; Charles S. Miller and Natalie J. Ward, *History of America: Challenge and Crises* (New York: John Wiley and Sons, 1971), p. 742.
10. Alonzo L. Hamby, "The Liberals, Truman, and FDR as Symbol and Myth," *Journal of American History*, LVI (March, 1970), p. 867.
11. Stone, *Truman Era*.
12. Phillips, *Truman Presidency*, p. 404.

13. Goulden, *Best Years*, p. 113.
14. Richard S. Kirdendall, ed., *The Truman Period as a Research Field* (University of Missouri Press, 1974), pp. 101, 102.
15. Barton J. Bernstein and Allen J. Matusow, eds., *The Truman Administration: A Documentary History* (New York: Harper and Row, 1966), p. 86.
16. *Ibid.*
17. Phillips, *Truman Presidency*, p. xi.
18. Rosenberg, *Our Times*, p. 34.
19. Goulden, *Best Years*, p. 233; Eric F. Goldman, *The Crucial Decade: America, 1945-60* (New York: Vintage, 1960); Hamby, "The Liberals," p. 861.
20. Phillips, *1940s*, p. 345.
21. Arthur S. Link, *American Epoch: A History of the United States Since the 1890s* (New York: Alfred A. Knopf, 1967), p. 665.
22. Richard Hofstadter et. al., *The United States* (Englewood Cliffs: Prentice-Hall, 1976), p. 643.
23. David Burner et. al., *America: A Portrait in History* (Englewood Cliffs: Prentice-Hall, 1974), p. 599.
24. Robert R. Jones and Gustav L. Seligmann, *The Sweep of American History*, Vol. II (New York: John Wiley & Sons, 1970), p. 471.
25. Herbert S. Parmet, *Eisenhower and the American Crusades* (New York: Macmillan, 1972).
26. Link, *American Epoch*, p. 865; Goulden, *Best Years*, p. 427; Dean Albertson, ed., *Eisenhower as President* (New York: Hill and Wang, 1963), p. 40.
27. John Gunther, *Eisenhower: The Man and the Symbol: (New York: Harper and Row, 1952.)*
28. Albertson, *Eisenhower*, p. x.
29. John A. Garraty, *Interpreting American History: Conversations with American Historians* (New York: Macmillan, 1970), p. 271.
30. Albertson, *Eisenhower*, p. xix.
31. Jones, *The Sweep*, p. 510.
32. Goldman, *Crucial Decade*, p. 243.
33. Charles S. Miller and Natalie J. Ward, *History of America: Challenge and Crisis* (New York: John Wiley & Sons, 1971), p. 768.
34. *Ibid.*, p. 776.
35. Aida Dipace Donald, *John F. Kennedy and the New Frontier* (New York: Hill & Wang, 1966), p. 12.
36. Evelyn Lincoln, *My Twelve Years with John F. Kennedy*

(New York: David McKay, 1965).

37. Henry Fairlie, *The Kennedy Promise: The Politics of Expectation* (New York: Doubleday, 1973), p. 180; Arthur M. Schlesinger, Jr., *A Thousand Days'* (Boston: Houghton, Mifflin, 1965), p. 740; John M. Blum et. al., *The National Experience* (New York: Harcourt, Brace & World, 1968), pp. 822-23; James David Barber, *The Presidential Character: Predicting Performance in the White House* (Englewood Cliffs: Prentice-Hall, 1972), p. 315.

38. Schlesinger, *Thousand Days*, p. 214.

39. Theodore C. Sorensen, *Kennedy* (New York: Harper and Row, 1965), p. 389; Harold Whitman Bradley, *The United States From 1865* (New York: Scribner's, 1965), p. 427.

40. Barber, *Character.*

41. Fairlie, *Promise*, p. 82.

42. John F. Kennedy, *To Turn the Tide* (New York: Harper and Row, 1962), p. 6.

43. Fairlie, *Promise*, p. 68.

44. *Ibid.*, p. 12.

45. Mowry, "Uses of History."

46. Schlesinger, *A Thousand Days*, p. 290.

47. *Ibid.*, p. 104; Maranell, "Evaluation of Presidents."

48. Lincoln, *My Twelve Years*, p. 354.

49. Stone, *Truman Era*, p. 165.

50. Kennedy, *Tide*, pp. 82-83.

51. *Ibid.*

52. Jones, *The Sweep*, p. 521.

53. Schlesinger, *Thousand Days.*

54. *Ibid.*, p. 725.

55. Barber, *Character*, p. 87.

56. Franklin D. Mitchell and Richard O. Davis, ed., *America's Recent Past* (New York: John Wiley, 1969), p. 429.

57. Barber, *Character*, p. 90.

58. *Ibid.*, pp. 90-91.

59. *Ibid.*, p. 91.

60. *Public Papers of Lyndon B. Johnson* (U.S. Government Printing Office, 1965), p. 704.

61. Sarah H. Hayes, ed., *The Quotable Lyndon B. Johnson* (New York: Drake House, 1968), p. 112.

62. Norman A. Graebner, *A History of the American People* (New York: McGraw-Hill, 1975), p. 866.

63. Lyndon B. Johnson, *A Time for Action* (New York: Atheneum, 1964), p. 7.

64. Eli Ginzberg and Robert M. Solow, eds., *The Great Society*

(New York: Basic Books, 1974), p. 213.

65. Bradley, *United States*, p. 439.
66. Rosenberg, *Our Times*.
67. John F. Heath, *Decade of Disillusionment: The Kennedy-Johnson Years* (Bloomington: Indiana University Press, 1975), p. 213.
68. Hayes, *Quotable Johnson*, p. 277.
69. Hofstadter, *United States;* Barber, *Character*, p. 38.
70. Heath, *Disillusionment*.
71. Doris Kearns, *Lyndon Johnson and the American Dream* (New York: Harper and Row, 1976).
72. Eric F. Goldman, *The Tragedy of Lyndon Johnson* (New York: Alfred A. Knopf, 1969).
73. Garraty, *Interpreting American History*, p. 274; Jonathan Schell, *The Time of Disillusion* (New York: Random House, 1975); Ginzberg, *Great Society*, p. 213.
74. Kearns, *Lyndon Johnson*.
75. Robert Liebert, *Radical and Militant Youth* (New York: Praeger, 1971); Seymour Martin Lipset, Gerald M. Schaflander, *Passion and Politics: Student Activism in America* (Boston: Little, Brown and Co., 1971).
76. Lipset, *Passion*, p. 106; Kenneth Keniston, "The Sources of Student Dissent," *Journal of Social Issues*, 23 (1967).
77. Keniston, "Sources."
78. Keniston, "Sources"; Richard Peterson, "The Student Left," in *American History: Recent Interpretations* ed. Abraham Eisenstadt (New York: Thomas Y. Crowell, 1969), p. 568.
79. See also Julian Foster and Durward Lang eds. *Protest: Student Activism in America* (New York: Morrow, 1970).
80. James Simon Kunen, *The Strawberry Statement: Notes of a College Revolutionary* (New York: Random House, 1969).

# THE PSYCHOGENIC THEORY OF HISTORY

LLOYD DEMAUSE

## OVERGRAMS FOR A UNIFIED PSYCHOHISTORY

> "Theories are nets:
> only he who casts will catch."
> —Novalis

1. That psychohistory is the science of patterns of historical motivations and is based upon an anti-holistic philosophy of methodological individualism.

   1A. Psychohistory is a science, not a narrative art like history.

      1A. 1. All psychohistorical research must be comparative, striving toward lawful propositions.

      1A. 2. Psychohistory advances like any other science, by the discovery of new paradigms and attempts to disprove them.

      1A. 3. Like psychoanalysis, psychohistory uses self-observation of the emotional responses of the

researcher as its prime tool for discovery; nothing
is ever discovered "out there" until it is first felt
"in here."

1B.  Psychohistory is individualistic, not holistic like sociology
and anthropology.

    1B. 1. The holistic fallacy that the group exists as an
entity over and beyond its individual constituents
presumes what it should investigate—the fantasy
that the group is really the mother's body and has
goals and motives of its own.

    1B. 2. Sociology, whether Parsonian or Marxist, is based
on the holistic statement of Durkheim that "social
facts must be treated as things, that is, realities
external to the individual" and is, as Parsons
admits, "inherently teleological."

    1B. 3. Anthropology is based on a similar holistic concept
of "culture," so that when Steward states that
"Personality is shaped by culture, but it has never
been shown that culture is affected by personality"
the tautological form of the assertion is dependent
upon not noticing that the term "culture" has no
meaning beyond the term "personality."

    1B. 4. All statements of the form "X is socially (or
culturally) determined" are tautological and assume
a holistic entity beyond the individual.

    1B. 5. Terms such as "society," "culture," "state," "social
structure," and "power" are all holistic; their
individualistic replacements are "group,"
"personality," "government," "group-fantasy," and
"force."

    1B. 6. The central method of sociology and anthropology
is to establish correlations between two facets of
adult personality and then claim causal connection;
the central method of psychohistory is to establish
causes of motivational patterns in prior personal
events and their restructuring within the adult
group.

1C.  Methodological individualism is the principle that group processes may be entirely explained by (a) psychological laws governing the motivation and behavior of individuals and (b) descriptions of their current physical historical situation, which itself is only the outcome of prior motivations acting on physical reality.

IC. 1.  The diagram below is sufficient to explain all historical processes, "group reality" being the term for shared fantasies of individuals when in groups.

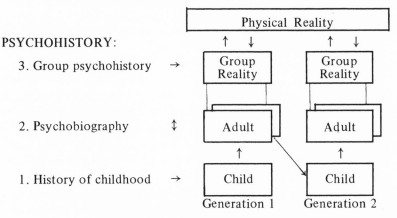

PSYCHOHISTORY:

3. Group psychohistory →

2. Psychobiography ↕

1. History of childhood →

IC. 2.  Durkheim's sociological rule that "Every time that a social phenomenon is directly explained by a psychological phenomenon, we may be sure that the explanation is false" is replaced by the psychohistorical rule that "All group phenomena have psychological explanations; individuals in groups act differently than individuals alone only because they split their psychic conflicts differently, not because some 'social' force is acting on them."

IC. 3.  With the disappearance of the deathless entity "society" all groups values are revealed as tentative and subject to change each generation; what now seems problematic is not change but constancy.

1C. 4.  It is not only the irrational in history that is susceptible to psychohistorical explanation; all of history, its strengths as well as weaknesses, integration as well as disintegration, has childhood determinants and group dynamics.

2. That the ultimate source of all historical change is psychogenesis, the lawful change in childrearing modes occurring through generational pressure.

   2A. Psychogenesis depends upon the ability of parents and surrogates to regress to the psychic age of their children and work through the anxieties of that age better the second time than in their own childhood.

      2A. 1. The regression-progression process stems from the innate biological desire of both parts of a previous dual-unity to relate to each other, and thus is the only historical theory to posit *love* as its central mechanism for change.

      2A. 2. The regression-progression process is identical to that which produces change in psychotherapy; thus history can be viewed as the psychotherapy of generations.

   2B. The evolution of childhood procedes at different rates of progress on both individual and population levels.

      2B. 1. Individual level variations in rates of psychogenic evolution occur because of (a) biological differences (both genetic and uterine events), (b) birth order differences (the later the birth, generally the less intense the parenting), and (c) chance (early loss of parent, injury, other personal life variations).

      2B. 2. Population level variations in psychogenic evolution occur because of (a) selection and isolation (emigration of a narrow range of parenting modes), (b) immigration (the infusion of new parenting modes into a larger population), (c) non-reproduction (psychotic, unfit, or other lower psychogenic modes not as often raising children), (d) culture contact (reinforcing emergent parenting types, providing surrogate parents), (e) material conditions (only as they affect child rearing), and (f) group-fantasy factors (wars and revolutions as they affect children, share of work by mothers, father's share in child rearing, etc.).

2C. The evolution of childhood is a series of closer involvements between adults and children, each advance tending to heal splitting, reduce projection and reversal, and increase empathy.

2C. 1. The six psychogenic modes and their dates of evolution in the most advanced countries are:

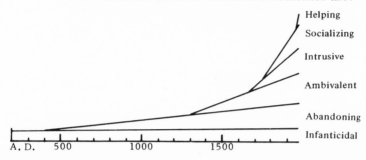

| Mode | Parental Wish | Historical Manifestations |
|---|---|---|
| Infanticidal | Mother: "I wish you were dead, to relieve my fear of being killed by my mother." | Child-sacrifice and infanticide, child as breast-penis, intolerance of child's anger, hardening, ghosts and magic, child sale, child sodomy |
| Abandoning | Mother: "I must leave you, to escape the needs I project into you." | Longer swaddling, fosterage, outside wetnursing, monastery, nunnery and apprenticeship |
| Ambivalent | Mother: "You are bad from the erotic and aggressive projections I put in you." | Enemas, early beating, shorter swaddling, mourning possible, child as erotic object precursor to empathy |
| Intrusive | Mother: "You can have love when I have full control over you." | Early toilet training, repression of child's sexuality, end of swaddling and wetnursing, empathy now possible, rise of pediatrics |
| Socializing | Mother and Father: "We will love you when you are reaching our goals." | Use of guilt, "mental discipline", humiliation, rise of compulsory schooling, delegation of parental unconscious wishes |
| Helping | Mother and Father: "We love you and will help you reach your goals." | Children's rights, de-schooling and free schooling, child therapy, birth without violence |

2C. 2. The "ambivalent mode" is a watershed in the evolutionary series, because up until then progress is achieved by internalization and repression of previously projected parts of the personality (magic), whereas after ambivalence is able to be tolerated (the Kleinian "depressive position"), progress is achieved through the reduction of repression and the increase in ego autonomy.

2C. 3. Progress at each mode depends on overcoming anxieties specific to that mode; for instance, a shortage of wetnurses will have a greater effect when abandonment is the crucial modal issue than at another time, and so on.

2D. The end result of man's biological evolution produced a helpless baby whose instinct is to form an intensely personal relationship, challenging the parent to regress and relate rather than repress and be alone.

2D. 1. Freud's idea that civilization procedes by "progressively greater renunciation of instinct" was precisely backward; civilization procedes only through progressively greater acceptance of the drives of children, allowing them to mature without defensive distortion.

2D. 2. Hegel's idea that history is "man's nature achieving itself" is closer to the truth, but only because each generation tries to help their children achieve their own desires, so that new values are generated evolutionarily rather than teleologically.

3. That the evolution of new psychogenic modes produces new psychoclasses which threaten the group fantasies of earlier psychoclasses and are expressed in historical periods of rebellion, triumph and reaction.

3A. Group-fantasies are formed in order that individuals may play roles to defend themselves against childhood anxieties.

3A. 1. Intra-psychic defenses are not effective in groups, so group-fantasies are substituted as shared defenses which prevent regression to childhood traumas.

3A. 2. The larger the group, the more the threatened regression, so the earlier the source of group-fantasy and the more primitive the splitting.

3A. 3. Man does not, in a group, become an animal—he becomes a frightened baby.

3B. What is usually called "social structure" is actually the splitting of large groups into smaller delegate-groups which play specific roles within group-fantasies.

3B. 1. Delegate-groups act out ambivalent feelings common to all members of the larger group but which the rest of the group wish to deny and project into them.

3B. 2. What are usually called "social institutions" are historical delegate-groups: the Church as a group-fantasy of dependency, the Army as a group-fantasy of birth, the Government as a group-fantasy of nurturance, Capitalism as a group-fantasy of control, Revolution as a group-fantasy of counterdependency, the Class System as a group-fantasy of obeisance, the School as a group-fantasy of humiliation.

3B. 3. Delegate-groups are made up of individuals who share defensive styles, and form themselves into hierarchies in order to contain fantasied group violence.

3C. Leaders are personalities able to become containers for the bizarre projective identifications of group-fantasies.

3C. 1. Projective identification, the central means of communication in group life, is the fantasied forceable thrusting of repudiated parts of one's psyche into another.

3C. 2. Leaders are not just parents—they play the defensive roles required by whichever stage of group-fantasy is operative, becoming stern fathers when group violence is being denied, nurturant mothers when abandonment is defended against, rebellious sons when authority is decaying, and paranoid siblings when group violence is being projected.

3C. 3. Leaders are always containers for the group's feelings of humiliation—the depersonalization or stripping away of intra-psychic defenses which occurs in a group producing the threat of being made a helpless baby again—so leaders always conduct foreign policy while filled up with feelings of near-humiliation.

3D. Historical group-fantasies result from the interaction of different psychoclasses.

3D. 1. Psychoclasses are groups of individuals with the same childhood mode within a given population.

3D. 2. Psychoclasses require different group defenses, and these are often intolerable to other psychoclasses.

3D. 3. The wider the range of psychoclasses in a given population, the more the conflict between their defensive styles.

3D. 4. The higher the psychogenic mode of the psychoclass, the less it is necessary for it to act out its conflicts.

3D. 5. Psychoclass is only partially related to economic class, depending on historical period.

3D. 6. Political and religious movements correlate more closely to psychoclass than to economic class.

3E. Each generation brings a new psychoclass to the historical stage, disturbing the group-fantasies of the older psychoclasses and producing periods of rebellion, triumph and reaction.

3E. 1. Only that portion of the new generation which shares the new child-rearing experience makes up the new psychoclass.

3E. 2. A period of rebellion occurs when the new psyhoclass is young, first mainly in the artistic spheres.

3E. 3. A period of triumph occurs when the new psychoclass becomes dominant in the group's goals, even though they are still a numerical minority.

3E. 4. A period of reaction occurs when the older psychoclasses clamp down on the goals and life-styles of the newest psychoclass.

3F. Psychogenic change is the ultimate source for all technological change; technological change is not, as often assumed, automatic, nor does it drag the psyche in its wake.

3F. 1. The reason childrearing styles correlate with technological levels somewhat is that the former produce the latter, not the reverse.

3F. 2. Low level parenting is always disfunctional to all technological levels—early toilet training did not help early capitalists accumulate money, it made them neurotically unable to invest it productively, as it does today.

3F. 3. No economic system "requires" any specific psychogenic types—capitalism and socialism have both functioned with both sadistic and mature personalities—and no economic system "requires" any specific childrearing.

3F. 4. The invention and spread of new technologies occurs when new psychoclasses reduce the projective identification of parts of their psyches into things—so that deep plowing can replace scratch plowing when "mother Earth" is decathected, gears can be invented and used when they are separated emotionally from teeth, and the whole of modern science can be invented when the Aristotelian notion of "real essences" is discarded.

3F. 5. Economic systems change when new psychoclasses can reduce the use of the group for projective identification—so that early market economies can develop when earlier reciprocal gift-giving is less needed as a defense against primitive death-wishes, late medieval expansion of commerce could come about when feudal bonds were not needed as defenses against abadonment, and capitalistic ownership of goods could appear with the decathexis of property from its "historical" (group-fantasy) ties.

3F. 6. Even supposedly "purely physical" historical phenomena turn out to be determined psychogenically—even plagues are dependant on the Christian love of dirt to sustain the rats whose fleas were its carriers.

3F. 7. Psychogenesis, not "social need," defines the order of invention—otherwise, scientific astronomy would not have preceded the invention of the flush toilet.

3G. Primitive tribes are not magical thinkers because they are technologically primitive—they long ago experienced psychogenic arrest and thereafter did not develop technologically, but only elaborated their group-fantasies.

3G. 1. Primitive tribes lies somewhere in the first two psychogenic modes of childrearing, as evidenced by the lack of depressive (guilt) illnesses which are the achievement of the ambivalent mode.

3G. 2. Primitives did not adapt their personalities to their harsh environments—they migrated to harsh environments because they matched their inner life.

4. That psychogenic modes determine the level of personality which can be attained, and establish the typical conflicts and defenses of each historical period which sustain the art, religion, politics and economics of each age.

4A. Psychogenic modes correspond to specific sets of personality types, using typical defensive patterns and growing in ego strength with each mode:

| Infanticidal Mode | Schizoid Personality | Primary-process thinking, symbiotic omnipotence, gender/zonal confusion, splitting and projective identification, sado-masochistic disorders |
|---|---|---|
| Abandoning Mode | Autistic Personality | Unrelated, narcissistic, exploitive, parasitic, distrustful, oral rage, self weak or grandiose, psychopathic, unable to tolerate delay, lacking in remorse, idealized mother, timeless |
| Ambivalent Mode | Depressive Personality | Guilty and depressed, insatiable in needs for love, status, sex, enormous superego demands, reality of time |
| Intrusive Mode | Compulsive Personality | Pseudorational, cold, detached, self-critical inwardly, phobic, obsessive-compulsive and conversion symptoms |
| Socializing Mode | Anxiety Personality | Less rigid character armor, free-floating anxiety and dissatisfaction with life due to delegate-living, loss of individuality in group, incomplete feelings |
| Helping Mode | | None yet adult |

4B. These personality types can range from "normal" to "abnormal" within each mode, depending on the degree of integration within the personality and the degree of support given by others in the historical period:

RANGE OF PERSONALITY TYPES BY PSYCHOGENIC MODE

|  | Infanticidal | Abandoning | Ambivalent | Intrusive | Socializing |
|---|---|---|---|---|---|
| Normal | Schizoid personality | Autistic personality | Depressive personality | Compulsive personality | Anxiety personality |
| Neurotic | Impulse disorders and sado-masochistic defenses | Anaclitic (neglect) depressive disorders and psychopathic defenses | Introjective (guilt) depressive disorders and manic defenses | Obsessive-compulsive disorders and conversion defenses | Hysterical disorders and psycho-sexual defenses |
| Psychotic | Catatonic and hebephrenic | Paranoid schizophrenia | Manic-depressive psychosis | | |

4B. 1. The leaders of every historical period—those who launch wars, repression and revolution in a considered and careful manner—are only those most integrated into the group-fantasies of the age.

4B. 2. Those considered "neurotic" in each age may often be a higher psychogenic mode than those considered "normal", only they must stand the anxiety of not sharing the group-fantasies of the age.

4C. The master group-fantasies of each historical period correspond to three defensive levels:

4C. 1. The Calamitous Fantasy—coresponding to the basic trauma of each childhood mode.

4C. 2. The Defensive Fantasy—denying this basic traumatic fantasy.

4C. 3. The Desired Fantasy—a further denial, providing the ideal group-fantasies of the age.

EVOLUTION OF FANTASIES IN THE WEST

| | Fantasy Level | Personal Level | Historical Level |
|---|---|---|---|
| Infanticidal (to 8th c.) | Desired | Father will save me from death. | Reincarnation, salvationist religions, kinship systems and economic reciprocity as counters to death wishes. |
| | Defensive | Father will kill me. | Sacrificial religions, Isaac, Christ, blood feuds. |
| | Calamitous | Mother will kill me. | Striga, Medea, slavery, wars of extermination. |
| Abandoning (8th to 14th) | Desired | Father-mother has not abandoned me. | Feudal bond, Great Chain of Being, Mariolatry, growth of Church system, mystical union with Christ. |
| | Defensive | I have abandoned father-mother. | Monasteries, crusades, pilgrimages, acidie. |
| | Calamitous | Mother has abandoned me. | Excommunication, being "lordless" witchcraft, devils. |
| Ambivalent (14th to 17th) | Desired | I love father-mother. | Growth of national sovereignty, divine kingship, merging of church and state, decline of magic. |
| | Defensive | Mother loves me if I am good. | Protestantism, purification of church, good works, calling, humanism, compact with God. |
| | Calamitous | Mother hates me. | Predestination, vengeful God, Renaissance melancholy. |
| Intrusive (18th c.) | Desired | I am the controlling father. | Nationalism, imperialism, capitalism. |
| | Defensive | I will take control from mother. | Revolution as counterdependency, utopianism. |
| | Calamitous | Mother controls me. | God as Watchmaker, true class system, child labor. |
| Socializing (19th to 20th) | Desired | I am now free. | Liberalism, free market system, ideal of schooling. |
| | Defensive | I will make group my delegate | Growth of nation-state and bureaucracy. |
| | Calamitous | Mother makes me her delegate. | Bourgeois as superego delegate, bohemian as id delegate, life as "role." |

5. That groups, whether face-to-face or historical, induce a "fetal trance state" in their members, reawakening specific physical memories from uterine and perinatal life.

5A. Man is a political animal, as Aristotle said, because for most civilized people only life in a group can re-establish contact with repressed fetal emotions.

5B. Only individuals in fetal trance states are able to form group-fantasies, which follow specific rules of fetal life such as:

5B. 1. Life gets continually more cramped, and growth always requires more physical space through actual expansion of territory (even though any fool can see that the resulting opposition to expansion destroys the group's growth.)

5B. 2. Other groups are either nurturant or blood-sucking, poisoning placentas (even though it is obvious that all groups are made up of individuals who have all shades of attitudes towards one.)

5B. 3. The proper attitude toward a nurturing placenta is awe toward its "power flow" (even though it may in fact be harming you.)

5B. 4. The proper attitude toward a blood-sucking, poisoning placenta is to suck its blood and to poison it in return (even though this may in fact involve your own death through retaliation.)

5B. 5. The primary purpose of any group is to preserve its womb-surround, regardless of the cost to individuals within the group (even though a war kills most Americans, it is worth it to preserve "what America stands for.")

5B. 6. The "skin" of one's womb-group wholly determines one's relationship to events (even though there is an epidemic in a nearby country, your morning paper features what your leader had for breakfast.)

5B. 7. Individuals are connected by umbilical cords to leaders, alternately being fed by and feeding them (even though the leader may be wholly inactive, or detrimental, to the group, power and obeisance "flows" on.)

5B. 8. Groups are connected by umbilical cords to other groups, placentas, and must fight for dear life for the "vitality" which flows between them (even though it may be beneficial for two groups to both reduce their armed strength, they cannot do so because it would affect the "balance of power," and so must "stem the turning of the tide" to "prevent the loss of vitality to its system.")

5B. 9. Disturbances to one's womb-surround are always the fault of a poisoning placenta, whom one can harm by "putting pressure" on it (even though you in fact increase your neighbors' hostility.)

5B. 10. When the group-fantasy of an intact womb-surround fails ("the fabric of society stretches thin, then tears"), the group inexorably slides into a war-as-birth group-fantasy (even though the actual reasons for war at that moment may be minimal.)

5B. 11. During the war-as-birth group-fantasy groups pump feelings into their placenta-leaders of being too crowded, asphyxiated, starved and strangulated (even though their economic condition may be in fact excellent.)

5B. 12. Groups go to war in order to overcome the helplessness and terror of being trapped in a birth canal, through means of a sadomasochistic orgy in order to "hack one's way out" of the mother's body (even though in fact the most logical solution to most war threats is to do nothing, nevertheless violent action is always most compelling.)

5B. 13. Once others plunge into a war-as-birth experience, neighbors feel sucked into a similar fetal trance state (even though Americans realize European wars are irrational, once they start they get picked up by "a force they cannot resist" and jump into their own birth primal.)

5B. 14. After successful wars, groups feel "reborn" and have a period of vigorous, optimistic cooperation which is viewed as "The Best Years of Our Lives" (even though they are actually economically depleted.)

5C. The extent to which a group sinks into a full fetal trance state is determined by the ability of its current group-fantasy to create the illusion of an intact womb-surround which can contain the traumas of childhood.

*Lloyd deMause is Director of The Institute for Psychohistory, Editor of* The Journal of Psychohistory, *and Editor and an author of* The History of Childhood, A Bibliography of Psychohistory *and* The New Psychohistory.

# INDEX

90417

D
16
D32

DAVIS, GLENN

CHILDHOOD AND HISTORY IN AMERICA.